Bobby Dazzler

Bobby Dazzler My Story
Bobby George

with Lance Hardy

First published in hardback in Great Britain in 2006 by
Orion Books
an imprint of the Orion Publishing Group Ltd
Orion House, 5 Upper St Martin's Lane,
London WC2H 9EA

10 9 8 7 6 5 4 3 2

A CIP catalogue record for this book is available
from the British Library.

ISBN-13: 978 0 75288 555 1
ISBN-10: 0 75288 555 3

Printed in Great Britain by Clays Ltd, St Ives plc

The Orion Publishing Group's policy is to use papers that are
natural, renewable and recyclable and made from wood grown
in sustainable forests. The logging and manufacturing processes
are expected to conform to the environmental regulations of
the country of origin.

www.orionbooks.co.uk

Contents

Acknowledgements

I would like to thank Lance Hardy, a good mate and a fine writer, for helping me tell the story of my life.

Bobby George
George Hall, Essex
November, 2006

Thanks to Bobby for his honesty, trust and remarkable life story; to Marie for her help and hospitality; to our agent David Luxton for pulling this whole project together; to editors Ian Marshall and Ian Preece, assistant editor Lorraine Baxter, designer Laura Brett and all at Orion; to photographer Steve Double, to my good friends Patrick Barclay, Stuart Clarke and Frank Wurzbach for their advice and assistance; and, most of all, to my mum and dad for their love and support.

Lance Hardy
Barnes, London
November, 2006

I dedicate this book to my wife, Marie,
the woman who changed my life.

1 Kenny the Mouth

Anyone who was around at the time will never forget the long, hot summer of 1976. England was having its worst drought in years. There were hosepipe bans and ladybirds everywhere, and that dreadful 'Combine Harvester' song by The Wurzels was number one in the pop charts and in your head every bloody day.

I was a 30-year-old builder back then, a real Jack of all trades, working from a rented garage in Ilford, east London. My life looked mapped out for me. I had a wife, two kids, a steady wage and my own house – not bad for a boy who left school hardly able to read or write. Then again, I was never going to be able to live those dreams of fame and fortune, and all the trappings that go with the lifestyle, that I'd had as a kid – or so I thought.

Darts was a popular pub game at the time but it didn't interest me. Fishing was my sport and it was fishing that introduced me to darts, with the help of a local man called Malcolm Ellis and a touch of sea-sickness off the southern coast of Ireland.

Malcolm had tickets for a fishing event near Kinsale, 20 miles south of Cork. I didn't know him that well, just from the local pub, but I could always find time for fishing. So when he mentioned it, I agreed to go along. On the very first day, the conditions out at sea were terrible. I suffered quite badly and was grateful when Malcolm, who didn't feel too clever himself, suggested knocking it on the head and retiring to dry land. By the next morning, the thought of going fishing appealed to neither of us and so we adjourned to a nice little pub we had spotted nearby, called the Lobster Pot, for a few pints.

When we walked in, two blokes were playing darts and everyone else was watching. I knew that Malcolm was a tidy player but I had never even picked up a dart and didn't fancy doing so now. I told him that as we headed for the bar, but as the beers flowed, Malcolm borrowed some darts from the landlord and somehow, suddenly we were next up to play, taking on a couple of locals at 20p a game.

I didn't have a clue about any of it – what I was meant to do, what to aim for, how to score or anything. I had absolutely no idea how the game worked. Malcolm had to guide me along. 'Get a twenty, Bob,' he told me and, for some reason, I found it easy to hit the target. Soon Malcolm was asking me to aim for treble 15. When I hit it, he whispered to me, 'You've got a gift.'

I have always believed that if you have a gift for something, it comes easy, and if you get praised for something, you enjoy it more. I remember the feeling as a boy at school – not that much praise ever came my way apart from the odd time in art or woodwork – and I had the very same feeling in that little old Irish pub.

We ended up playing darts all day and all night. It was 'winner stays on' and we never came off the board. No one came close to beating us and we didn't have to buy a drink from the moment we picked up our darts in the afternoon until closing time. As we left the Lobster Pot, a little the worse for wear, and headed back to our digs at the Marina Hotel down the road, Malcolm told me that he thought I had a real talent for darts and tried to persuade me there and then to take up the game seriously. All I wanted to do at that moment, though, was get to bed and go to sleep. I thought nothing more of it. The weather in Kinsale improved and we spent the rest of the week fishing. By the end of the holiday, Malcolm had become a close friend.

I often went to the pub for a pint after finishing work. The Old Maypole in Barkingside, which was next door to my garage, was a real spit and sawdust place. Darts was an important part of it, even if there was just the one board with fungi growing out the top and a leaking roof above it! Malcolm played for the pub team. One night, several weeks after the Ireland trip, I went into the Maypole for a quiet drink and came up close and personal with a real mouthy bloke called Kenny, who was known locally as 'Kenny the Mouth'.

Kenny was at the dartboard with an old boy called Jock McKean. Jock couldn't stand up never mind throw a dart, but he apparently owed Kenny a lot of money and was trying to pay off his debt. Now, as it happens, Kenny was a pretty useful darts player. He played in the pub team along with Malcolm and told anyone who could be bothered to listen that he was the best player in Essex. Kenny liked to settle his arguments with a game of darts, often against people who either couldn't play or were in no state to play. He always played for money – his usual stake was a pound – and he always won.

Jock had had a fair few drinks that night and offered no competition but Kenny wouldn't let it go. He started shouting, and the old boy looked frightened and upset. That is when I got involved. I got off my seat and told Kenny to leave Jock alone. At 6ft 4in tall and weighing in at 17 stone, with a 50in chest and 17in biceps, I could more than handle myself. Unsurprisingly, Kenny wanted to sort things out with me on the dartboard rather than in the car park, and challenged me to a game of darts.

I hadn't played the game since that one and only time in Ireland, but I told him that I was happy to accept his challenge, on the understanding that I would play him in a week's time. I wasn't ready to take him on just yet.

'That's fine,' he said. 'I'll beat you whenever you fancy it.'

I was determined that he wouldn't and suggested upping the stakes to a massive £50. It really was game on. Kenny agreed and a date was set for our duel the following week. I wasn't worried about losing the cash. It was the principle that mattered to me.

The next morning I went out and bought a dartboard and put it up in my house. Malcolm loaned me a set of silver-plated darts made by a local toolmaker and I practised with them for hours on end. For seven days and seven nights I ate and slept darts, learning how to group the arrows together and consistently make big scores. Counting was a big problem but I had Malcolm to help me with that.

I had to beat Kenny the Mouth. I just had to. I really disliked him. He got on my nerves and riled me.

A week later I found Kenny up at the dartboard in the Maypole, showing off with his custom-made brass darts and up to his old tricks. I went straight over and told him that I wanted to take him on right there and then. We played 1001 best of three legs, which is a long race in darts, but it was no contest – I won easily. He asked for 'double or quits' to save face and I beat him again. Everyone in the Maypole saw it. Kenny the Mouth was probably the pub's best darts player – he was comfortably the loudest – but he suddenly decided he'd had enough of playing me. I wasn't having that, though. Looking around the pub, I told him, 'No way. You've taken their money for years and so now I'm taking yours.' After that, Kenny soon stopped going to the Maypole and started drinking – and mouthing, no doubt – somewhere else.

Malcolm, who was with me that night, couldn't believe it. 'Kenny Edinburgh's a very good darts player, Bob, and you wiped the floor with him. You've got a rare gift and you really have to think about taking up this game.'

I still couldn't see what all the fuss was about. There wasn't any money to be made in darts and money was the absolute key for me. As long as I was earning, I was happy. I saw everything else in life as a waste of time and while darts was fun it wasn't going to pay for my keep – although I did enjoy taking a few bob off Kenny the Mouth.

A few weeks later, Malcolm persuaded me to accompany him to a darts night in Chigwell, featuring all the top players in the area. I wasn't impressed at all by what I saw and told him so.

'Malcolm, if this lot here are really the bollocks, then one day I could be the best player in the world.'

Malcolm grabbed me by the arm, looked me straight in the eyes and said, 'Bob, I've been trying to tell you that for months.'

2 Francis Robert George

I was born in a flat above a garage at 927 Romford Road, Manor Park, east London on 16 December 1945, just after the end of the Second World War, and given the names Francis Robert. Well, at least, that is what my birth certificate says!

Francis and Robert are popular names in the George family tree. My father and grandfather were both called Francis and my uncle's name was Robert, but my name was a mistake. My parents wanted to call me Robin. The old man called me Robin until the day I left home, and some people who have known me from a very young age still call me Robin today. Thinking about it, Robin would have been quite an appropriate name for a darts player, with Robin Hood and all that, but my birth certificate clearly lists my name as Francis Robert George.

It isn't really that much of a mystery. The old man had bad eyesight. He was certified blind when he was in his late twenties, and he could hardly see at all when I was born. He registered my birth and wouldn't have been able to read a single word on the certificate. What a mess! Whoever wrote it down didn't even get the names in the right order.

Anyway, by the time I went to school I had discovered that my name was actually Robert and that is what I have used ever since. I never went much on the Francis bit and dropped that as soon as I was able to talk.

The George family name hails from Boston, Massachusetts, USA, and literally hundreds of them are listed in the telephone book there. My grandfather was born in the States and was some character. His family earned a fortune from the Californian gold rush. When he moved to England, he met Henrietta. They married and settled in Barkingside, east London, which is where my old man was born in 1924.

As broad as he was tall, my grandfather was as hard as nails and used to love to tell me how he had lost an eye in a knife fight on a ship. He had a good brain for business but was undone by a love of gambling. In between the wars, he owned two restaurants in London and lost both of them separately in games of cards. In his later years, he worked as a chimney sweep and, despite his glass eye, rode around Barkingside on a motorbike, carrying his ladders. He was known locally as 'George the Sweep'. He worked well into his seventies, ending up as a hod carrier and still downing 15 pints of Guinness in the pub every night after his shift until the day he packed it in.

My grandfather was a gentleman and a grafter and a real inspiration to me. I see a lot of myself in him, but hard work seems to have missed a generation with his son. Now, the old man could talk a good game but he rarely got his hands dirty. In his defence, that could have been due to his health and the problems he had with his eyesight.

During the Second World War, the old man was sent away to an army camp in Shrewsbury, where he met my mother – my first mother, that is. That part of my life is complicated as well. You see, I had two mothers. The first gave birth to three children, including me, but sadly died when we were young. She was replaced in our lives by a woman who took on the job of bringing us all up. I have always referred to that woman as 'Mum' because she is the only one I can remember.

My first mother, Jessie, was born north of the border in Aberdeen. She stood over 5ft 9in tall and had bright red hair. Her mother also died at a young age, from tuberculosis, and her father, who was a policeman, then committed suicide. This meant that she and her sister moved all over Scotland while they were growing up, staying with various relatives here and there.

During the war, Jessie enlisted in the Army Training Service in Glasgow and was moved down to Shrewsbury. She met the old man in 1943 and by the end of that year was pregnant. They married in January 1944 and seven months later my sister Heather was born at Retford army hospital, in Nottinghamshire.

After the war, the family set up home in Manor Park, which is where I was born the following Christmas, delivered by the bare hands of the old man himself. In those days, before the National Health Service was established, midwives charged to come to your house and so the old man thought nothing of doing it himself to save some dough. He was very much his own man like that. I was lucky to survive, though. Born with the umbilical cord wrapped tightly around my neck, I was so blue that the old man genuinely feared I was going to die. For the rest of his life he used to tell me that I had taken all his luck from him that day. I was a big baby too, and he nicknamed me 'Big Buddha' throughout my early years. The incident must have affected him quite badly because when my brother Kevin arrived in October 1947, he did so at East Ham Memorial Hospital. I was the only one of the old man's three children to be delivered by his own fair hand.

My mother was very sick when Kevin was born. She was suffering from the early stages of tuberculosis – the disease that had killed her own mother – and her health steadily deteriorated. She lost a lot of weight and was soon admitted to hospital.

It was a difficult time for the old man. He later told us that when my mother was allowed to come home for a few days during her illness, he used to stand me next to Heather on the kitchen table to show her how much we had grown since the last time she had been with us. They both knew she was dying and that must have been terrible for both of them.

My mother passed away in June 1949. The only lasting memory I have of her is being pushed around in a big black pram with Kevin when I was hardly more than a baby. We were all so young when she died. I was three, Heather was four and Kevin was just one.

The old man never had what you would call a proper job and back in those days he often got involved in protection rackets in the pubs and clubs of the East End to earn a few bob. Shortly after my mother died, we had to leave our house suddenly for some reason or other that was never explained to us. We travelled only ten miles or so back to the old man's roots in Barkingside, but that was a fair old distance in those days and far enough away to start a new life.

We moved into my grandfather's home on Neville Road. He had a lady friend staying with him at the time. She had won his heart after my grandmother's early death and had soon brought her mother along for a bit of company. My uncle Robert and his wife Mary were also living there with their baby daughter, Sylvia. In total, ten of us lived in that house, six adults and four children.

The old man just couldn't cope with three young children and he asked Ilford Borough Council for a home help. Relief arrived in the shape of Ruby, who then changed her name to Phyllis because she thought it sounded better. Whatever her name was, she was soon having an affair with the old man and within just a few months had replaced our mother in every single part of our lives.

Phyllis was some 20 years older than the old man, making him the original toy boy lover. Born in 1904, she was 45 years old when they got together and he was just 25. I don't blame the old man for that. As a family, we had to survive and he didn't have many choices open to him. He could either find himself another woman to help in the house or send the three of us off to Doctor Barnardo's. I am glad he decided to do it in the way that he did, but what was hard was never being allowed to mention the name of our dead mother.

He was very secretive about where she was buried and whenever Heather asked him about it, he would tell her, 'It's none of your business, so shut up.' Apparently, she lay in an unmarked grave in the grounds of Holy Trinity Church in Barkingside. We were never told which grave was hers and were never allowed to go there to try to find it. In fact, I don't know where my mother's grave is to this day. A few years ago a fire destroyed all the church records so I doubt that I will ever know. The old man lived with that secret all his life. He just wanted us to forget about our mother and love Phyllis instead.

Heather found that very difficult, which made the old man furious and Heather often got a smack from him as a result. I think that the 15-month age gap between the two of us made a huge difference to how we coped with our mother's death and the arrival of Phyllis in our lives. Kevin and I accepted the change just as the old man wanted us to, but Heather was that much older and suffered a lot more than we did. Perhaps it was due to being a girl as well.

The old man was horrible to Heather. He often called her names and made derogatory remarks about our late mother, knowing that they would cause her pain and upset. He once said to her, 'You're a slut, just like your mother was.' Of course, this is not the sort of thing any father should say to a young girl who has just lost her mother, but the old man could be cruel and nasty like that, particularly with his own flesh and blood.

I think he found difficulty in dealing with the fact that Heather was a girl. He treated her in a very masculine way and regularly refused to take her out of the house when she was young because he couldn't cope when she needed to go to the toilet. He was very much a man's man and my sister often took the brunt of that.

For all his faults, the old man was very loyal to Phyllis, staying with her until the day she died at the grand old age of 86. They never married but she took the name of George and he always regarded her as his wife.

By the end of the 1940s, the council re-housed the new George family at 5b Hamilton Gardens, Gants Hill in a flat above a bookshop. It was nothing special by any means but it seemed like Buckingham Palace to us at the time. The rooms were massive compared to what we had been used to. I shared a double bed with Kevin and we thought we were living in luxury.

The old man used to stay at home all day, spending most of his time in bed. When he did work it would be outside in the small garden that came with the flat. Phyllis was the worker of the two of them and earned what little money she could at a beetroot farm in Barkingside. Her job was man's work really. She unloaded lorries, skinned beetroots, washed celery and then prepared and packed them for markets. With so little money around, Phyllis would bring any leftovers home and every day would feed us on beetroot and celery. That is all that we ate and I am sure it is connected to me having rosy cheeks today! Our treat was a daily spoonful of malt syrup – free on the National Health Service – and I loved that.

There was one catch with Phyllis moving in with us and that was that she brought her 14-year-old son, Ronnie, with her. He became a sort of stepbrother to me but was bloody hard work at that age. His surname was Pain and that just about summed him up. Ronnie was over ten years older than me and would later join the Royal Air Force.

He was always smartly dressed and I remember him putting paper clips in his trousers to lose any creases when he hung them up.

Whenever Ronnie came home on leave, Kevin and I had to share a bedroom with him. That had one advantage in winter. It used to get very cold in that house but Ronnie – being a real mummy's boy – was allowed to have a gas fire whereas, when he wasn't there, we just had to shut up and freeze our nuts off.

Every Sunday morning, Ronnie would wake us up, give us some money and send us off to the shop to buy him a copy of the *News of the World*, a Wilkinson blade, 20 fags and a Mars bar, which he then ate in front of us while lying on his bed. Ronnie made us go for him in all weathers and never paid us a penny. He even blackmailed us by threatening to tell lies about us to Phyllis if we ever tried to say no.

Phyllis had two daughters as well – Daphne and June – but they were a lot older and didn't have much to do with us. It is a shame that Ronnie couldn't have done the same. The old man had actually dated Daphne when he was in his teens but that didn't stop him falling for her mother.

June and her husband, Ron, were very good to Heather, Kevin and me and became like an aunt and uncle to us. I think they just felt sorry for us because we had to go without so much. The only Christmas presents we ever got as children were from June and Ron. One year, courtesy of the Salvation Army, they bought Heather a doll and gave Kevin and me a cowboy suit to share. Those gifts made it the best Christmas ever.

Christmas was particularly hard. The three of us would hunt around the flat looking for something that we could nick, to give ourselves a treat. Heather once found a tin of the old man's Quality Street and we devoured the chocolates and then pushed all the empty wrappers up the chimney. We got away with it until the old man went to light a fire and all the wrappers fell down on him. He was livid. We got a good hiding for that and were sent to our rooms and left to starve throughout the rest of Christmas.

With so little money in her purse, Phyllis had no choice but to get most of our clothes second-hand from cheap jumble sales. She didn't do things by halves either and once bought me some leather breeches – real yodelling trousers they were, a few sizes too small for me. They showed off all of my thighs. I had to wear those bloody things all the time, even in the winter.

She wasn't proud at all. Worn-out y-fronts would be washed and hung out to dry on the washing line, for all the neighbours to see. It was embarrassing and I used to plead with her, 'My underpants have had it, Mum,' but she would just shout back, 'Shut up, they're clean, aren't they?'

No one could see my underpants when I wore them but everyone could see my shoes. Phyllis made me clean and polish them every day so they looked smart and presentable, even if the soles were riddled with holes and let in water.

Phyllis took a lot of pride in her own appearance and would save every spare penny so she could go to the hairdresser once in a while. She always used to say to me, 'Make sure you comb your hair, have a wash and tidy yourself up before you go out.' She instilled a pride in my appearance, which has stayed with me. How I look in public has always mattered to me. I never go on stage wearing dirty shoes, for instance. They are always clean and shiny. If my shoes are dirty, I feel dirty and so I make sure I clean them, even if they have got holes in them. That has remained with me as well.

Phyllis was an industrious person and it is fair to say that her language, and the old man's, was industrial too. They swore all the time at home and shouted a fair bit too. Heather, Kevin and I grew up with that as part of our daily lives and were brought up to accept swear words as a figure of speech. It became the language that we used. I have spoken like that myself ever since, even around my own children.

Phyllis would leave notes all over the place with swear words on them. If we ever came into the house with muddy boots on she would leave a piece of paper with the words 'Wipe your fucking feet' written on it. That is how she enforced her house rules on us.

For a giggle, Kevin once wrote 'Bollox' underneath her handwriting, spelling it incorrectly on purpose so that, knowing I wasn't too hot in the dictionary department, she would think it was my handiwork. I got two clips around the ear for that, one for writing down a swear word in the first place and the other for misspelling it!

Kevin regularly did that sort of thing. He knew that I would always be the one to get the blame and be on the receiving end of Phyllis' wrath. I would go to school to get away from all the shouting at home but when I got there the teachers would shout at me, too. It is a wonder I wasn't deaf by the time I was ten.

My first school was Gearies Infants School in Gants Hill and I absolutely hated it. In the years that immediately followed the war, most schoolteachers came from military backgrounds and were extremely tough individuals. Some of them spoke like they were still in the bloody army, and the kids with them. They seemed to enjoy dishing out punishment, both mental and physical, and I hated them, both for what they stood for and how they treated me. It was 'George, do this' and 'George, do that' all day bloody long. Whenever the old man was called by his surname, he would immediately respond, 'I am Mr George to you.' I learned that from him and answered the teachers back in the same way, saying, 'I am Mr George to you,' but all I got was more abuse and the slipper.

Academically, I wasn't the sharpest tool in the shed, a fact not lost on my classmates. The other kids quickly realised that when it came to words and numbers I was a bit thick, to say the least. This had a massive negative impact on me. I soon lost all my confidence and developed a stutter that was to stay with me throughout my school life. Added to a pitiable home life, I didn't have much going for me.

Never in my life has the difference between money and the lack of it been so apparent to me as it was in east London just after the war. And for children like me it was severe. There was a strong Jewish community in Gants Hill and a lot of the children at my school came from wealthy families. They would turn up at school looking nice in brand new clothes and I would be dressed in army surplus stuff. It was embarrassing. Sitting next to boys who were clean, smart and tidy was very hard for me. They would talk about having nice warm baths every night and we didn't even have any hot water at our house.

Once a week the old man would bring in an old tin bath from outside, fill it up with water and place it next to the fire. He would get in and get washed and then Heather – as the oldest child – would follow suit before it was my turn and then finally my brother's. By the time Kevin got into the water, it was freezing cold and the tub was completely full of scum. I dreaded getting into that tin bath and always spent as little time as possible in it. All these years later, I still wash very quickly and I am sure that is the reason why.

3 Pulling weeds and killing turkeys

By the time I was seven, the old man's eyesight had deteriorated so badly that he was placed on the blind register and we had to move to a new home at 3 Duke Gardens, Barkingside. The old man loved the outdoors and always wanted a bigger garden, where he could grow his own flowers. He was now able to realise that dream, although he could hardly see the results of his labours.

I would spend hours outside with the old man, listening to him, looking at him and learning from him. It wasn't easy for him, not being able to see, and a lot of his thoughts and ideas had to remain in his head. As I got a little older, he started to use me as his 'eyes' and to do things for him. That used to make me feel about ten foot tall and was just the tonic I needed with all the difficulties I faced at school.

One of the first skills the old man taught me was weeding. He showed me the difference between a Sweet William plant and a weed. Of course, when you are a small boy everything in the garden looks the same but there is a difference between a plant and a weed and eventually I was able to see that for myself and separate the two. The old man always offered me encouragement. 'Well done, Robin,' he would say. 'You're great at this you are, just like a grown-up man.' Those words meant so much to me. I totally idolised the old man and was never happier than when I was in his garden working for him.

By contrast, Kevin always got it wrong. He would come outside, pull all the flowers out of the ground and leave the weeds alone. The old man got very angry with him and wouldn't allow him anywhere near the plants. 'Get fucking out of it, Kevin,' he would bellow.

When it came to work, the old man had little time for Kevin. 'I wouldn't allow your brother to make my coffin,' he once told me, 'because when the coffin bearers go to pick me up, all the handles would fall off.'

That sort of comment always used to make me feel better about myself. I was the one who was able to help the old man. Kevin couldn't do that. I was the intelligent son. A few years later it dawned on me that Kevin wasn't stupid at all and he messed up on purpose just so he never had to do any work in the garden. Meanwhile, silly bollocks here stood outside in the rain saying, 'I know the difference between the weeds and the plants, Dad. You can rely on me.' I was working my nuts off while my brother was playing with his mates.

The old man was a one off. This is a bloke who would pull out his own teeth with pliers wrapped in cotton wool, just so he could save a few quid. He never went to a dentist and would happily walk around town with holes in his gums and lumps of flesh hanging out of his mouth. He loved nature, though, and adored animals and birds. He regarded them as kind and trustworthy creatures, the total opposite of how he saw mankind. 'Always trust your dog and always trust your birds. Those friendships are for life,' he told me. 'But don't ever trust human beings, they are deceitful and cunning and they will always let you down.' The old man was an environmentalist well before his time and often drilled into me that 'Mankind is destroying the world and polluting everything.'

His speciality was birds. He kept them all his life and knew everything there was to know about them, whether caged or wild. He knew where they would nest, what their eggs were like and the songs that they would sing. He was like Doctor Doolittle in that respect, trying to copy the birdsong so he could sing along with them. Every single bird in our garden knew him. I swear they did. That was his hobby, his life. When he was at school he taught all the other children birdsongs. He would test me on them, too, giving me a rollicking if I ever got one wrong.

The old man also bred rabbits and turkeys to make money, and this led to a particularly hard and painful lesson for me. I used to love having those rabbits and turkeys in the garden. We had dozens of them and I looked after them all, cleaning them out and feeding them. I got to know them all, considered them my friends and talked to them and stroked them as any young boy would do with his pets.

Then, just a few days after my eighth birthday at Christmas 1953, the old man told me to fetch some turkeys, break their necks and bag their heads. I didn't want to kill them but he answered me sharply, 'If you don't kill, you don't eat. That's life. Grow up.'

So the old man showed me how to kill them. He picked up a turkey by its legs, held on to the wings and then broke its neck by placing its head in the palm of his hand and pulling it down sharply while twisting his arm upwards. Then it was my turn and it was horrible. The poor bird's wings flapped about and its neck snapped as I killed it.

I had to learn how to keep hold of the wings carefully so that the meat on the legs would not bruise. Then I had to pluck them, truss them up, put plastic bags over them, suck the air out and then deliver them to his customers in the neighbourhood. The whole experience upset me greatly but I also felt very proud that I was doing something to please the old man, and that was the most important thing.

He taught me how to kill the rabbits too. I had to put my hand underneath the chin, my thumb over the back of the ears and then pull down and lift up sharply to break the neck. It was awful at first but I had to do it for him. I totally idolised him. I was very attached to those rabbits and once thought I had managed to save the life of one of the little fellows – my favourite – by placing it carefully to one side. The old man had seen what I was doing, though, and killed it right in front of me. 'Look, you've missed one,' he said, as he placed his hands around its neck.

Shooting those animals with a rifle would have been a lot easier for me – bang and it is dead. But to look after a creature for months, become a friend and then kill it with your bare hands – that is a lot harder.

Many people kept chickens, geese and turkeys at that time and on Christmas Eve the man of the house would go outside with a broom handle or something and kill the bird. Children would usually be spared the sight of that, but not at our house. Selling rabbits and turkeys was a business for us. We sold a lot of meat but there were no freezers in those days and so we were often left to eat all the leftovers ourselves. It would be turkey for a fortnight and then rabbit for a fortnight. That is what we kept, so that is what we ate. At least it made a change from the beetroot and the celery!

Maybe the fact that I found reading, writing and arithmetic so difficult at school made me want to impress the old man more, and the more I put into it, the more I got out of it. I was very good with my hands and the praise I received from him made the work enjoyable. If you are good at something, it comes easily to you. I never experienced that too much at school and so helping him outdoors meant much more to me. It gave me a bit of confidence and that suited the old man down to the ground.

He didn't believe in the education system anyway and never allowed any of us to do any homework. When I got home, he used to say to me, 'School's nine to four. Home time is time to work in the home.' He would rip up our homework and burn it on the fire. Once I was sent to detention class after school and then got clobbered by the old man for getting home late. That only happened once and then the old man put his foot down.

'Don't ever go to any detention class again,' he told me. 'If those fucking teachers can't teach you between the hours of nine and four, then they can't teach you afterwards either. If they don't like it, send them over here to see me.'

I told the teachers what the old man had said but they never took him up on his offer and I never had to do detention again. If ever the old man needed me to help him, I would just take two or three days off school. All my schoolwork was done in the yard at home for him.

The old man did allow Heather, Kevin and me some form of education by sending us all off to Sunday school every week. He was not religious in any way – in fact, he was an atheist – but maybe he saw it as a good opportunity to get his leg over on a Sunday morning. The man in charge at the Salvation Army, where we went, was Mr Meyers and he was the man who baptised me, which didn't go down too well at home.

Mr Meyers also showed me how to paint. I had a real talent for it and quite fancied myself as an artist for a while but, of course, there was never any chance of my parents being able to afford to send me on to further education after I left school. So I had to knock that dream on the head right there and then.

Later, when I had proper oils to paint with, I once created a piece of work featuring two cocker spaniels with really sad eyes. I used the oils to give depth to the painting and shaded the colours of the dogs for contrast. I was very pleased with the result and it was later sold to raise money for charity. For someone else to enjoy your work is a great thrill and they obviously liked it enough to buy it, whoever they were. I felt very proud about that, like I had really achieved something.

The Salvation Army was very good for me and, above everything else, it taught me how to respect things. I regularly cleared away rubbish from old people's gardens and mowed the lawns for them. I enjoyed doing all that much more than going to school.

Mr Meyers was a great influence on me. He taught me how to play the trombone and encouraged me to sing Christmas carols around the local streets. He also got me to take a pledge not to drink, smoke or go in to public houses, but that one was short-lived!

Although he had his ways, there is no doubt that the old man was a clever bastard. His mind was full of all sorts of information and a lot of what he knew was down to Phyllis, who would spend each and every night reading encyclopaedias to him. He couldn't see for himself and so he just listened to her and took in everything she said. Phyllis had tremendous patience and the old man had a tremendous memory. Together, they made quite a couple.

Unlike Heather, I now regarded Phyllis as my mum and was happy to call her such. She brought me up from the age of three and my birth mother is just a photograph to me. That hurts my sister, but it is the truth.

One day, I was looking out of the window at home and saw some boys riding pushbikes. I wanted one, too, so I said, 'Mum, all the boys around here have got pushbikes and I haven't. Can I have one please?'

She looked me straight in the eyes and gave me her answer. 'I haven't got the money to buy you a pushbike, and sitting there thinking about it isn't going to get you one, either.'

In those days, three or four quid would buy a pushbike but that was a lot of money, particularly for a family that didn't have two halfpennies to rub together.

'If you want a pushbike,' she added, 'you better get off your fucking arse right now, get outside and get yourself a job. Then you can buy one for yourself, can't you?'

So that is what I did. I knocked on doors and asked for work. I trimmed hedges and cleared out yards every day for two months. I would do anything just to earn some money.

My main money earner was horseradish. I collected horseradish plants from the side of the railway track and took them home to scrub and grate, piling the result into jars, which I sold for sixpence each. I soon earned enough money to buy myself a pushbike, and that is how I learned the true value of things. That pushbike cost me two months' hard work. Other boys down my street didn't have a clue how much their bikes cost. They were just handed them as presents, but my push-bike mapped out my life for me. Mum taught me that if you wanted something, you had to go out and get it. Any drive I have, I got from her, completely. I didn't inherit it, I was taught it. It was the way she lived her life until the day she died and I am exactly the same.

My parents had different attitudes but they each taught me so much. The old man showed me how to work and Mum gave me a working ethic, the 'get out and do it' routine. Together, they made me what I am today. Mum gave me hope when I was young, particularly when I struggled at school. Her philosophy was that I should better myself at every opportunity, which was totally different from the old man, who couldn't care less what happened.

My friend Johnny Smith, who lived across the road, came over to our house for dinner every now and again and once told me that if he could find a wife like my mum, then he would be made for life.

'Your mum's a proper mum,' Johnny told me. 'She does things other mums just talk about. When your mum says dinner will be at four o'clock, dinner is at four o'clock. I like that about her.'

His own mother had died when he was a young boy and his father didn't live much longer either, poor sod. Johnny was a loyal friend but he lived on his nerves. He was a few years younger than me and I treated him like another younger brother and took him everywhere with me. I think I was almost a father figure to him, especially after he lost both his parents. We had some good times together.

Mum was very strict when it came to food. If you ever missed a meal, you had to go without. She thought nothing of heating it up and serving it again the next day until you ate it. We weren't allowed to delve into the pantry if we were hungry, either. Her methods worked. She brought us up well and no one ever missed a meal in our house.

Now and again, we got cheese as a treat. We all loved cheese and Mum once handed a chunk to me and asked me to cut it into three pieces. Kevin asked for an inch, then Heather asked for an inch, which meant I was left with hardly any cheese at the end. Mum saw all this and hit me across the head, just for being plain stupid. Life was very tough for her and with so little money in our house we had to go without a lot as a family. I soon learned to cut portions within our limits.

By the time I moved to Newbury Park Junior School, my stutter was so bad that I was often too embarrassed to open my mouth and dreaded the thought of even going into school. I became withdrawn and began to keep myself to myself. The old man tried to help me with the stutter, advising me to breathe in slowly and think about every word I said, but whatever I tried I just couldn't get rid of the damned thing.

At Newbury Park I found to my cost how cruel children can be. Some of them took the piss out of me for having no money, for the second-hand clothes and cheap shoes that I wore, but mostly, of course, they made fun of my stutter. I couldn't answer them back without making it worse and I had to put up with a lot of mental bullying. That continued until the day I learned to put my hands up and hit back.

Luckily, I had a stuttering mate in Eric Pratt, and he endured as bad a time of it as I did. I got to know Eric through going to various markets and we became good friends, particularly when we realised that we both had a stutter. Eric knew a lot about nature and he taught me how to catch birds, which really pleased the old man. The two of us regularly played in the woods together. We would take a couple of hard brooms covered in a sticky resin, and place them next to a piece of wood that we had carved into the shape of a bird and painted like a goldfinch. We had a real goldfinch in a cage nearby and waited for it to sing its little heart out. This would attract plenty of birds and when they came over, bingo – they would get stuck to the brooms and we would cage them up. I took them home and the old man used them for breeding. Eventually, he would then sell them on or swap them for goods.

Despite my friendship with Eric being a profitable one in that way, our stutters became really bad. The old man tried to stop me from seeing him and Eric's old man tried to stop him from seeing me. They thought we were bad influences on each other's speech problems, and they were right. When we were on our own in the woods, it didn't matter so much, but in public we came across as a right pair of idiots. In fact, the old man used to call us such to our faces.

We tried so hard to crack it but just couldn't. We practised by trying to pronounce Eric's surname but neither of us could ever manage it. Looking back it was hilarious, but at the time it was difficult and very frustrating for both of us, and our families.

Eric eventually managed to lose his stutter – as I did mine – and now owns a pet shop. Let's just hope that we never meet up again because I am sure our stutters would come back to haunt us both again. They were always there when we were together.

Football was the number one sport at my new school but I never went a lot on it myself, despite the efforts of our headmaster, Ken Aston, an exceptionally nice man who was to become a dear friend to me. Mr Aston was an absolute giant of a bloke with great big ears, which made his head look just like the FA Cup. That was appropriate because he went on to forge a very successful career as a referee and was in charge of the 1963 FA Cup final between Manchester United and Leicester City at Wembley Stadium. He also went to three World Cups, refereeing in Chile in 1962 and officiating for FIFA in England in 1966 and in Brazil in 1970.

Mr Aston is especially remembered for two matches that have gone down in World Cup folklore. In 1962, he sent off two Italian players – Giorgio Ferrini and Mario David – during Italy's bruising and bloody encounter with hosts Chile, a match now infamously known as 'The Battle of Santiago'. Mr Aston was right there in the thick of it, and said later, 'I wasn't refereeing a football match that day, I was acting as an umpire in military manoeuvres.'

Four years on, in the World Cup quarter-final between England and Argentina at Wembley, Mr Aston became a national hero when he came down from the stands to escort Antonio Rattin to the dressing room after the Argentine captain had been sent off but refused to leave the pitch. My old headmaster could speak Spanish and because of this – and probably his size – he was able to talk sense into Rattin and get him off the pitch, ending over ten minutes of appeals and arguments.

Rattin's excuse was that he didn't know that he had been sent off. The next day, Mr Aston found a solution to this problem when he came up with the idea of introducing red and yellow cards in football matches, while he was sat in his car at some traffic lights on Kensington High Street.

Mr Aston had a brilliant mind like that and always made his classes fun at school. He often asked us to help him plan his journey to football grounds, working out railway timetables and things. I used to love doing that. We calculated distances and trips, such as how long it would take to get from London to Liverpool with a change at Manchester. He always said this was a big help to him. He used to referee a match in the old First Division on most Saturdays.

When it came to playing football, I never had any kit of my own and always had to borrow it. The shorts were usually two sizes too small and the boots two sizes too big. The leather ball we played with was so big and heavy that when you kicked it your knee almost fell out.

Mr Aston knew I didn't like football and so he always put me in goal. Apparently, I had the perfect build for a goalkeeper but I think he just said that to get me interested. One day he took me to one end of the pitch to show me how to save penalties. Mr Aston – a grown man of 6ft 6in – placed the ball on the penalty spot and told me which corner he was going to kick it towards and where I should dive. I dived correctly, went to catch the ball and ended up dislocating my finger. He drove me to hospital, explaining on the way that, when it came to penalties, I should always punch the ball or push it away and never attempt to catch it. The pain was quite bad and a doctor had to straighten out my fingers before he could strap them together. From then on, I always had a cold when it came to football lessons.

Mr Aston was a true gentleman and in later years I often rang him up at home for a chat and to ask how things were going. He and his wife Hilda always called me 'Our Robert' and loved to watch me playing darts on TV. He used to say that our trip to hospital made me a better darts player. I damaged my throwing hand that day and he always joked that the injury gave me more flexibility when I threw.

Mr Aston always treated me with respect and shortly before he passed away a few years ago he told me that I was still the same as the boy he had taught in the 1950s. 'You always did things your own way and now you've made a success of your life,' he said.

He always asked how the old man was, too. Of course, the old man never visited my school. 'Fuck parents' evening,' was how he responded whenever I handed him an invitation to talk through my education with the teachers. But Mr Aston loved flowers. He lived in the same house all his life and always bought flowers from us, which he remembered well. 'He was a very tough man, your father,' he told me. That bloke was a true diamond, and the best teacher I ever had.

Something I did enjoy at school was dancing, which was somehow on the curriculum in those days. We had lessons every week and I found that I was quite good at it. Mavis Smith was my dancing partner and together we won our age group in a regional competition, held at the Ilford Palais.

I never regarded Mavis as being particularly pretty but a few of my mates were quite jealous of me dancing with her, so obviously the girl had something going for her. Mavis could definitely dance, I will give her that, and she was very much the talented one of the two of us. She had all the proper dancing gear, too, while I just wore a dress shirt and a pair of ordinary trousers.

Away from school, my childhood was quite a productive time. I made sure that I took advantage of everything that was around me, particularly outdoors. One of the best things about growing up in London was being able to use the underground. By the age of ten, I was going on it all by myself, catching a train at Gants Hill and arriving in the city centre less than an hour later. All the museums were free and I regularly visited the National History Museum and Imperial War Museum for the cost of just a few pennies on the train. Londoners don't know how lucky they are to have the underground system.

It was around this time that I fell in love with fishing. My friend Bob Prue got me into it and we regularly walked to Hainault Forest, more than three miles away, to fish in the lakes there.

Bob was the eldest of five children – four of them boys – and my best mate when I was growing up. His family's house became a second home to me and we had some rare old times together until we both got hitched and settled down. We spent a lot of time down at the aerodrome in Barkingside, where we played around with any old junk, burned tyres and pored over pictures of women in naughty magazines such as *Titbits*. I made my first fishing rod from an old tank aerial that I found there. After the war you could easily get hold of tank aerials. I put a handle on it and an eye for the line. I never caught much with it but I just loved fishing, sat out in the fresh air surrounded by nature.

Another boy, Geoff Meader, would fish at the lakes in Hainault Forest, too. Geoff always arrived nice and early and if ever you asked if he had caught anything, he always replied, 'Oh yes, I've got some perch, roach, and a couple of pike already,' but when you looked in his net, there was nothing there. 'They were so big, I had to put them all back in the lake,' he would say. I never saw Geoff catch anything.

When I wasn't with Bob, I was usually messing about at the aerodrome with another mate of mine, Mickey Steele. Mickey lived close by and we used to spend hours making tree houses and playing about in old air-raid shelters and wartime bunkers. One day the two of us went behind a bush to do what little boys do and as we were stood next to each other, Mickey looked down at mine and said, 'How come you've got the oak tree and I've got the acorn?' He still reminds me of that today.

By the time I arrived at Gearies Secondary School at the age of 11, I realised that I was very slow academically. All that 'add five to make ten' bollocks just did my head in. I never got into reading or writing and didn't stop to consider what I was going to do about that when I left school. I never wrote letters or lists. All that I was sure of was that I couldn't do it. It was like looking through a window and everything being black.

Most of the teachers at my school gave up on the thick kids and threw them on the rubbish dump. They just concentrated on helping the brighter ones, which obviously didn't include me. Times have changed for the better and these days children who struggle at school are generally given more help and advice, but back then the education system was harsh. It was definitely a case of once a dunce, always a dunce.

I had a natural talent for sport, though. Whether it was running, jumping or throwing, I used to love to get involved and always looked forward to school sports days. I excelled in running, both on the track and cross-country, and enjoyed the javelin and shot-putt.

Of course, any young athlete who wants to get on needs the right gear – the shirt, the shorts, the socks, the spikes – and there wasn't much chance of that in the George household. I have always believed that if you look the part, you act the part, and going without so much as a child had a lot to do with me dressing up when I became a darts player. I badly wanted to look the part and it felt so good. I also found that when I felt good about myself, I played better darts.

The school sports ground was about five miles from my house and I would get over there on my own two feet. I would run to the sports ground, run a race and then run back home afterwards, to save the bus fare. Well, you can't be doing that, not if you want to do well anyway. I was knackered before I started and, unsurprisingly, my athletics career never got off the ground. My parents never came to school to watch me participate in those sports days, just like they never came along to any of the parents' evenings at school. Neither of them showed any interest in my schooling at all and that hurt me a lot, particularly at that age.

I soon discovered that I had another physical talent – I was a good fighter. Although I still struggled with a stutter, within a few months of moving to the new school I was no longer subjected to having the piss taken out of me. This was in no small part due to Bob Prue. Three years older than me, he was the guv'nor at Gearies by the time I arrived. No one messed with Bob, not even the teachers, and Bob looked after me. First years usually get picked on by boys three or four years older but there was none of that with him around.

Bob taught me how to hold my own against the older boys. I was developing very quickly physically – by the age of 12 I stood 6ft tall and weighed over 14 stone – and the time seemed right to fight back against the bullies. When they poked fun at my stutter, I struggled to answer them back verbally and so I just started hitting them instead. That soon sorted it out and from then on anyone who laughed at me in any way got beaten up. I was a big boy now and I'd had enough. Fighting came very easily to me and soon the bullying and torment that I had suffered at the other schools was a thing of the past. It was simple really. I just had to learn to put my hands up. I didn't have to say a word, which was just as well because I still found a lot of difficulty in doing that.

I had to become aggressive to survive. I have never thrown the first stone in my life but my mum drilled into me that 'kindness is a weakness' and she was right. I had to look after myself, and I had to sort my mum out, too. She was a tough old bird and regularly bullied me herself.

I had longed to learn to play the guitar for quite a while – I fancied myself as the new Elvis Presley – and as a young teenager I decided to save up all my money and buy one. It took me a lot of toil and trouble and I absolutely treasured that instrument. Of course, I didn't have a clue how to play it and it must have sounded bloody awful as I tried to pick out the chords, but that was the only way to learn.

Late one night, Mum charged into my bedroom and screamed at me, 'Stop that fucking row now.' I told her that I had to learn how to play and the only way was to keep trying.

'Don't you ever fucking answer me back,' she shouted. She picked up my beloved guitar and smashed it over my head. It broke into tiny pieces and all the strings dangled around my neck. I was heartbroken. I was furious. I snapped. I wasn't going to take this sort of treatment from anyone any longer, not even her. As a child I had learned how to throw knives and kept a few long ones in my bedroom. I picked one up and held it to her throat.

'If you ever hit me again, you'll get this between your fucking ribs,' I told her.

She rushed downstairs to tell the old man and then got rid of every single knife in the house except one. She was left with just one kitchen knife, which she always kept hidden from me. From that day on until the day I left home I had to eat all my meals with just a fork. I was never allowed to use a knife and had to have all my meat cut for me.

I sorted out her son, too. Ronnie was horrible to Kevin and me when we were young boys and whenever he returned home, he behaved like an arsehole. Heather disliked Ronnie as well and once she secretly stuffed some holly into his pillowcase. It scratched his face something rotten and caused him a fair bit of pain, but that was nothing.

By the time I got to 14, I was a different boy. Ronnie, who was now in the army, came home on leave one day and started going off at me, as he always did, but I'd had enough. He was 24 years old and a grown man, but I told Kevin to lock the door and then offered Ronnie a fight.

'You're an army boy, right?' I said. 'So, let's see how you rate as a soldier.' I put him on the floor with my first punch and every now and then, Kevin put the boot in. At the end, he was pleading for us to stop.

From that day on, my relationship with Ronnie changed. He suddenly became a decent bloke. I didn't show him any malice and we got on fine. He later lent me his driver's licence so that I could teach myself how to drive.

I mainly wanted to drive so that I could help the old man train his pigeons. He needed someone to take the pigeons out and release them a long way away so that they could find their way back home. Those birds were his life and he was very protective of them. A cat once got into his shed and tried to get at them and he got out his rifle and tried to shoot it on the spot. He took aim but being such a blind beggar he hit the neighbour's car door instead. The old man eventually caught up with the cat in the greenhouse and when it went for him with its claws, he got hold of it and pulled its head right off, killing it on the spot.

I learned to drive by borrowing a friend's Morris Eight from a local yard. I just put it into gear and off I went, driving it up and down the same road for weeks on end. I learned how to reverse and turn corners down by Barkingside tube station and I was out on the road in a few weeks.

School started to become more enjoyable. My favourite time of the day was always lunchtime and I adored the dinner ladies. They could see that I was a big boy and would hand me second and third helpings to try to fill me up. I was also milk monitor and this meant I took crates of milk to all the classes and then collected the empties later. I would take all the straws out and finish off the bottles myself until I couldn't drink any more. It was much better than anything I was going to get at home and so I made the most of it.

During my last year at Gearies, I began to show an interest in girls. Some of the boys brought dirty magazines to school and we would sit by a tree and learn all about the birds and the bees. I am sure it was well written but, of course, I could only look at the pictures!

We played kiss chase with the girls and one of them – a fat lass with glasses – really fancied me. She never even bothered to hide and would just stand there and wait for me to find her and kiss her. 'Can you see me, Robert?' she would cry out. Well, I wasn't having any of that. I pretended to be as blind as the old man and totally ignored her. She never did get a kiss out of me.

I was very good at metalwork and often took the class when our teacher, Mr Tucker, had to nip off to the staffroom to do something. I made a lot of things in metalwork. My speciality was ashtrays and I could knock one out in less than an hour. It would be a proper job as well. Some of the other pupils needed a whole term to make an ashtray and it would be rubbish. It used to take me a lesson and then I would flog it for a couple of bob.

My mate Johnny Smith wasn't too good at metalwork and once when Mr Tucker asked us to make an ashtray, he pinched the teacher's and put his own initials on it. When Mr Tucker gave out his marks, he gave Johnny four out of ten. We looked over at each other and couldn't stop laughing but Mr Tucker had the last laugh. He had realised what was going on because that ashtray was the best one in the class.

For all my talents in art and metalwork, I was absolutely hopeless at English. I hated the subject and once tried to do a deal with my teacher by offering to make her an iron gate in return for not going to her class. She was unimpressed but I tried anything and everything in the hope of missing an English lesson.

Mr Tucker was one of the good guys and I got on well with him. He was one of the few teachers to show me any form of respect during my final years at school. Most of them looked down on me because of my difficulty with anything academic. They thought I had no intelligence.

The worst treatment came from my woodwork teacher, Mr Saunders. He had been a Sergeant Major in the war and I think someone must have forgotten to tell him that it was all over. He would scream so loud that I nicknamed him 'Hitler', and he obviously disliked me. He wasn't on his own.

With my schooldays coming to an end, I eventually decided to take no more of this crap from the teachers, and after sorting out the bully boys, I moved on to one of the bully men.

I was messing about one day in art class – a subject that I actually enjoyed – and some relief teacher caught me red-handed. He came over and started having a go at me in front of the whole class. He spoke to me more man-to-man than teacher-to-pupil. It was the sort of conversation that I would be getting into on a Saturday night down the boozer in a few years' time.

After failing to make his point, he started saying things to wind me up. 'You really think you're a big boy, do you, George?' and 'You really think you're a strong man, do you, George?' When he suddenly suggested getting out some boxing gloves and having a fight, I was well up for it. I'd had enough of him. He told me he had boxed before but I didn't care about that. I might have been just 14 years old but I was already the size of a man and knew I could take care of myself, particularly against the likes of him. We went straight down to the school gym and I knocked him out in front of the whole class. It was a fantastic feeling.

I left school the following week.

4 Going underground

I left school hardly able to read or write. One reason for that was my stutter. I never felt comfortable opening my mouth at school and if you don't want to speak, it is difficult to ask questions and learn. Once you miss the first step in anything, you get left behind and that is exactly what happened to me with reading and writing.

Remarkably, I have always had beautiful handwriting – maybe it is an artistic talent – but it went to waste for many years until I became famous and started signing autographs. Anyone who knew me at school would never have imagined that I would go on to work for the BBC one day. Ken Aston and I used to laugh about that and I still have to pinch myself whenever I appear on the box and speak to the nation.

I left school in the spring of 1960 at the age of 14 with not one qualification to my name, little confidence and a stutter I couldn't get rid of. Somehow I had to find a way of making some money and I had to do it quickly. My parents were struggling to keep their heads above water themselves and were in no position to help me. Life looked as though it was going to be a pretty rough ride, but within weeks it all turned around. Eric Pratt, my stuttering soul mate, got me a job working at George Abbott's flower nursery near Mawney roundabout in Romford, and I soon discovered that I was much more suited to working for a living than I had ever been to education.

Eric got me the break that I needed. I took to working life right away and absolutely loved it. I found the job easy because the old man had grown flowers for years and Mum sold them. I cycled ten miles to work and then grew flowers and bedding plants all day long, before taking them into town to be sold at the big markets. It was such a transformation for me. I was in control of what I was doing and felt as though I belonged at Abbott's.

I also found that the more educated boys from my school weren't as clever as I thought they were going to be in the big, wide world. That shocked me at first but it also gave me a massive boost of self-confidence. I only really competed with those boys at school on paper and I always came off second-best in that game. Now I was competing with my hands and the only time that I had really done that at school was in the playground, when I had my fists up. I soon realised that those boys weren't that much brighter than I was after all. They had just been better at reading and writing. That is all. There are more ways of judging someone's intelligence than what they can do on a bit of paper and I was finding that out for myself down at the nursery. For all their education, when it came to the work yard, some of them were completely lost.

It was a fantastic time for me. It was like I had discovered wings and could fly. I had found a path. All I needed was to be good at the things that interested me and to work hard at the jobs that paid me.

Abbott's paid quite well for boys of my age and the work introduced me to real London life with weekly trips to Covent Garden every Wednesday night. Once we got there, we could earn a further ten shillings for ourselves by working as barrow boys and unloading lorries for men who had come from out of town.

In those days, old Covent Garden had two great big gates. I soon learned to wait at the back of the queue until those gates were unlocked and then shoot around the side to pick up the best barrows – which made off-loading easier and quicker – as all the grown men pushed like hell and struggled to get through.

When my work was done, I was often asked to join the lorry drivers and market traders for a pint but, although it was nice to feel like one of the men, I was far too interested in making money to join them in the pub, and would politely decline.

Any fiddles that were going on, I would be in on them. Some old boy would tell me to go and grab some flowers and quickly take them to a certain stall, making sure no one saw me. I picked up a lot of half crowns doing stuff like that on the sly and I was soon regularly earning about £3 per night, which for 1960 was pretty decent dough. The bees and honey were already my main focus.

I loved the smell and touch of money from a very early age – maybe because there was so little of it about in our house – and so when I started earning I was in my element. I collected florins – two bob bits in old money – and carefully stacked them up to a certain height on a shelf in my bedroom before taking them down to the post office to pay into my savings account. Sometimes it took ages to build up that pile of florins and that confused me, until the day my brother Kevin told me he was pinching them off the shelf. I never noticed, but as daft as I had been, I learned a big lesson and never made that mistake again. Overnight I became a lot smarter where money was concerned.

A few months after starting at Abbott's, I was approached by two men in the Fairlop Oak pub in Barkingside with the offer of some decent money to model clothes in a photo shoot. I was very wary of them and feared that they may be a couple of homosexuals – who were coming out of the closet in their droves in London at that time – and up to no good. I rejected their offer without giving it any consideration.

The old man thought I was an idiot for turning down such an opportunity to make some easy money but I was genuinely scared of what I might be letting myself in for. I suppose if I had gone along with it, I could have had an entirely different career mapped out in front of me. Who knows? Instead, I stuck with the flowers before eventually moving into the building game.

For all that the old man didn't want me to pal around with Eric Pratt, there is no doubt that my mate played a massive part in my early working days. It was due to him that, after 18 months of growing flowers, I took my first steps into properly working with my hands. Eric told me about a job that was going at B. Finch Ltd, in Barkingside, working on building maintenance, which involved bricklaying, joinery, painting, plastering and plumbing. He put in a word for me and I got it. The job offered a proper trade, doubled the money I was getting at the flower market and allowed me to live the life I wanted.

Cars were always my passion, much more than birds. I loved cars and spent a lot of my money on them. I was still a year away from being old enough to take my driving test but I was already a capable driver and had been driving up and down the country for a couple of years.

My first car was a Ford Popular. I bought it at 16 and insured it in Ronnie's name. It cost less than a tenner but gave me my own set of wheels. When I turned 17 I had to take a test so I could get my own driver's licence – I had been using Ronnie's since the age of 14 – and after passing me the examiner asked how long I had been driving. I told him a week or so. The honest truth was well over two years.

After passing my test, I splashed out on a Vauxhall Cresta. It was a nice-looking car but I looked far too flash in it and wrote it off any-way when I hit a tree in Ongar. I replaced it with an Austin Healey 3000, which really was the business.

There was a lot for me to learn at Finch's but I found the work easy and very satisfying. I wanted to learn and possessed a real energy for working hard, so I would happily graft around the clock, both for my employer and for myself. I soon became a real Jack of all trades. I did a lot of jobs in my spare time to earn a bit of extra money, at the end of a long, hard working day or at weekends. Every Sunday I worked for a painter and decorator in Ilford called Geoff Lynge. I once painted all the houses down Netley Road – £14 for the front and £7 for the back. I worked as hard as I could for Geoff to earn as much money as I could for myself.

With a variety of jobs coming in I decided that my next motor should be a van. As soon as the old man heard about it, he roared, 'We'll get a lot of pigeons in that, son.' The van put a twinkle in his blind eyes and soon I was loading the pigeons up by the dozen and driving up to Peterborough to release them all for him. By the time I got to the Midlands, I desperately wanted to get rid of the bloody things but the weather conditions had to be right before I could do that. It was cloudy and that meant the pigeons could easily get lost, so I had to sit and wait for the rainstorm to come and go, and when it was fine, let them out for their return trip. I clocked the time the pigeons left Peterborough and with the recorded times of when they arrived back in London, we could work out which birds were the fast ones.

Kevin also went on pigeon duty in my van but, being a clever bas-tard, he just drove around the corner and played cards at his mate's house. He would let the birds out and call up the old man, saying he had released them an hour or so earlier. He worked all the timings out so that they matched and spent the day gambling. When I trained the pigeons, I tried to do it properly, even if it meant sitting in the Peterborough rain for two hours.

I was happy, though. I was earning decent money and I was playing hard as well – young, free, single and out to enjoy myself. I made sure that I always had a good night out with my mates on a Saturday. Everyone lived for Saturday night. It was the night to put on your best suit and let your hair down. My favourite suit was made of mohair with bright red lining, and I had paper collars and cuffs. I used to wear it with a pair of winkle pickers.

I usually went out on the town with the Prue boys. We would jump in my car and hit the pubs and clubs most weekends. Sometimes we would get into a row on the road before we had even had a drink.

Old man Bobby Prue was the main cause of the trouble. He played the piano and we always seemed to end up at some pub with him banging out a tune on the old Joanna. Usually, after everyone had had a few drinks, someone would have a go at him – over the music or someone's seat – and a big row would start up. We would all pile in and the fists would fly.

For a young man in his late teens in the East End back then, Saturday nights were more about fights than birds. It was just the way it was. Unless you ended up with a black eye you didn't feel as though you'd had a proper night out. I am sure that was how the Prue boys saw it, and I was just the same. In the early 1960s it was easy to find a spot of bother. The Fiddlers in Dagenham provided good entertainment most weekends. It was a crazy time but good fun. Everyone was on rum and black and out of their heads.

Apart from that, most of my time was spent at work, where I could stay out of trouble and focus on making money. Finch's was a good place to be and I managed to get Kevin a job there when he left school. He repaid me with bells on, by introducing me to my first wife.

Betty was dark-haired and came from Barkingside. She was a couple of years younger than I was, about the same age as Kevin, and began working at Finch's at the same time as he did. The three of us soon started going out together as a group with a few others from work.

Kevin had known Betty since they were both 14 and in some ways I thought she was more suited to him than to me. He was more outgoing, quite forward and a lot louder, and I think she liked that sort of thing, but Betty was more interested in me. She used to walk past me at work singing that Susan Maughan record 'Bobby's Girl', which was a big hit at the time. It used to drive me up the bloody wall. Then she started turning up at the house, knocking on the door and asking me to go out with her.

I had never really had a proper relationship before. I was just too busy making what money I could and enjoying myself to think about having a girlfriend. Girls weren't a priority in my life. I was much happier spending my spare time fishing.

Don't get me wrong. I wasn't behind the door. I had slept with a few birds but I didn't class any of them as girlfriends. I was too young and too busy to get serious. I was quite shy, too, and as soon as girls began to put any pressure on, suggesting dates and stuff like that, I would give them the elbow. Things can change in your life, though. You leave school, learn how to drive, get a car, get a job and then get a bird, I guess.

Betty was persistent. She had lost her dad when she was young and I think that made her need a man in her life, someone who could give her financial security and support. I went out with her on and off for years and after a while we got engaged. I can't remember ever asking her, so maybe she asked me. It is my nature to go along with things sometimes so that would make sense. I never once thought about marrying her. I just put all my energies into work and let the other side of my life look after itself.

By the time I was approaching my 18th birthday, Finch's had really taught me everything it could and, although it paid well, I knew I could earn more money elsewhere – at Kenny and Moody for instance. They were tunnel construction specialists, working on the proposed Victoria Line for the London Underground.

I got a job with them through a chap called Brian Rose. He was lying on his back in my street one day, playing around with the brakes of his car. I asked him if he needed a hand and ended up fixing his car for him. He told me about the underground project and said he was an agent on the lookout for tunnel workers. I was immediately interested. It promised massive money and sounded like a challenge. It was also an opportunity for me to do something that would last forever underneath the streets of London.

I went along to the firm's head office for a chat and was asked if I had any experience in that game. The answer was none but I made it clear that whatever I was asked to do, I would handle, and I was offered a job. The Victoria Line kept me busy for a few years. It was very good money and attracted interest from a lot of men, but you had to be fit and strong to do the job. Any fakers soon got found out.

At first I was a ganger on the night shift. We operated from a deserted aerodrome and I was put in charge of eight men. Our task was to prepare gigantic metal moulds, tighten them up and grease them. When ten segments were ready, they were transported in sections to where the tunnel was to be dug. Concrete was poured around the metal and when it had set, the moulds were taken apart, cleaned up and greased for work to be carried out on the next section.

We were meant to break the moulds with spanners but they were so frustrating to work with that I replaced them with automatic air guns. That saved us a lot of time. We undid each of the moulds in less than a minute with those power tools and completed that part of the job within hours.

I let all the boys go home early. I never told anyone about it but workers never forget things like that. I just used my loaf and got the job done quickly. That earned respect and friendship. We paid for those tools out of our own pockets and they were worth every single penny.

Building the rings took us about six months in all and was easy money compared to what came next – digging the tunnel. My gaffer explained to me that I was rather young to work underground but said he would turn a blind eye to that if I really wanted to do the work. I was dead keen and very confident that I could do a good job for him, despite having no experience in that line of work.

I started off at the pit bottom, more than 80 feet underground. To get down the shaft, you either climbed down a ladder, which could be quite frightening, or a crane would lower you down in a big bucket. Once down there, you were faced with another choice – walk to the face of the tunnel or get on a small battery-operated locomotive that took you there.

Accidents were common and sometimes horrific. One man, a big strong fellow who loved to play rugby, had his hand cut off by the rams as he tried to turn the tunnel. A lot of the locomotive drivers lost fingers when they put their hands out to the sides of the tunnel. Many workers, myself included, would regularly do double shifts because the money was so good, and tiredness sometimes affected concentration. That was often fatal. Working with a winch and all sorts, you were always aware that if someone didn't do their job properly, part of the tunnel could end up falling on your head.

Once, I carelessly put my right hand into a cement mixer and had to be rushed to hospital, where the first diagnosis was to cut off my finger from the knuckle. I felt sick and asked if there was nothing that could be done to prevent this. A young Indian doctor examined it and said he could try to sew the finger back together. Thankfully, the operation was a success and the finger, which is on my throwing hand, has been as good as new ever since. I still have the scar to remind me how daft I was. I was very lucky and without that doctor's intervention and skill I wouldn't have had any sort of career in darts.

We were digging out virgin soil from the actual face of the tunnel at this time, with the permanent threat of water rushing in. London happens to be full of dry, blue clay, which breaks up like coal. This all had to be shovelled out with a spade and that is how we extended the tunnel, bit by bit as we went along.

There is no denying that digging the Victoria Line was a dangerous job and the risk of a disaster occurring was high, but a lot of that was due to the era in which we were working. Regulations in the 1960s were nothing like they are today. Health and safety? Forget it! I wore a pair of shorts and baseball boots – no shirt, no hard hat, nothing. There were no toilets down there, either. If you wanted to go to the toilet you had to go in the tunnel near to where you were working. Just get it done and get back to work. Over 40 years on, there is no way tunnel workers would be asked to work in those conditions.

I made some good mates while I was digging those tunnels. There was a great team spirit – a lot of good boys and a lot of good drinkers – but we had to get on together. We had no choice. We were pissing, shitting and eating in the same spaces with nowhere to wash our hands and no toilet paper. You had to wipe your arse on your hand and then wipe your hand on the tunnel wall. When you work hard in conditions such as that you don't necessarily have the urge to urinate because you sweat so much, but your bowels are working overtime to compensate. It didn't make for a pretty sight or a pretty smell, for that matter. It used to stink down there, but what else could you do?

I worked 16 hours a day but I was a young, fit man and found that all that shovelling was good for my muscles as well as my bank balance – but I won't ever let it be said that we were paid too much money. I saw men lose limbs down there and working in such squalid conditions was no fun for any of us.

Like all underground tunnels everywhere in the world, the Victoria Line has different depth levels and lines decline over certain distances. It is difficult and dangerous to dig deep without doing so gradually. Some tube stations in London have lines three and four deep where different lines meet, and it is truly mind boggling to try to understand how it works. Believe me, it isn't much clearer to me and I have been down there.

The route and direction of any line is worked out mathematically but it is far from simple. You can dig blue clay 80 feet underground at one end of the line and a few miles on you will be into ballast, or another underground line or water. This all has to be worked out by surveyors and engineers before the workmen can start.

I helped dig the Victoria Line from Tottenham Hale to Green Park. That is a fair old stretch, so spare a thought for me should you ever make that journey in the future. I did do some work a little further along the line at Blackhorse Road too, but we hit a pocket underneath a reservoir and water came rushing in, completely flooding the face of the tunnel into a ready mix. We had to run like hell to get out and, thankfully, no one was injured.

I worked on the Victoria Line for the best part of three years from start to finish and once it was completed, I was offered a job digging tunnels in Hamburg, Germany, through a fellow tunneller, Phil Page. I declined the offer but Phil went over to Hamburg and got very badly injured when a shaft snapped. Many of his colleagues were crushed to death in the disaster.

I had done the job long enough to know how dangerous it was and that incident in Hamburg convinced me that it was time to move on and do something else with my life.

5 Pubs, clubs and knuckle-dusters

It was great to grow up in the sixties. That decade really was how it has been written about on the fag packet – sex, drugs and rock 'n' roll. The changing of attitudes made my teens and early twenties a special time for me. Suddenly, anyone from anywhere could achieve anything. For me, that meant working as hard as I could to make money, and I worked my nuts off.

I left home in 1966 after a row with the old man and went to live with a mate, Melvin Burpitt, in Fairlop Road, Barkingside before moving into my own rented flat in Ilford. Of course, one moment sums up that time more than any other in England and that is when our national football team won the World Cup in 1966. Everyone remembers where they were and what they were doing on that day and I am no different. I was painting a bloke's front room in Chigwell with my back to the TV set!

There were no cars on the road that day and all the shops were completely empty. There was not a single soul about. It is the only time in my life that I can ever remember the whole country just switching off from their normal routine. The old man told me that World Cup final day was similar to the Queen's Coronation in 1953, but more people owned TV sets by 1966 so I guess it was even quieter than that.

The match attracted a record TV audience. I was probably the only person in the entire country who was working that day and that just about summed me up. I was far too busy earning a crust to bother with some football match.

West Ham United captain Bobby Moore was already a local legend and he became a national hero when he collected the World Cup from the Queen that summer, but that didn't stop me giving him a mouthful when he cut me up in his S-type Jag on Gants Hill roundabout shortly afterwards. I don't know how he missed me. I caught up with him and we had a good old row about it. World Cup captain or not, Bobby was from the same area as me and we both spoke the same language!

Music was a big thing in my life in the 1960s. I liked The Beach Boys, The Kinks and Frank Sinatra. They were all big pop stars in their day but The Beatles were the biggest and the best. How those boys wrote so many brilliant and beautiful songs still staggers me to this day. When 'Twist and Shout' came out, I bought my first ever leather jacket. That was the look back then. Everyone wanted to be a Beatle, or to look like one anyway. I paid £15 for it and it probably came off the back of a lorry, but that was a lot of money in those days. Almost overnight, shirts and suits went out of fashion and leather jackets and polo-neck jumpers became all the rage. What was so fantastic about The Beatles was how they transformed themselves, in terms of both music and fashion, to mirror the changes of that time. They were really something special.

Working on the underground had done no harm to my physique and I was now in better nick than I had ever been. It was only a matter of time before it got around that I was a naturally strong man and able to handle myself. So it was no surprise when I started to get asked to work on the doors of various pubs and nightclubs as a bouncer.

I knew some boys who were already employed in that line of work and it seemed right up my street. I was big, fit and strong and not afraid to put my hands up. I was a good fighter at school but I wasn't a bully and never went looking for trouble. I just knew how to look after myself. I was never the type of bloke to start a row but I always knew how to finish one. It is human nature that the best way to make a living is by doing something that you are good at. Not everyone can sit behind a desk. We all have to earn a crust and take our chances in life, whatever they may be and wherever they may come.

I worked on the door at a number of establishments throughout east London, including Barkingside, Chadwell Heath, Dagenham, Elm Park, Ilford, Manor Park and Newbury Park. I never knew the Kray twins. They were obviously very well known in the area but by the time I came on the scene, they had both gone to prison.

Nightclubs are generally nice places frequented by nice people and today things are not much different from how they were 40 years ago. By the second half of the sixties, when boys reached their late teens – especially where I come from – all they wanted to do on a night out was impress the birds and have a few beers with their mates, and if they had to put their hands up during the evening, that is what they did. Bouncers are generally nice people, too. They are just doing a job like everyone else. When I did it, I tried to be nice most of the time. Well, as nice as I could be!

My first job was comfortable work at the Green Gate in Newbury Park. Mike Reid, now famous for playing Frank Butcher in *EastEnders*, was a very successful comedian and used to do a regular turn there. I got on well with him. There was also a disco and a few stand-ups. It was a good night out with not much bother going off at all.

Then I moved on to the Room At The Top in Ilford, a much bigger place with far more potential for trouble. Some nights it could be relatively quiet – a few pints, a bit of aggro and fish and chips on the way home – but usually some sort of incident blew up and it was my job to sort it out.

There was no such a thing as a body search back in those days. That sort of business just didn't exist back then, which made things interesting to say the least. A big strong man should be able to handle himself against anyone with his fists, but weapons – especially knives – can level the odds in an instant. A few punters carried knives and every now and again they would get pissed up, get angry and start causing trouble. Some geezers would think nothing of using bottles or glasses to settle a row. This could get very ugly. I witnessed a few people being glassed in the face and it is a gruesome and sickening sight.

Each of the bouncers at the Room At The Top looked after a corner of the club and when there was any sign of trouble a button would be pressed and a light would go up in that particular corner. All the boys then headed off in that direction to help sort it out.

I always tried to talk to any possible offender before using force, but sometimes I just didn't have a choice and had to wade in. It was usually over in seconds but that can be a very long time in certain situations, so we had baseball bats behind the bar and knuckle-dusters in our pockets, just in case we needed them.

If a bloke has a knuckle-duster on him, it is like having a machine-gun. You shouldn't mess about with tools like that. I only used a knuckle-duster once and it scared the life out of me. I honestly thought that I had killed a bloke with it. He came at me with a beer bottle. I was on my own and so I slipped my hand into my pocket, put it inside the knuckle-duster and hit him firmly on the forehead. He went down immediately and didn't move for minutes. I never used that weapon again. I didn't feel clever having used it. I was young and stupid and just panicked. Such weapons are illegal now, which is a good thing because they are bloody ridiculous tools.

We had to have some form of protection, though. There weren't many of us working at that place and it was a very rough environment. Nowadays it isn't that simple and there are laws that prevent bouncers from hitting out like that. You have to restrain the offender today, which makes it much more difficult for the doorman.

Bouncers must get on and stick together. I became good mates with a lot of the boys who did the job with me. To survive in that type of environment, you have got to be able to operate as part of a team and put your total trust in your workmates. Friendship and loyalty have always been important to me, and when someone from that scene – especially at that time in east London – calls you a mate, it means a lot, believe me.

After the dirt and grime of the Victoria Line and the bottles and bruises of the nightclubs, I decided to learn a totally different trade. I was flicking through the local newspaper one day and saw an advertisement for a window-cleaning round in Wanstead. I fancied a change, so I rang up this bloke and bought it, there and then. I got myself a van and some ladders and started my own business.

Wanstead is full of detached Victorian houses with big windowsills. I quickly mastered the art of propping a ladder at each end of a road and then stepping from sill to sill, cleaning the windows at the tops of all the houses without ever needing to set foot on the pavement. That speeded up the whole process and I cleaned windows in no time at all.

I didn't quite experience the capers of the film *Confessions of a Window Cleaner* when actor Robin Askwith hit it off with all those birds. I did get invited in for cups of tea, but that was mainly by lonely old ladies who wanted a chat. In fact, I had some of the worst tea I have ever tasted doing that job. I managed to throw a few away but sometimes ended up drinking over 20 cups in a single round.

One old dear waited for me every week. 'Hello, Mr Window Cleaner,' she would say. She told me how her son hadn't visited her in years. It was quite sad to hear. She would make me a cup of tea, which wasn't too clever at all, and before I knew it, half-an-hour had gone before I had even put my ladders up.

On the other hand, one very posh lady used to make cakes for me. I always looked forward to eating cream cakes and chocolate gateaux at her house, but most of the time it wasn't like that. Comments like 'You've missed a bit by the corner, Mister' and 'You'll have to clean that up before you earn your half a crown,' were much more common.

I used to charge half a crown for the front of a normal house and a couple of quid for the larger ones, particularly if I was asked to clean up the woodwork too. Cleaning the wooden frames made the windows look cleaner and maintained the wood.

Window cleaning isn't difficult but it can be hard work and your arms and legs ache at the end of the day. It is difficult to get the bees and honey, though. I would push my card through the letterboxes, with a note saying I would collect the money later, and spend most of Friday afternoons trying to do just that. Some people were never in and so they never paid me, which was frustrating.

The only plus point to window cleaning is that you get a day off when it rains. I don't understand how some people do it for 20 years or more. It was just a gap job for me until I decided what I wanted to do next. I lasted six months in that game and then sold the round back to the chap I had bought it off in the first place.

Granite floor-laying was my next vocation. A mate of mine, Gordon Branscombe, suggested it to me. He explained it was physically demanding but sold it to me on how much money I could make from it. Lovely jubbly. It was right up my street.

Floor-laying is hard graft. Laying a factory floor requires you to put down about six inches of concrete, wire the floor, coat it with granite cement and then trowel it so it doesn't wear. An industrial floor needs to last for a long time. A man has to be very strong to be a floor-layer. It is just one of those types of job, although it is slightly different today because power tools have replaced the skills of the tradesman.

I had to work on my hands and knees all the time and completely relied on my physical strength and a very strong back. I did that type of work for a long time and although I enjoyed it immensely, I have no doubt that shovelling concrete, laying floors and working on my hands and knees for all those years caused my serious back problems later on in life.

By my early twenties, I had made a name for myself due to my size and power and I soon began to make a name for myself as a floor-layer, too, as someone who could work effectively but quickly. A surveyor by the name of Keith Pickett heard about me and asked me to do a job underneath some railway arches in Camberwell. The problem was that he needed it doing in one day and, so he told me, that was why he called on me to sort it out.

'You're the only man I can think of who could do it in a day, Bob,' Keith told me.

I asked my brother Kevin and some trusted mates, Bernie Bradstock and Johnny Smith, to come along with me. The four of us apprehensively went over to Camberwell, where we were met by over 30 tonnes of sharp sand, which had to be mixed with 150 bags of cement. The catch wasn't that we had to do the work in a single day but that there wasn't a bloody mixer to do it with! So Bernie and I mixed the cement with our own hands, Kevin and Johnny barrowed it and I laid it – and all in one day as requested by Keith. He was ecstatic that we managed it, and labelled us the 'Human Mobile Digging Machine'. Keith loved to tell his friends that story but for me it was just another day's work and another day's pay.

My natural strength earned me money in all sorts of ways. Away from hard, gruelling building work, I would happily lift things for show to earn a bit of extra cash. That game started with my mate Mickey Porter. We laid floors together and usually lifted 25 tonnes of cement first thing in the morning before we even got started.

Mickey was small and weighed about 10 stone, but he was very strong. He used to demonstrate his strength by lifting a hundredweight (112 lb) bag of cement above his head ten times. Word got around about Mickey's party trick and other workmen used to pay money to see him do it. One day, for a laugh, he mixed it up by telling them that I could lift a hundred-weight bag over my head ten times with one hand.

I was twice the size of Mickey, so the boys asked me to lift two hundredweight bags of cement above my head. This became a winner and soon I was doing it for bets and earning good money from it. Then I moved on to lifting both bags above my head ten times in a row. I was an immensely strong young man – lifting 280 lb bars and 165 lb dumbbells with one hand when I was at 16 – and this was like food and drink to me.

My shape was entirely natural and I never once worked on it. My mate Wag Bennett had a gymnasium at Forest Gate. He invited me down one day and told me that with my very strong basic body shape, I should become a body builder but I couldn't be doing that and shovelling concrete at the same time. Body builders have to eat the right foods and do proper training, and that wasn't my scene at all. I didn't have the time or inclination to dedicate my life to it in that way. I wasn't going to work for 12 hours a day and then go to a gym to pump iron.

My size and strength have always attracted attention. Once, on a building site in Aylesbury, a workmate, Richard Cowen, was pushing metal bars half an inch thick into some concrete, and he set me a challenge. 'I bet you can't bend one of these, strong man,' he said. So I picked up one of the bars, placed it around his neck and bent it good and proper. He asked me to get it off, but I couldn't. Bending something is easy if you have got the proper leverage, but it is totally different when you come to undo it. Richard had to walk around all day with a big metal bow tie around his neck until someone was kind enough to cut it off with a hacksaw. He never challenged me again.

Strength is a gift I was born with. The old man, who was much bigger than me and very powerful, showed me the value of strength. He also used to arm-wrestle with me when I was a boy. He always beat me but he was a good man to learn from. There is an art to it and the old man taught me about timing and that your power is in your back and not your arm. You don't need to have massive arms, even small men can arm-wrestle well if they have got good technique.

Arm-wrestling was very popular in a lot of pubs in the area at that time – properly done with buzzers and everything – and one night I went for a drink and found Canada's arm-wrestling champion sat at a table, beating everyone in sight. I took him on and beat him. It took me 20 minutes and it was a hell of a tussle. By the end of the contest, the table was on the floor. He told me that I was the first guy off the street ever to have beaten him.

My brother Kevin was also a good arm-wrestler. He once went along to a promotion night in Barkingside and won a contest against a local professional arm-wrestler. Kevin used to arm-wrestle with the old man, too, so I guess it ran in our family. It was another good way for us to make a few quid because there were always plenty of people who fancied taking you on at that game for money.

While I was granite floor-laying, I learned how to plaster. My uncle Bob taught me and soon I was off plastering ceilings and toilets and learning yet another trade. Plastering is an essential skill if you need to cover up a balls-up. If bricks have been laid improperly or a wall isn't right, plastering can superficially cover up any mistakes.

I soon found that if you can plaster and render, you are able to build anything. Rendering is important because it can sort out irregularities and plastering finishes off the job. A lot of builders can lay bricks but can't plaster to save their lives and are therefore unable to complete a job by themselves.

I learned to weld while working for German firm Demag. They made overhead cranes at their plant in Banbury. Demag had the best welding gear in the world and hired out equipment to government training centres to teach people how to do it. A chap called Harry worked there as a teacher and he taught me how to weld in my spare time. He was a good personal tutor.

I enjoyed welding and was soon making gates and mending lawn-mowers for local people, just to master the skills involved. I did a lot of stuff like that. Spraying was the same. I offered to spray cars for free, just to learn how to do it. People couldn't really complain when it was done for them free of charge, even though some of them tried to. I had one bloke walk around his car, inspecting every inch of my handiwork.

I learned early on that you can't be the captain of a ship until you have worked your way up from being a member of the crew. I had to do my time on deck in all those different lines of work before I could begin to call the shots. My time would come.

Before the end of the sixties I was a married man. Betty and I married in our local church in Barkingside in 1968. I was 22 years old and looking back I think I made a big mistake. As I have said, Betty was much more pushy than any of the other girls I had known and she pushed me all the way down the bloody aisle. My nature is to follow and I followed her on that one, all right. I was young and naïve and just went along with it all.

Our relationship was never steady. We would regularly split up and not see each other for weeks and then she would turn up at my local with her sister or my brother and we would just seem to get back together. Marriage fell down on me without me realising what was happening.

A man can think he is in love when he is young but generally he doesn't even know what the word means or what the rules are. Most men are stupid in that area until they are over the age of 40. The dick rules the head completely. That is definitely true where I was concerned.

I really don't know why I married Betty and I really don't know why she married me. I suppose in those days a lot of people got married when they shouldn't have. It just seemed to happen back then, particularly in the late 1960s and early 1970s, and maybe that is why so many couples from that era later split up. For me, marriage was like buying my first car. I thought I would drive it for ever and I thought I would love it for ever, too. Then, after two years, the novelty wore off and I just wanted to get another one, quick!

Working as a floor-layer meant I had to travel all over the country and the fact I was away from home a lot of the time probably helped to keep Betty and me together for so many years. In truth, my marriage didn't last long. On paper it might look like it did, but not in terms of a real marriage and the vows that we took. We went our separate ways early on and did our separate things. Betty loved to go to nightclubs and I loved to work and earn money.

We were married for well over two years before we had any children and that was all a bit late in 1960s Barkingside, too, so that tells its own story. Nicola was born in 1970 and Shane came along three years later. There is no doubt that the kids kept us together. I'd had two children with her and I didn't think it made sense for their sake for us to split up.

Interestingly, Betty and I never used to row. Arguing is not really my style anyway and I don't think she cared that much to try to work anything out. So there were no cross words, no shouting and no bawling. There was just nothing.

I suppose with me working away from home so often the marriage was always going to fail. We just made the best of what was a bad job. I let Betty do her thing and tried to make my life as good as it could be. We lived together in that way in Ravensbourne Gardens, Barkingside for the best part of 20 years.

Despite the house not being very big, I gradually turned it into a four-bedroomed palace. I was always trying to improve that place. I would take old, used bricks from sites I worked on – whatever I could get without paying for it – and set about making improvements. We constantly had a lorry outside our house with all sorts of stuff in it.

I built a 25-foot extension and put a bar in it, adding an extra bedroom, a shower room and a utility room upstairs. A personal dream was to have my own outside swimming pool. I built it for the kids and had to dig it out by hand. That was a big job for me to undertake. I had help from a young lad called Mark Furlong but it took us two years of shovelling and barrowing to finish the pool. It was a nightmare operation but once you begin a task like that you just can't go back. I had to do it bit by bit in my spare time. I made it triangular-shaped, with the deep end at the smallest part and the shallow end at the largest part. It measured 36ft long and took up one-third of the garden.

Maintenance was the biggest problem. All the family loved to use the pool but none of them ever cleaned it out. I would go away to work and when I came back it looked like a cesspit. It gradually declined into a state of disrepair, which was very sad, but the state of the swimming pool was nothing compared to the state of my marriage. Nothing was working and the relationship was over. We lived under the same roof and had the same kids from the same marriage but, for all intents and purposes, we were both single.

We made an agreement. Betty soon had a regular boyfriend and I had girlfriends. Looking back, I suppose it was a bit weird but there had been no marriage as such for a very long time and it all just made sense in the end. It was the best option for all of us.

6 The Maypole Master

By the mid-1970s my life was full of a lot of work and a lot of grief. I was in an unhappy marriage, had two unhappy kids and wasn't happy in myself at all. I realised that I needed some sort of escape and darts provided it. After my fishing trip to Ireland with Malcolm Ellis, putting Kenny the Mouth in his place and then being left unimpressed by what I saw at that finals night in Chigwell, I decided to give the game a go.

I already had my own set of darts – Malcolm let me keep the silver-plated brass set he had loaned me to beat Kenny. They were the business and I still have them today. Malcolm was the inspiration I needed to try to succeed. He always told me that I had enough talent to become one of the best players in the world. His opinion was good enough for me and the least I could do for him was to try to prove him right.

I was never going to be content with being just another pub player anyway. I wanted to be the best in the pub, the best in the region, then one day the best in the country and after that, the world. That was my ambition but achieving it was not going to be easy. I encountered problems in the Old Maypole before anyone could even shout, '180'. It may have been my local pub, next door to the garage I rented and used for welding and spraying cars, but that did me no favours when it came to trying to get into the pub's darts team.

One drawback was my inability to count. Another problem, for some of the regulars anyway, was that I threw differently from all the other players in the pub. I was also not registered as a player with the British Darts Organisation (BDO).

The way I throw darts is unique – across my face, from left to right – and although I throw right-handed, I sight the dart with my left eye. It isn't illegal but it is different. I have always played like that from the first day I picked up a dart. It is just my natural throwing action. My brother Kevin throws in exactly the same way as I do, although not quite as well! He is left-handed, so he throws from right to left. It is a bit like watching myself in the mirror.

I didn't realise how unusual our throwing action was until I saw myself playing darts on TV a few years later, but it was a big issue down at the Maypole right from the very start. Maybe that was because I came out of nowhere, with a totally different style from everyone else. It got some backs up, that is for sure.

Obviously, I wanted a place in the pub team. I was confident that I was good enough to be in it but I had to earn my stripes first. Darts could be a closed shop back then and it used to drive poor old Malcolm crazy. He had so much faith in my ability and was concerned that a special talent might easily go to waste, but he couldn't get me a game for the Maypole, however hard he tried.

Reg Taylor was the main stumbling block. He was in charge of the team that played in the Barkingside Summer League. Reg was also in the process of putting together a team for the larger area of Hainault, which was to play in the much bigger, newly formed Essex Super League. I desperately wanted to be part of it – any of it, all of it. It seemed to me that darts was just about to take off and that excited me, particularly as I had a taste and a talent for it.

Malcolm took me up to the Alfred's Head in Hainault to enrol me as a BDO member. This was the first hurdle and a necessity for any player who wanted to play darts seriously at any level, and had hopes of getting on in the game. The BDO registration was easy but acceptance by Reg and his sidekick Johnny Squires was a lot more difficult. It didn't matter to them what I could do with a set of darts, the big news that had now filtered through was that I couldn't count. They both had a big view on that.

Johnny was at the Alfred's Head when I signed up with the BDO and called me over.

'I've heard about you,' he said. 'A few questions: can you count? Can you call a game? Can you chalk?'

I felt like saying, 'Can you piss off?' but, on this occasion, I remained calm, kept my top lip buttoned and walked away from him. Malcolm assured me that both chalking and counting were immaterial and the main thing was I had the potential to be a very good player.

He told Johnny that it was ridiculous to leave me out of the Maypole team and he felt so strongly about it that, if I wasn't included, he would resign. Malcolm was by now probably the best player at the Maypole and everyone knew that, including Reg and Johnny, but the two of them were adamant that if I couldn't count and couldn't chalk, then I couldn't get a game for either the Maypole or the Hainault Super League team they were putting together. It was a pretty big blow for me at the time. I was beginning to find my way in darts and needed someone at the next level to help me get a foot in the door.

Counting was the big problem for me. Malcolm was doing his best to help but he was being frustrated by politics every step of the way. I know 'rules are rules' and I was nothing more than a beginner, but I just needed a break. I thought about trying to join another pub team but didn't fancy moving to another district, and the Super League was going to be the way to the top.

Reg and Johnny announced that the Maypole was to have two places in the Hainault Super League team and that there would be a play-off between 16 invited players to find them. Malcolm once again pleaded with them on my behalf and this time they relented. To this day, I don't know why they had a change of heart, but I had a chance and that was all I cared about.

It wasn't a popular decision. I felt a great deal of resentment from a lot of players on the night because I still hadn't played a game of darts for the pub and here I was getting an opportunity to play for Hainault. I had to put all that to one side and just get on with my game. It was sad and quite unnecessary but that is how darts can be sometimes. It is still the same today. Nothing has changed in that respect in over 30 years.

The play-off matches took place up on the stage in the back room at the Maypole. This was the best induction to big-league darts I could ever have hoped for – a raised oche, PA system, spotlights and an MC. I was in heaven.

I played well enough to get through and secured my place in the

Essex Masters with little bother at all. I still needed some help when it came to counting, of course, but my natural throwing ability could speak for itself and I was never in any danger of not doing the business that night.

To make things even better, the other player to qualify was Malcolm, who patiently stood beside me throughout all the shenanigans, telling me which doubles and trebles to hit. I was very fortunate to have a friend like Malcolm. He tried his damnedest to get my talent recognised and I have got a lot to thank him for. Malcolm's faith in me and his never-say-die attitude were the things that kept me going in the early days. If faced with such a situation alone, my instinct would have been to pack it in, but Malcolm saw something exceptional in me and wouldn't allow me to do that. His support got me over that first important hurdle. Without him, you wouldn't be reading this book.

A month after our play-off successes, Malcolm and I drove over to Westcliff-on-Sea to represent Hainault in the Essex Masters championship of 1976. All the knockers at the Maypole couldn't quite believe that I could be competing at such a level in darts so quickly. But Malcolm wasn't in any doubt and neither was I. It was just the next step up. I still hadn't seen anything or anyone to worry me.

Players representing 32 Super League teams from across the county took part in the Essex Masters, all aiming to win the title and claim a place in the coveted Winmau World Masters tournament – the jewel in the BDO crown – at Wembley later in the year.

Malcolm and I travelled to the venue with Charlie Argue, an Irishman who drank in the Maypole and, as his name suggests, liked a row. When we arrived we were surprised to discover that two places for the World Masters were up for grabs and there were to be two Essex Masters champions as a result. All the players felt that was strange but there were no complaints from any of us. The World Masters was one of the game's two big tournaments and the chance to compete in it was the ambition of every BDO player in the country.

The Essex Masters was a straight knockout competition between 64 players – five wins and you would claim one of those two top prizes. It would have been fantastic if both the Maypole boys could have won through but unfortunately Malcolm went out in the first round. He was gutted but he put his time to good use – he spent the rest of the evening taking bets on me winning the competition. He was also on hand, along with Charlie, to help me with my counting.

I got myself into the last four where I had to beat Harlow's Roger Everington for a place at Wembley. Just like me, Roger had an unusual throwing style and that earned him one of the game's first nicknames, 'The Bowman'.

A lot of darts fans came up to offer support that night, including Roy Gow, who told me that I had hit more 140s than 100s in the early rounds.

'There's no way you can lose playing like that,' Roy said. What he didn't know, of course, was that I still couldn't count to save my life. I was faced with a 90 out-shot to beat Roger and win the title but I didn't have a clue how to go about it. Luckily, Charlie was on hand to help me out.

'Treble 18, Bob,' he shouted from the floor. Well, I hit treble 18 but my mind was still a complete blank about what I should do next. Nerves sometimes make moments like that even worse and I just stood at the oche bewildered, looking for help. Charlie shouted out again, 'Just ask, Bob, ask.'

MC Derek Ransom told the audience to be quiet but mentioned to me that if I needed to know what was left, I was entitled to ask him. I never knew I could do that – I was still so new to the game and had lots to learn. So I asked him what was left, he told me 36 and I went bang, double 18. That is how I won the Essex Masters and with it a place in the World Masters. Just like that!

It is no wonder some of the older players at the Maypole despaired of me. I admit it was a bloody ridiculous state of affairs and I could be murder at times, but the important thing was I did the business and put the name of Hainault on the darts map.

Derek raised my arm aloft and told the crowd to remember my name. I have never forgotten that moment. It was my first taste of the limelight and I can still feel those goosebumps all over my body as he said those words.

I shared the title with Kenny Russell of Barking. We were both given trophies, which was a bit odd. Being one of two Essex Masters champions was an unusual experience and it became unique. The following year the rules were changed. In future, two Essex players would again go forward to the World Masters but there would be a play-off to determine the Essex Masters champion, which made much more sense.

I couldn't wait to get back to the Maypole and shut up all the doubters. It is only 35 miles back to Barkingside from Westcliff-on-Sea but it seemed to take for ever that night. As soon as I walked through the door with Malcolm and Charlie, Johnny came over and asked, 'Who won it, then?'

Malcolm immediately piped up, 'Bob won it. I told you he would. He was fantastic,' and then I went outside to get the trophy out of the car. Johnny only had one tooth and it almost fell out that night through shock!

We locked the doors and had a great night. It was brilliant and suddenly I felt accepted by everyone at the pub. At long last, I was finally one of them. All the talk of me being unable to count or chalk was over. I was now a champion, off to represent my county in the World Masters. The funny thing was I still hadn't played a game for my local pub team.

Malcolm gave me two names when I asked him who the best players in the area were – Dave Brown and Ronnie Hayward. They both played for pubs in Ilford, Dave at The Bell and Ronnie at the King George V. I wanted to play against them.

Dave was a quiet bloke, happy just to play darts for his pub. He helped me a lot but we weren't exactly peas from the same pod. He never entered competitions and I couldn't see the point in that. He once told me, 'The difference between us, Bob, is that all I want is to be a big fish in a little pond while you want to go out to sea and swim with all the sharks.' He was spot on.

I vividly remember meeting Ronnie for the first time. I walked into the King George, saw a group at the dartboard and shouted over, 'Which one of you lot is Ronnie Hayward?' Ronnie was a few years older than me and probably wondered what he had done to upset me. When I explained why I was there and asked if he would give me a game of darts, he was as good as gold and obliged. Before we started,

Ronnie said that he would rather help me than beat me, which was just as well because I beat him.

Ronnie – whose sister Lil Coombes was the top ladies darts player at the time – was an inspiration. He helped me immeasurably and taught me a few little tricks of the trade along the way. One tip concerned throwing down the middle. He told me always to offer to go first when throwing for the bull and to aim for the top of the 25, almost on the wire, thereby obstructing your opponent's view and the path of his dart.

Ronnie has sadly passed away. My fondest memory of him is of two successive legs that we played at the King George, when I checked out both times in nine darts. Incredibly, Ronnie, who threw first in both legs, was on for two nine-darters himself. It was an amazing couple of legs but I was so new to the game that I didn't realise it at the time.

Ronnie missed a nine-darter in the first leg by narrowly failing to hit double 18, and I then sunk a nine-darter. He was so excited by this that he suggested doing it again.

After six darts we were again both on for nine darters and after Ronnie failed with his seventh attempt at a treble, I hit it. He was now almost shaking as he told me, 'Bob, you've got to believe me, mate, that just doesn't happen.' I now know that for myself.

Darts was a gift I never knew I had for 30 years, and I still found some parts of the game difficult. I continued to struggle to get my head around all the numbers on the board, for instance. Ronnie taught me a lot of out-shots. I beat Joe Britton in an early Super League match in Ilford with a 158 checkout, courtesy of two treble 18s and the bull. Ronnie put his thumb up when I looked over towards him. It was one of his favourite shots.

Ronnie was a diamond, Malcolm was brilliant and Charlie had been on hand to help but, deep down, I knew that I had to rely on myself to progress. So I came up with my own scoring system and, just like my throw, it was pretty unorthodox. Another Essex player, Glen Lazero, and I worked out each and every possible permutation. Glen's girlfriend typed them all up and I worked at memorising them, just like the old man would have done. My game improved almost overnight.

I saw how trebles and singles that sit next to each other on the board can work in your favour. I have always liked 121 as an out-shot for the simple reason that there are so many ways to hit it. Just think about it. Numbers 14 and 11 are next to each other so immediately there is one large treble target to hit. After that, there are lots of options – treble 14 leaves you treble 19 and double 11. Treble 11 leaves you treble 20 and double 14. Single 11 leaves you treble 20, bull, and single 14 leaves you treble 19, bull. You can never have too many options in darts. A lot of my out-shots have been copied and are now used by other players, but for some reason 121 remains exclusive to me. I have never once seen anyone else attempt it.

As I have said, I was never any good at mathematics at school but I found that darts is more about remembering numbers and combinations. I had to crack this and it took some time but in the end, practice made perfect for me. I memorised every out-shot like numbers from a telephone book. To this day, I don't do any form of arithmetic when I play darts. I just know how all the numbers work. They are in my memory bank now and don't ever leave me.

Working out all those permutations gave me more confidence and an extra gear. It also confused TV commentators a little later on and led to comments from them that I didn't know what I was doing. I knew what I was doing, all right. My system was just different from everybody else's. I accept that I came up with some pretty wild formulas but they worked for me and they still do.

For example, I don't involve treble 20 much on my finishes. With so many options, I find the best way to play is to keep as many of them open as possible. If I require 94, I aim for the bull first. The tried and tested route is treble 18 and double top, but not for me. My reasoning is simple. Bull and 25 offers a much bigger target than treble 18 for a kick-off, and if I get the bull, I can try single 12, double 16. If I get 25 – and, let's face it, if you can't hit either the inner or the outer bull, you shouldn't be playing darts – I can go single 19, bull. To a man, everyone else would aim for treble 18 first off, and should they miss, they would need a treble and a double with the next two darts to finish.

It is obvious to me that my way gives you a better chance, but it wasn't the regular way and plenty of people soon had a view on that.

If I ever checked out on those finishes, I supposedly did it by chance. I was never given any credit for it. My out-shots upset darts traditionalists but there was really nothing to them. I was just a rotten counter who didn't want to take risks. I needed as many options as possible.

Floor-laying helped me a lot with those finishes. I had a fair amount of time on my hands as I waited for the concrete to set and so I took my dartboard with me on certain jobs, and practised all the different permutations and possible finishes. Other times, I played darts in a local boozer while the concrete set. Later on, I paid men to work for me so that I could spend even more time improving my skills. If I hadn't been a floor-layer, it is unlikely that I would have made it as a darts player. The sheer nature of the job allowed me the time I needed to improve my game. If I hadn't spent so much time away from home, it would have been impossible.

My work also opened my eyes to another world. I was very much a London boy up until then but floor-laying took me all over the country and I enjoyed that part of it very much. I used to like working in Aylesbury because the John Kennedy pub rewarded any darts player who hit a maximum with a free pint. I would hit six or seven at lunchtime and could hardly walk back to work.

The John Kennedy had a decent dartboard but a lot of pubs that I visited didn't. I got fed up with this and used to take my own board along to play on. No one seemed to mind when I put it up, and it improved my game no end.

At this time, I was driving a 1600E Ford Cortina automatic with no seats in the back. I took them all out so that I could put my shovels in there. This car was as vital to my darts in the early days as anything. I would often survive on just a few hours sleep by kipping in that car, or – if I felt like it – grabbing 40 winks lying on the warm cement with a sheet of polystyrene over it.

Most of the building sites that I worked on had a canteen and as long as I had a full English breakfast inside me, I could last all day without food. Breakfast is the most important meal of the day for any builder, and for years I lived on bacon, eggs, sausages, tomatoes and a slice of fried bread. Death on a plate it may be but it was a lovely way to start the day.

Darts had to fit around my work, which was still the biggest thing in my life, and even though I was Essex Masters champion. I never lost sight of where I came from and always maintained that I had to be a better floor-layer than darts player to ensure that I could make a living. My reasoning was simple – if I played a bad game of darts, I still got paid, but if I laid a bad floor, I certainly wouldn't be paid.

My life away from work was now totally dominated by darts, though. If I wasn't working out permutations, I was playing. I soon added the regional Monday and Thursday night league trophies to my Essex Masters crown and was proving that I was no flash in the pan. I hardly ever saw Betty or the children, and spent even less time with the old man, Mum, Heather or Kevin.

Kevin helped me out with work from time to time and once came to the rescue where darts was concerned. My brother was a tidy player himself. One night, I was off doing a job for someone out of London and couldn't take my place in a darts final that I had qualified to play in, up at the Alfred's Head. So I asked Kevin to stand in for me. I wasn't that well known in Hainault and Kevin and I look so similar that I doubted anyone would notice the difference. Well, not only did he stand in for me, Kevin won the bloody competition and no one clocked it, even though he throws darts with the other hand from me. In fact, top Essex player Dave Brown was so impressed with how Kevin played that night that he later congratulated me on the performance!

'Bloody hell, you're some player, Bob,' Dave told me. 'I never knew you could throw left-handed as well!'

Fitting darts around work meant I often played matches looking a right sight, as far removed from the image that I now have in the game as you could possibly get. There was no glitter or jewellery in those days, just a filthy vest, dirty jeans and a great big pair of red Doc Martens boots covered in concrete. However, there was a dress code for the 1976 World Masters and I had to make a bit of an effort by wearing a white T-shirt with a maroon rosette pinned on it, displaying my name and my county.

The World Masters was in its third year and the size of the event was a reminder to me of what I had achieved in such a short space of time. It was still only nine months since that fishing trip to Ireland

and less than four months since the Essex Masters. The tournament started on a Friday night with hundreds of us playing off to get the competition down to 64 players. The real deal came on Saturday, when we had to play to find the winner. It was best of five legs, all the way to the finish.

Although the World Masters was a big event in darts, the competition had yet to catch the imagination of the media. There was no radio or TV coverage and little news of it in the newspapers. Darts remained very much an underground sport at that time and, while all the top names were at Wembley that weekend, I didn't have a clue who any of them were. Alan Evans was the defending champion and favourite to win the title again, but his name meant nothing to me.

Come the Saturday afternoon, I was still in the competition, having managed to get through the Friday night matches. I finally went out at the last 32 stage and was delighted with the dartboard I was given for getting so far.

Kenny Russell – the guy who had qualified from Essex with me – also got through to the Saturday rounds and came up against a player from Derbyshire, called John Lowe. This was the first time that I ever set eyes on the man who was to become one of my biggest rivals in the game. Kenny had two darts at double 18 to beat him, missed them both and John went on to win the tournament.

Other stars of the future at Wembley that year included Cliff Lazarenko, Leighton Rees and Jocky Wilson. I feared none of them, partly because I didn't know who the hell they were and partly because I didn't think any of them were any better than I was. It is incredible to think that within three or four years all six of us – Alan, Cliff, Jocky, John, Leighton and myself – would be household names.

However, that was many moons away and all I could think about when I left Wembley that night was how much better I could have played. I wanted to turn around, go back into that arena and do it all over again. Only this time, I wanted to win. I had gone from the dullness of the Maypole to the bright lights of the Wembley Conference Centre in a short space of time and, having discovered what it was like to play in a totally different environment, I wanted more of it.

Within just a few months of taking up competitive darts, I had realised that there were only so many tournaments to play in and that the available prize money was next to nothing. Darts could pay well but you needed to know the right people and in Charlie Argue and Tommy O'Regan, I had two mates who knew a thing or two about the lucrative world of money races. I never once thought about talking to Betty about it. She showed no interest in what I was up to. I didn't think she would be too keen on me being in the pub so much, either.

I worked with Charlie on the Victoria Line project. He was a locomotive driver in the tunnels and one night he fell asleep at the wheel and lost a finger in an accident. Luckily, it was on his left, non-throwing hand. Charlie played darts at the Maypole and would often throw matches on purpose and then ask for a re-match with money at stake. Once the money was on offer, he would wipe the floor with the opposition. Charlie knew how darts worked from top to bottom and would do anything to put his opponent off, from stepping over the oche to lighting up a fag during a throw.

I played him once in a competitive match and he was murder, the worst player for barracking that I have ever come across. He was given a warning. That experience introduced me to the bad side of darts, which did me a big favour. It taught me how to guard against barracking and I will always be grateful to Charlie for that.

Tommy was a character as well. He hailed from Walthamstow and became famous in darts for captaining both England and Ireland. He led England in the first-ever recognised international match in 1973. No selection committee existed back then so the best players in the country were able to represent England, regardless of their nationality. When the BDO was formed the following year, the county system was introduced and with it came a proper selection process for national honours. As a result, Tommy started to play for and captain his country of birth, Ireland.

Tommy was one of the best players in the world in his day and won the National Darts Association (NDA) singles title three years running. He was a nice, generous man who loved a drink, and he taught me a few tricks, mainly that there was more than one way to win a game of darts.

I often played with Tommy down at his local, the Swan in Walthamstow. He called me 'The Big Fella' and nicknamed himself 'The Great Regan'. We would take the punters on for 20 quid a game and earned a fair bit from that.

Tommy was also a real wind-up merchant and loved to play tricks on people. His favourite gag was to stand a man in front of the dartboard and then knock a lighted cigarette out of his mouth with a single dart, nailing it into a double on the board. One night, during an exhibition at Chigwell, an old boy volunteered for the trick. He stood by the dartboard, lit up and demanded Tommy do his party piece, right there and then. So to shut him up, Tommy threw a dart right into the side of this old boy's nose. He was in so much pain that Tommy shouted out for a brandy. Tommy picked up the brandy, dipped his finger in it and dabbed the old boy's nose before downing it in one. It was quality entertainment and everyone roared with laughter.

Tommy had a gentle soul, though, and got me doing charity exhibitions, which can be such rewarding work and raise much-needed money for good causes. One of the first exhibitions we did together was to help out the firemen when they were on strike at Christmas 1976. We raised a fair amount of money for them.

The most emotional charity nights I ever did were at the King George for a little girl who had tragically lost her hand in an accident. A lot of money was needed to pay for an artificial hand, and once I heard about her plight I decided to help. I played charity darts for months and eventually the target was reached to pay for the operation.

Some years later, an attractive young lady stopped me on Ilford High Road and asked if she could shake my hand. She then told me why. The little girl had grown up into a young woman, and she looked so happy.

Things like that mean so much more to me than any darts trophy or cheque ever could. I have had great pleasure playing exhibitions over the years and have earned the best part of a million pounds for charities and good causes like that one.

Charity nights became very popular in the 1970s and up-and-coming players were very keen to get involved. A teenager from Stoke Newington turned up at a few. His name was Eric Bristow.

I first came across Eric in a BDO tournament at Margate. After the competition, the players took each other on in a good-natured contest at a pound a go. I was on the board enjoying a bit of a winning streak with a long queue of people lining up to play me. Eric was one of them. He waited patiently but when he got near the front he suddenly shouted out, 'I've seen what you've got mate. I'll beat you, wait and see.' This wasn't in keeping with the relaxed game of darts we were enjoying. Eric was very young at the time but it was already apparent to me that he was a cocky sod.

Coincidentally, Malcolm Ellis was next in line to play me, so I let him win, just so I could wind the mouthy youngster up a bit more. Eric played Malcolm and lost. Eric had waited all that time to play me and prove a point, and he never got his chance. He was furious. He got the hump and left, shaking his head and muttering under his breath as he went. But in his own way I think he respected what I did that night, just for the crack.

It wasn't long before Eric and I became good friends. We kept bumping into each other at various tournaments here and there and I soon realised that the two of us were alike, particularly our sense of humour. We got on well and we had a lot in common. We came from the same part of the world and we both loved darts and a giggle.

It took me a little while to realise just how good a darts player Eric actually was. He was so mouthy in his early days that I didn't see the talent the boy had. He was a lot younger than me – by far the youngest player on the scene at that time – and had started playing the game when he got a dartboard for his 11th birthday. We began to play pairs together and I used to drive Eric and his father, George, all over the place. Unlike my old man, George took a big interest in his son's darts.

Once, during the Sussex Open in Gatwick, I was so ill with the flu that I had to withdraw from the competition but, not wanting to let my young friend down, I drove over to his house and picked him up so that he could still compete. When we got to Gatwick, Eric went inside to play but all I could do was lie back in the car and sleep. He woke me up by banging on the door to tell me that he had got through to the final and needed me to go indoors and support him. I dragged myself inside, stood on a chair and cheered him on to victory. We split all our winnings in those days and Eric won £500 that night, which worked out at £250 each. That more than paid for the petrol.

Splitting was very common on the darts circuit in the early days – much more than it is today – and, once agreed, it was an unwritten rule to stick by it, with not a hint of greed or nastiness. Eric and I split our earnings from the word go. We were mates and we trusted each other. Where darts tournaments were concerned, what was mine was his and vice versa. He was always as good as gold when it came down to dealing with the dough.

Yes, he could be arrogant at times, both on and off the oche, but I think he needed that for his game. There was never any malice there. If he had something to say, he would always say it to your face and I respected him for that. He was blunt but he was also honest and I never once heard him bad mouth anyone behind their back.

In 1977, Eric and I won the pairs at the Crayford Open and almost met each other in the final of the singles. I reached the final and Eric got to the semi-finals where he lost to Peter Chapman, a darts veteran and former *News of the World* champion.

Peter had a big hairy chest and used to love to show it off by playing darts with his shirt open all the way down to just above his navel. Eric was never shy in coming forward and mentioned the chest hair to Peter, asking if he grew an extra hair every time he lost a match. When Peter asked why, Eric replied, 'Well, you're playing my mate in the final and you've just grown another one. Look!' He could be a saucy bastard at times.

The two of us had some great times together, particularly in the early days, winning lots of tournaments and causing havoc all over the place with our money races. We always had a laugh too. I once played Eric in St Paul's Way, east London. I went up to the oche and hit the wire under the treble 20 three times in a row. No score. Eric was in hysterics until he got up to the oche and did exactly the same with his three darts. No score.

Six darts hit six wires. It was incredible, I have never seen or heard of anything like that before or since. Some drunk in the crowd heckled us and told us we were rubbish. Quick as a flash, Eric went over, offered him his darts and said, 'Go on then, you do it. Hit the wire three times.' It was a priceless moment.

At that time, money races were the only way to earn good money from darts, and if you were a decent player, this was normally easy money, too. Eric and I were normally so confident that we carried little cash on us because normally we won. I say, normally.

One night I drove Eric to the Mother Hubbard pub in Loughton, where he took on Bob Wood in a money race for £200, which was a great deal of money back then. He lost. Eric came up to me at the bar and asked me to lend him the money to cover his debt, but I had nothing like that amount of cash on me. We were both flummoxed for a moment, until Eric went over to Bob and offered him a game of 'double or quits' against me! Suddenly, I was the one in the firing line. If I won, we were in the clear and if I lost, we somehow had to find £400.

The match was played over seven legs of 1001 and at one stage I was in serious trouble against him. With little money in our pockets, Eric and I were about to get lynched by the locals, and we were out-numbered by about 30 to one. At the end of one leg, I walked over to Eric and handed him the keys to my Ford Cortina, parked outside. I told him that if I looked like losing, he had to get outside, start up the engine and leave the passenger door open for me. In the worst-case scenario, we would have to make a run for it. We would have no other choice. The money race would probably turn into a car chase.

I went back to the oche and no sooner had I played my first three darts of the next leg when Eric shouted out with the keys in his hand, 'Bob, I can't drive.' I couldn't believe it. Talk about waking me up! Our only chance now was for me to win the match. I pulled out several maximums and nicked it on the final leg. I was wet through with sweat at the end, and that was just to cancel out a bet that Eric lost. We left the pub without a penny between us, and never went back.

That was our apprenticeship but there is no doubt that such experiences improved our darts. My game was improving all the time. The cheques and the trophies were proof of that.

Eric and I became the game's version of Butch Cassidy and the Sundance Kid, and we stuck up for each other through thick and thin.

I will never forget that about him. Most of the others just looked after themselves but he wasn't like that.

I did an event for Marlboro cigarettes in the West End with a few of the boys in the summer of 1977 and we all had to dress up in the sponsor's red shirt and red trousers. A big white Rolls-Royce was booked to pick us up in Chingford, so that we could arrive at the function in Leicester Square in style. I was the last one in line and by this time there wasn't much room in the car. Quick as a flash one of them said to me, 'No room at the inn. You'll have to get the train, Bob.' He shut the door in my face and the Rolls drove off. I couldn't believe it. I had no choice but to walk to Chingford train station, looking like a fag packet, and make my own way to the heart of theatreland. It was embarrassing and degrading. I felt like a right prick.

A few years later when I owned a Rolls-Royce of my own, I was driving in Walthamstow and passed the same guy standing at a bus stop. He put up his hand and asked me for a lift. 'Sorry, no room at the inn, mate, you'll have to get the bus,' I said and pulled away. I may be stupid at times but I never forget things like that. He got the message.

Darts was now my life and it was oozing out of every pore. In the summer of 1977, Malcolm Ellis and I came up with an idea to get the game, and our names, into the *Guinness Book of Records* – set the highest-ever total scored in ten hours. The BDO sent a director down to the Grove Social Club in Chadwell Heath and we threw 451,273 in front of all the officials, properly and professionally.

We didn't drink and we didn't go to the toilet, that was how committed we were to setting a record and getting our names in that book. It was a difficult and tiring task but it worked, and a few weeks later we both received signed certificates from Norris McWhirter, the editor of the *Guinness Book of Records*.

At the end of the year, I once again entered the Essex Masters and this time won it outright. At Wembley I improved on my performance of 12 months earlier by getting into the last eight of the World Masters, where I lost to Paul Reynolds. Progress was steadily being made and I began entering tournaments left, right and centre. I entered Opens galore, often with Eric, and played in the singles, pairs and sometimes even the triples. I would go anywhere in the country to play darts.

I won the Essex Champion of Champions title in both 1976 and 1977 and beat all the top Super League players in the county in the process, including the one and only Reggie Carter. Reggie was a true character and made a bit of a name for himself by taking off his clothes at darts matches and presentations just for the hell of it. Eventually, Essex officials found out about this caper and banned him from county darts. Apparently, Reggie wasn't banned for dropping his trousers but for dropping his trousers while wearing the Essex county shirt!

I once played pairs with Reggie in a friendly against Suffolk at my mate Kenny Harris' pub, the Ram in Brandon. He required double two for the match and told me the only way he could be sure of hitting it was if he took his clothes off. I told him he had better take his clothes off then. He hit double two with his first dart while all his clothes were strewn across the oche. I had never seen anything like it in my life.

By the late seventies, darts was beginning to become very popular. More and more people were playing the game and paying to watch tournaments. Entrance fees were going up and so was the prize money. Suddenly, much more coverage was appearing in the news-papers and Eric and I started to feature regularly in the *London Evening Standard*. To get publicity for the game and for ourselves, we started whipping up a pretend rivalry between us by making comments about each other. It didn't really matter what we said. We were as ambitious as each other and desperately wanted to win matches and big events.

I'd had a little sip of success – it was hardly a taste – and my eyes were open, not only to darts but to all the possibilities that the game could bring. Obviously, I was happy with my performances in the 18 months that I'd had in the game – coming from a total novice to the last 32 and then last eight in the World Masters isn't too shabby. Now I wanted a top prize to call my own.

The *News of the World* (NOW) championship was the top honour in darts, and that was the one I wanted. The NOW championship was the original world darts competition and the BDO rules were based on it, including straight darts, double finishes and the no-score rule.

It began, funnily enough, in my own backyard. The very first championship was held in 1928 at the Ilford Palais on Ilford High Road and was won by Sammy Stone, who came from nearby West Ham. For 20 years, it wasn't a national event never mind a world championship. The competition was for the London metropolitan area until the Second World War and then, in 1948, it became darts' first world tournament.

It was very popular from the start. In 1939, nearly 15,000 spectators turned up at the Royal Agricultural Hall in London to watch Marmaduke Brecon shock the legendary Jim Pike in the final. After the war, over 300,000 players regularly entered the championship every year from their pubs. It was a long, old tournament. Any player in any pub in any town could enter and it would take the best part of a year to find the eventual winner.

I first heard of the competition in rather unusual circumstances. Ronnie Hayward was a smoker and one day he produced a magnificent silver cigarette lighter from his pocket. I immediately liked the look of it and noticed the words *News of the World* on it. Ronnie told me that if anyone owned such a lighter, they were a real darts player.

Ronnie had been presented with the engraved lighter when he got to the county finals of the competition. I fancied one of those lighters for myself but to get one, I had to win one. I couldn't just go out and buy one from a shop.

I had just missed the entry date for the 1977 competition and so had to wait another 12 months before I could enter the 1978 event. All of the other major tournaments required an invitation to compete but this one was different. The NOW championship was for anyone who fancied having a go. It was free to enter. All you had to do was write your name on the board at your local pub and you would be in with a chance.

It was a competition for the people and that is why it was so popular. It also had a very short format – best of three legs, 501, from the first round to the final. Games were played from 8ft, and who threw first was decided on the toss of a coin.

It was the one that every player wanted to win but it was a long, hard process. The first hurdle was to win your pub competition. Each pub had its own winner and that player competed against all the other pub winners in the area finals. Then came the county finals and the regional finals. Eventually, just 13 were left and they would play on stage at the Wembley Empire Pool, challenging for the original and – to my mind – still the best trophy in the game of darts.

At the first time of trying, I won the pub competition at the Maypole, the Hainault district, the county of Essex, and then the Eastern Counties final. The hardest part for me was the first round at the Maypole. Playing against my mates over such a short format for the right to progress was difficult. Similarly, there were a few familiar faces at the district final. Once I got to the Eastern Counties final, my opponents were unknown to me and I was able to shut off and concentrate on my darts. I always played better darts when I didn't know anything about my opponent because I just played against the board. Knowing someone can bring extra pressure.

So, some ten months from the start of the competition, I was in the grand final at Wembley with 12 others, vying for the most famous trophy in the game. Both Eric and his father came along to support me and sat in the front row cheering me on. I was made joint favourite with Tony Brown, of Dover.

Minutes before I took my place on stage I was told I had to change my shirt. Darts manufacturers Durro had sponsored me throughout the regional rounds and I had played every match in a T-shirt bearing the company name, but the NDA put a stop to that at Wembley and suddenly decided it was against the competition's rules.

Paul Durrant, the owner of Durro, wasn't too happy about it and neither was I. With no change of clothes – I had travelled across London wearing my playing gear – I had to find someone, and quickly, who had a shirt on his back that would fit my frame. Luckily, a punter in the front row was exactly the same size and he loaned me his shirt for the day. He sat and watched the action in my Durro-sponsored darts number. It was ridiculous.

The odd number of finalists meant that three players received byes into the quarter-finals. Unfortunately, I wasn't one of the lucky ones and was drawn to play Scotsman Jocky Wilson. I recognised Jocky's face instantly – his toothless grin would soon become a darts trademark –

from my appearances at the World Masters, but I didn't know too much about him as a person or a player. Eric knew a lot more. He told me that Jocky was a bit on the fiery side and warned me to expect him to jump up and down and scream throughout the match.

It was the biggest match of my career so far. Jocky jumped and screamed, just like Eric told me he would, and he beat me fair and square. I really gave the match to him without playing anything like my best. When Eric saw me afterwards he called me a prat, and I felt like one. I had done all that hard work to get there and it came to nothing. To lose at Wembley without even putting up a fight was gutting. I was disappointed in myself more than anything else, and understood first-hand why the NOW championship was regarded as the hardest tournament in the world to win. Short games are exciting to watch but they can be so easy to lose, especially if you come off second-best in the toss, as I did against Jocky, and have to throw second.

I took a lot of positives from the day, though. The atmosphere was something else, much better than anything I had experienced before. This was definitely the one to win. I loved the tradition of the event and I thought the way in which the MC called out 'Men on the mark' at the start of each leg was fabulous.

Darts was getting bigger with every passing month and more and more tournaments were beginning to crop up, but for all the players in all the pubs up and down the country, this was the only one that actually mattered. If you reached the final stages of it, you earned the instant respect of all darts players everywhere in the world. I wasn't too bothered about a cigarette lighter any more. I wanted the trophy.

More than any other tournament, this one convinced me that darts was my future. Ronnie had told me that the NOW championship meant everything to him and that his one ambition in life was to walk out of Wembley Empire Pool with the trophy in his hands. Now I knew what he meant.

The honour of doing that in 1978 fell to Sweden's Stefan Lord, who created a bit of a stink along the way. Stefan qualified to play in the grand finals due to being the Swedish national champion, an event he had been seeded in and therefore invited to play in. This contradicted the NDA policy of everyone in the competition having to play from scratch. There were meant to be no invitations, hence the peculiar number of 13 finalists. Other countries had lengthy play-offs to find a representative for the grand finals but Sweden decided not to and the NDA allowed it.

There were complaints from far and wide but they came to nothing and Stefan lifted the trophy to catcalls and whistles from the crowd. He was the first overseas champion. I set my sights on winning it back for England.

7 Hello America

I had never considered setting foot on an aeroplane before I played darts but within two years here I was, at the age of 32, flying off with the BDO on a trip across the Atlantic to play some tournaments and generally spread the name of the game Stateside.

Paul Durrant wanted to put some of the best British players together under the Durro banner and take them over to America as part of the annual BDO expedition. Paul offered to pay for the flights but the players had to pay for their own keep and if any prize money was won, it had to come off the price of the flights. Paul was a Hainault Super League team player himself and was trying his hand in business. There was not much money in it for us but his sponsorship also supplied us with T-shirts and tungsten darts and flights with our faces on.

I desperately wanted to go to America and saved hard for the trip. I saw it as a chance of a lifetime and, fortunately, had an employer at that time, Roy Cottee, who was very understanding and allowed me to take a month off work to explore the opportunity.

'Have a crack, Bob,' Roy told me. 'You'll always be able to lay floors but you might not have an opportunity to make it as a darts player again.'

Roy was a diamond – as were all his family – who hailed from East Ham. I worked with all the Cottee family, including grandfather Will, and they were all top blokes. Former West Ham and England footballer Tony Cottee is Will's grandson and Roy's nephew.

If Roy hadn't been so understanding, there is no way I would have jeopardised my work and taken the risk. So I have a lot to thank him for.

Eric Bristow was part of the Durro team, along with Colin Baker and top female players Linda Batten and Pat Piper. The excitement was amazing as we boarded the plane at Gatwick Airport. Darts had given us all a new perspective on life. Tony Brown, John Lowe, Dennis Ovens, Leighton Rees and Tony Sontag also made the trip, along with BDO chief Olly Croft. Olly had good World Darts Federation (WDF) contacts in America and he arranged for us to stay with various families during our time over there, to save on cost. The Americans wanted to see the best darts players and we needed them to help us out with accommodation. The arrangement was a sensible one. It helped them, helped us and helped the game of darts.

We flew into Los Angeles and I just couldn't get over how many telegraph poles there were. On first sight, the States was just telegraph poles and car parks. The first stopping point was at the house of one of Olly's contacts, where Colin and I were to stay while we were in LA. It was to be a right scream.

We shared a room. We also shared a bed, a big squishy water number. Unbeknown to us beforehand, the owner of the house had a lady friend staying with him and she was one big old lady, standing over 6ft tall and weighing a good 14 stone plus. One night after a few drinks, both Colin and I were fast asleep when we woke up to find this giant of a woman climbing into the waterbed between us. 'C'mon guys, move over. There's plenty of room in here for me and you,' she said with a smile.

'Who the hell are you, darling?' I snapped and she said that she lived there.

Maybe Olly's American contacts wanted a bit more excitement than just watching us play darts. I wasn't interested and turned my back to go back to sleep, leaving young Colin to ponder whether it was worth his while.

One thing you can say about Americans is that they are not shy about coming forward. Within days of arriving I was approached by one of the nation's best darts players, Nicky Virachkul, about the possibility of staging a money race. I didn't have much money with me and anything I earned had to pay for my flights in the first instance, but I was up for playing Nicky and told him that if, at the end of the tour, I had got some cash to my name, we would definitely get it on.

I shouldn't have worried. The States was like a goldmine. The tournaments paid well, the British boys did well and the fact that we split the winnings meant that it was one long party for all of us. The camaraderie was good. There was a holiday atmosphere about the trip and a feeling that we were all in it together. It was brilliant.

I was still very much my own man, though, and sometimes that could work against me, particularly concerning darts politics, where I was a little wet behind the ears. A few of the older players took advantage of the fact that I wasn't afraid to speak my mind by selecting me as the players' spokesperson in a row with the BDO over shirt sponsorship.

The BDO were happy for England shirts to feature the name and logo of team sponsors Admiral, but drew the line on any other form of sponsorship. Undeterred by this stand, and the farcical sight of me having to change my shirt on stage in the finals of the *News of the World* championship earlier in the year, Durro and all the other sponsors wanted to get their own branding on the England shirt as well.

I was informed that a meeting had resulted in some of the players taking a hard line against the BDO on this matter and I was asked if I would speak to Olly Croft about it. So I approached Olly and put the players' case over, even though I hadn't been selected to play for England at that time.

Olly was suitably unimpressed by me suggesting such a notion and likewise so was I when the players suddenly ducked for cover and left the situation looking like it was a personal dispute between the BDO and myself. It was a naïve thing for me to do and I learned a big lesson about trust that day. I think I was just so keen to make friends and fit in. I had suddenly burst on to the scene from nowhere and I wanted to feel like I belonged with the rest of the players, but I was stupid to get involved and paid the penalty. I believe that the whole matter delayed my international career for some considerable time.

The first tournament on the tour was the Santa Monica Open, where there seemed to be about 20 Brits and hundreds of Americans competing for the prize. I got to the semi-finals in the singles, losing to Leighton Rees, and won the mixed pairs with Pat Piper by beating Colin Baker and Pat's teenaged daughter in the final. Colin and I were splitting so that was a nice way to start off proceedings.

We worked our way up the West Coast, playing various events before we got to the big one, the North American Open, which was played on the Queen Mary, moored in the beautiful setting of Long Beach.

The North American Open is a special event, not dissimilar to the NOW championship – best of three legs, 301, double-in and double-out. Nearest to the bull determines who throws first, each and every leg. That is what I call proper darts.

It was the main prize in American darts and the trophy told you so. It was absolutely massive. Alan Glazier had won the tournament the previous year and, as he wasn't defending his title, he had asked me if I would kindly take the trophy back for him. I agreed but when it turned up at my house I instantly regretted my decision. It was about 3ft tall and I had to dismantle it, wrap it in newspaper and pack it in its own special suitcase. Then I had to put it all back together again in America. It is fair to say it was a nuisance.

Some 512 players entered the North American Open. The draw was unique. Every player had a card with a number on it. Cards numbered 1 to 256 went in one pile and cards numbered 257 to 512 went in another. Both packs of cards were shuffled and laid face down. Then the top cards were taken off each pile and the players with those numbers were drawn to play each other. The tournament was a long one, played from start to finish in one day. The overall champion had to win eight successive matches to lift the trophy.

The draw seemed weighted towards the American players and the British boys had to play each other more times than not and therefore knocked each other out. History stated that there was always an American in the final and generally it was Californian Len Heard.

The British team spirit was fantastic. We cheered each other on throughout the day and, because there were so few of us, whoever was left in at the end was going to get the support of all his mates. It just so happened that the one left standing was me.

The Americans did exactly the same and that created a terrific atmosphere. It was a real us versus them situation.

I came up against Tony Sontag in the semi-final and that was hard because he was such a good mate of mine back home, but I beat him, and in the final I played an American called Pete Polinksi. Eric Bristow, who was knocked out very early on, offered to chalk the game and when I threw the winning dart he leapt up in the air like he had won the bloody thing himself.

That North American Open was a very tiring 18-hour event. There weren't enough dartboards to go around for a start and the hanging about that all the players had to do was mind-numbing, but I so badly wanted to win the tournament that I pushed myself through it. I put every ounce of energy I had into winning. Luckily, I was still a young man and could cope with it all, but it remains one of the longest days of my life. After that year, the organisers arranged it better and it was nowhere near as hard in the future.

Unlike Alan, I couldn't be doing with all the aggro of taking the trophy to pieces again so I just left it on the ship. I don't think it has ever left the States since. I did get a winner's plaque to keep and that remains one of the few prizes from that era that I still have in my possession today, taking pride of place on the games room wall at George Hall.

As well as that enormous trophy, some valuable world-ranking points and a winner's cheque of $4000 dollars, the 1978 North American Open title also earned me a trip to London and another invitation to play in the Winmau World Masters at Wembley. As I was also to win the Essex Masters, for the third successive year, I ended up qualifying twice and so represented both Essex and the USA. I didn't need the prize of the trip to London, either, because it only cost me a quid to get to Wembley on the underground. In hindsight, I think the WDF should have given the place in the World Masters and the trip to London to the American boy who was runner-up. That would have been a nice gesture.

We were all making so much money in the States that it was coming out of our ears. Colin and I were runners-up in the North American pairs to John Lowe and Tony Brown. Wherever we went, the British boys just cleaned up.

The final event on the Queen Mary was a Great Britain versus USA team event. We won it easily and after the match, posed for photographs dressed in official BDO shirts. The Americans had given me a cowboy hat when I had been crowned singles champion and I was so pleased with my performance throughout the tournament that I wore it for the snapshot. That didn't go down too well with John Lowe, who made a complaint to the BDO about my cowboy hat. He said it was disrespectful to the British team for me to be photographed dressed as an American, but I thought it was complete nonsense.

The North American Open was the biggest prize in darts that I had so far won in my career and I was delighted, but John could only give me stick about it, dismissing it as a 'Mickey Mouse competition'. I laughed it off but couldn't understand why he was trying to put me down. Perhaps he was just one of the old guard. He had been there right from the very start and was used to things being done in a certain way. Suddenly, this brash, young Cockney boy came along, who didn't seem to care about any of the rules, or anyone's status. I was ambitious, sure, but I wanted to have a good time and put a bit of fun into darts. He didn't seem to go on that one little bit.

As you have probably gathered, John and I don't get on too well. From the start, he didn't seem to like me and I didn't go a lot on him, either. At first, I tried my best not to take any notice of him, but it grated. I think John saw himself as the good guy of darts and me as some fool who brought no good to the game. I think that is what he has always felt, but God knows where the game of darts would be today had we all done it John's way.

The next tournament on the tour came in the shape of the Golden Gate Classic, in San Francisco. What a city San Francisco is – I absolutely loved it. We went everywhere, including the island of Alcatraz. I thought it was bloody horrible and no place to spend your life, but then I guess that is what it was there for.

San Francisco is just wonderful, though. The buildings, flowers and trams all make it what it is and then, of course, there is that bridge. To be honest, the Golden Gate Bridge disappointed me a little. Obviously, it is some sight and a magnificent piece of engineering, especially when you consider it has survived an earthquake, but I fully expected it to be gold in colour and it was more dirty brown. The Dirty Brown Bridge doesn't have quite the same ring to it and I don't suppose that I would fancy painting it much, either, but I was expecting a lot more than a bigger version of the Forth Bridge in Scotland.

Despite that, San Francisco remains my favourite city in the whole wide world. It is far more European than the rest of America, with lots of walkways and street entertainers, and it also has a very interesting science museum. Some players had no interest in seeing any of that, which staggered me. All they wanted to do was play darts and all they saw were the city's pubs and clubs. The same is true for many of today's players, but a dartboard looks the same in America as it does in England, and from that very first visit to the States, I have tried to make the most of any trips abroad and see the sights.

I won the triples, mixed triples and four-man team events in the Golden Gate Classic. I also got to the final in the singles but unfortunately lost to John Lowe. There was now a fair bit of needle between us and it was a great shame I lost that one to him. Nevertheless, by the end of that trip, I had 13 tournament wins to my name. I had earned some serious money – Eric even nicknamed me 'Bobby Dollar' – and felt like I had really put myself on the world darts map.

At the end of the tour, a few of us hired a big American convertible to drive up the coast and I was appointed driver. It took me a little while to get the hang of the car and it was an education to say the least when I did. One thing that driving in the States taught me was how to use one finger on the road whereas in England we use two. I lost count of how many times that one finger was directed at me by local drivers with the accompanying word 'Asshole'.

Another thing I loved about America was the food. Burgers are the Americans' speciality. If you order a burger in America, you get the works. One I had in Vallejo, near San Francisco, measured five inches by five inches square. It wasn't only the meat that was square, either. So were the onions and the tomatoes, which had been grown in square boxes. You have never eaten until you eat in the States. It is wonderful.

That trip was such a good crack and really summed up a time when darts was full of fun and friendship.

With money in my pocket, I left San Francisco and headed back down the coast to LA in search of Nicky Virachkul and his offer of a money race. Nicky couldn't wait to play me and suggested we used a British pub called The Crafty Cockney in Santa Monica. We both put a fair few dollars behind the bar and played out a mammoth match of

best-of-51 legs at 1001. I won and celebrated the next day by buying
a real American belt buckle, made of sterling silver and featuring an
American Indian headdress. I have worn it every single day since then,
whether I have been playing darts, mending a roof, wearing a suit or
fishing.

That win meant I really had hit the jackpot where the readies were
concerned. The landlord of the pub later congratulated me by buying
me a pint or a dozen and handing me two shirts with The Crafty
Cockney logo on them. The shirts, just one size, were far too small
for me, so I gave them to Eric. The Crafty Cockney became his trademark but Eric never came up with it himself and neither did it come
from London, as a lot of people think. Eric got the name from a pub
in Santa Monica where I beat Nicky Virachkul in a crazy 51-leg
money race. The famous red shirt was already complete with a logo of
the Union Jack flag and the cheeky policeman. All Eric had to do was
put it on his back.

8 Window to the world

By the time the *News of the World* championship came around again, I felt ready to win it. I had grown as a darts player – more gutsy and focused – and my triumph in the North American Open had topped off a successful tour of the USA for me.

The one low point of 1978 had been my performance in the NOW championship. I had been so desperate to win it and felt I hadn't done myself justice when it mattered. I was keen to make amends after that disappointment. It took ten months of tough darts to qualify to play at the Wembley Empire Pool and I nearly missed my chance before the 1979 competition had even started.

The Old Maypole had already staged its finals night while I was away in the States but luckily Ronnie Hayward's pub, the King George V, was due to have its play-off just after I returned home. So, I made the two-mile trip down the Cranbrook Road to Ilford and won a place in the Hainault regional finals by representing my mate's boozer. Ronnie was a great support to me that year. He was the one who had got me so excited about this competition in the first place, and I was thrilled to be playing for his pub.

Ronnie's sister, Olive, put us up the night before the Eastern Counties area finals and that evening when we were practising in a nearby pub, a fresh-faced young boy challenged me to a game of darts. I hammered him and was quite surprised when he told me that he was playing in the NOW area finals the next day as well. He hardly looked old enough to have left school.

That was my first meeting with Keith Deller. Four years later he was to take the world of darts by storm when he won the Embassy world championship title with a 138 checkout against Eric Bristow. He was still just a boy in 1983 – posing for the newspapers drinking a bottle of milk – so imagine how young he looked when I met him that night in Suffolk.

Keith was still learning at that stage and I beat him 2–0 in our first-round match but he did have shots to beat me in both legs. Other than that, the night posed few problems for me and I again won through to Wembley without losing a leg, beating veteran Eddie Brown, who won the NOW championship in 1962, in my final match.

I had done the hard part again and earned myself another crack at winning the famous old trophy but I wasn't going to Wembley just to make the numbers up. I feared no one. I had developed a real killer instinct. Concentration is key to winning the NOW championship. The format is so short that it is vital to be completely focused on your game.

My ambition went deeper than winning the tournament, though. I realised that I needed to claim one of the big titles to establish my name in the sport. The North American Open had been fantastic but it was an overseas event and wasn't shown on TV. The man in the street knew nothing about it or me. I had to win a big tournament in my own country and I had to do it in front of the TV cameras. If I did that, I would be made. It was my window to the world.

I made sure I dressed up for the occasion. I wore a bright, tight yellow and blue sports top to show off my muscles, and yellow sweatbands on my wrists. Sweatbands were all the rage back then. Bjorn Borg and Kevin Keegan had made them a top fashion accessory in tennis and football, and I was trying to do the same in darts.

Unlike the previous year, when I was made to change my shirt on stage, NDA officials were happy with how I looked. Paul Durrant wanted to get the Durro logo on my shirt, but I'd had that row and I wasn't going through that again.

ITV's *World of Sport* planned to feature the darts around that day's horse racing, but, by a stroke of good fortune, the horse racing was cancelled due to bad weather and darts was to be shown throughout the afternoon. The viewers were in for a treat. I even turned up with my own dancing troupe for the occasion. Betty, showing a rare interest in my darts career, and her sister Carol joined up with Kay and Sandra – daughters of the former landlord of the King George V, Gordon Croucher – and formed the 'Bo-Bo Girls' especially for the occasion. Dressed in jeans, pompoms and my name stitched in big gold letters on the seats of their pants, the girls were great for the game of darts. They caused a bit of a stir but all they were trying to do was put a bit of fun into the game and that was fine by me.

Again, due to the odd number of finalists, three players were to be given byes into the quarter-finals. We all stood on the stage as the draw was made from the giant trophy, each of us willing the word 'bye' to be called out next to our name. I was one of the lucky ones this year and got a passage straight into the last eight.

That was a big boost for me and when I played George Adams, from Somerset, I hit the right notes on the board with three 140s from the off. I defeated him 2–0, keeping up my record of not conceding a leg in the competition, to proceed to the last four.

Welsh champion Lance Richards stood in my way for a place in the final, and two bull finishes wrapped up another good win for me. My first-leg out-shot was 135. I hit 25, treble 20 and bull. TV commentator Dave Lanning called it 'unorthodox finishing' but there wasn't anything unorthodox about it as far as I was concerned. All those hours that I had spent working out and memorising the permutations while waiting for the concrete to set were now paying dividends.

It was very interesting that when I arrived on the national darts scene that day, in front of the TV cameras, my scoring technique was met with exactly the same response that it got when I was first starting out at the Maypole three years earlier. But I can tell you it was such a good feeling to hit that bull and to feel all the hard work paying off. If I could have heard Dave's words in my ears, it would have felt even sweeter.

I met Alan Glazier in the final. Alan, the man in black, was one of the true gents on the circuit. He had knocked out the controversial defending champion Stefan Lord in the first round and was playing very good darts. The match was billed as the 'Battle of London' even though Hampton Hill-born Alan had now moved up to Wetherby, North Yorkshire, and I was representing the Eastern Counties.

Alan was the clear favourite but that didn't bother me. Neither did the crowd of 7000 people packed into the Empire Pool or the millions watching live on TV. This was the one that I wanted. This was my chance to make a name for myself in darts. I had to take it.

I won the toss and four steady tons left me needing 101 for the first leg, which I wrapped up with a treble 20, a single one and double top. In the second leg, I hit the only 180 maximum of the entire day, and when MC Les Treble called it out pandemonium broke out in the arena. I had never witnessed a darts crowd reaction like that before and I absolutely loved the thrill of it.

Alan had one dart at double 18 to level the match but missed and that left me needing just 80 to claim the title. Two single 20s left me double top for the championship. I fixed my eye not only on the top bed but on a hole within it left by a previous dart, and fired my winning dart into that very same hole. I leapt up into the air in celebration and bounded towards the board to retrieve my darts. It was a beautiful moment and a wonderful feeling to be world champion. The crowd were up on their feet – and it was all on TV. I had done it. I had made my name in darts.

Actress Diana Dors presented me with the trophy. She was such a charming lady and told me how exciting she thought the whole day had been, how much she enjoyed darts and how excellently I had played. I remember telling Diana and the massive crowd – via a microphone – that it was the best day of my life. Actually, I was in awe of what I had just achieved. Those two 15-dart legs only lasted five minutes, but they changed my life completely. Later, I was told that I had created history by becoming the first man to win the NOW championship without dropping a single leg from start to finish.

To mark the occasion, some friends snatched the winning board off the Wembley stage and stashed it in my car boot, much to the dismay of the NDA. Ronnie Hayward lived his dream too, when he walked out of the Empire Pool with the trophy over his head. A drunken fan even congratulated him outside the arena on a 'great game of darts, pal'.

I celebrated in rather unusual style by attending a wedding reception in Southend-on-Sea. NDA president Johnny Ross, who was in his seventies and an old friend of the legendary darts player Jim Pike, had never missed the NOW championship final but that year it clashed with his daughter's wedding so he had no choice but to give it a miss. He invited me to the wedding reception, win or lose. In the circumstances, the least I could do was to take the trophy along with me. It meant a lot to Johnny, probably because he had seen Jim finish runner-up in the championship way back in 1936 and 1939, but never win it. The old boy was absolutely made up when I arrived in the hall and was choking back tears when he congratulated me.

Johnny had telephoned me the night before the finals to wish me luck and I told him that I had yet to drop a leg in the competition. 'Well, you can drop one tomorrow, Bob, but just make sure you don't drop two,' he said.

He couldn't believe it when I told him that I had become the first man to go through the entire tournament – all ten months of it – without dropping a single leg. I am proud to say that it was some achievement.

While Malcolm Ellis, Ronnie Hayward, Ernie Mott and I were at the wedding reception, the King George V was in true party mood, and when we turned up a little later on, the walls were bending under the pressure. The new landlord of the King George, Gabriel Nolan, who had taken over from Gordon Croucher earlier that year, was a huge darts fan and a big gambler. Gabriel apparently won a lot of money on me that day – much more than my prize money – and was more than happy to open a free bar for everyone inside. It was a blinding night and dozens of people ended up crashing on the pub floor until the morning. I was so pleased, not just for myself but for Malcolm and Ronnie and other close friends.

I was especially pleased for Malcolm. Without him, none of it would have been possible. He got me into darts in the first place and was the one man who believed in me from the start. I was Malcolm's protégé and had now delivered my promise to him that one day I would become the best player in the world. It was less than three years since I said those words to him and here I was, the 1979 *News of the World* champion.

But the way, did you know that the figure on the top of the trophy is throwing an arrow across its face, left to right, just like me?

In its day the NOW championship was the most important tournament in darts. Make no mistake about that. The rise of the Embassy and the BDO–PDC split has obscured that fact. It was also the hardest to win. A few months before my win at Wembley, John Lowe beat Leighton Rees in the final of the second Embassy tournament, but I wasn't there. Lots of players weren't there. We were still living in the days when that event was a closed shop for the invited élite. Very few players at that time considered it to be a true world championship. By contrast, everyone entered the NOW tournament. Both John and Leighton had played in it the year that I won and were knocked out, as was Eric Bristow.

I was the true world champion of 1979 and I don't think anyone disputed that when I lifted the trophy. Sadly, history now suggests something entirely different but for that moment and at that time, I was the best player in the world and recognised as such. Overnight, I became a star. Photographers came to my house and asked me to pose by my swimming pool, smoking a giant cigar.

I loved all the attention. Darts was becoming big news and I was now one of its biggest names. Fate – and the weather – definitely played a good hand for me that day. Suddenly, I had strangers coming up and congratulating me in the street. Even the old man seemed proud of me and that is saying something. I had gone from no one to someone and was in my element, drinking champagne and signing autographs all day long.

Everyone at the King George was so proud of me and I didn't buy a pint in there for years. I used to love ringing the pub up and when the barmaid answered, 'King George', replying, 'Speaking'. They were great times for me.

Within days of my Wembley triumph, I was guaranteed six months' worth of darts bookings. It wasn't difficult to take the plunge and turn professional. Roy Cottee had kindly kept my floor-laying job open for me during my month-long trip to America the previous year and even after winning the North American Open, I remained in full-time occupation, turning down a lot of exhibition work as a result. I had actually been working as a floor-layer at London Bridge, near to the offices of Courage brewery, the day before I won the NOW championship.

That day, I paid Courage a visit. Darts sponsorship was becoming big business and I wanted to see if there was any interest in me. I didn't bother making an appointment and had to wait in the reception area feeling a right scruff in my working gear of vest, jeans and boots, which were covered in concrete. I spoke to a marketing guy called Dave Clarke and explained that I was the Essex Masters champion, North American Open champion and was also in the final of the NOW championship that very weekend. A fair amount of exhibition work was coming in from pubs and clubs too, and so I asked him if Courage would sponsor me to the tune of £200 per week. Along with prize money and a few working jobs, I calculated that this would earn me a good living. Dave said he wasn't sure, wrote my telephone number down and promised to ring me by the end of the day. By the time I played at Wembley, he still hadn't called, but first thing on Monday morning, the phone rang.

'Hello, Dave Clarke here. Congratulations, by the way,' he said. 'You came to see me a few days ago about us sponsoring you at £200 per week.' I laughed at the cheek of him.

'It's gone up to £200 per night now,' I replied.

We struck a deal, and a good one too. I did things properly for Courage. I made a stage setting with electronic gear and employed London referee Phil Jones as an MC. I also got a lot of bookings in the North East of England. Those shows made good money and would be worth even more today when I tell you that my first MC up there was the comedian Roy 'Chubby' Brown.

Chubby had just started doing stand-up when I was booked for some darts shows through a mutual friend, Stuart Stamp. We became a bit of a double act. I would throw darts and he would call a few games before cracking some jokes. Sometimes we lasted about half-an-hour before Chubby got us thrown out due to his material being considered too blue. His jokes have always been near the knuckle and some of the things he used to direct at unsuspecting ladies back then were probably a bit too much and certainly unprintable.

I was probably the bigger star back then, but not by much. It is a shame we can't do it again today – Chubby performs in front of 5000 people these days and I would fancy some of that.

I never really sat down and thought long and hard about making a living out of darts. The game just snowballed and took over my life. Fate decided that path for me. Yet despite being crowned NOW champion in some style, I kept being overlooked when it came to international recognition, and was once again left out of the England team by the selectors. It was bewildering. Here I was beating the best players in the world and yet it wasn't enough. Maybe my face didn't fit. I didn't know what to think.

I was desperate to play international darts – all the top players were involved but I wasn't wanted. Representing your country is the aim of every sportsman, whatever the game, and darts is no different. I decided to look at my options and turned my attention north of the border. My mother – the one who died when I was three – had been born in Scotland. Maybe, I qualified to play for the auld enemy?

I rang Scotland selector Alistair Petrie and he immediately agreed to put me forward for selection for the Scottish team. I was more than happy with that, especially if it meant putting one over on the England side that didn't want me, but the BDO weren't having any of it and the rules regarding international registration were suddenly changed. From then on, a player could only take his father's country of birth to qualify, not his mother's. I ask you! It was farcical.

The Scottish boys understood the situation and were fine about it, but it was now a case of England or nothing for me. If I was ever going to play in a World Cup or one of the other big international tournaments, it was going to have to be for England. No other avenues were open to me.

The Scots have always been good to me where darts has been concerned. They came to my aid again more than 20 years after this incident, when I was badly let down by three English counties ahead of the Embassy qualifiers, but more of that later.

Luckily, within a few weeks of my conversation with Alistair, I was selected to make my debut for England in, of all places, Edinburgh. I had finally got international recognition.

Times were gradually changing for the better but sadly the annual trip to America that summer hadn't been a happy experience. Betty had decided she wanted to come and bring the kids with her. I went

△ My parents – they met during the war.

▽ It was difficult for the old man after my mum died. The photo below was taken shortly after that. My brother Kevin is in the pram; Heather, my sister, is beside me.

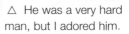

△ He was a very hard man, but I adored him.

◁ An angelic face, but within months I was killing turkeys and skinning rabbits.

▽ Struggling with my stutter and hardly able to read, I'd had enough of school by the age of 14.

◁ My money went on cars, not birds: Barkingside, July 1967, with my Austin Healey 3000.

▽ 1976, with the Old Maypole darts team. Malcolm Ellis (to my right) was responsible for getting me into darts.

◁ My first time on an aeroplane, off to the North American Open in 1978 (*Darts World*), where I'm pictured (opposite page, above) hitting the winning double. Eric Bristow chalked the match for me, then celebrated like he'd won the bloody thing.

▷ Still in America, John Lowe (standing to my right) clocks my headgear.

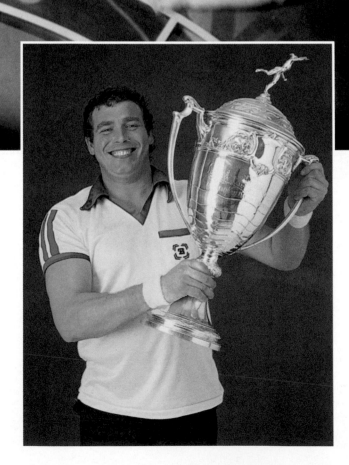

Beating Alan Glazier to win the *News of the World* championship in 1979 (*News of the World*).

▷ It was Ronnie Hayward's dream to walk out of Wembley with the *News of the World* trophy (Bill Perry).

▽ 'Bobby George' is born.

Some 'Mickey Mouse player'.
My trophy haul by the end of
the seventies (Courage).

△ A man will only ever have one dog that is unique. Buff was almost as big a star in darts as me.

△ A proud father, with Shane and Nicola.

△ The landlord of the King George, Gabriel Nolan, with King George.

◁ The end of an era – laying granite floors was a thing of the past, as I began to earn plenty of dough playing exhibition darts and winning trophies (the *Sun*).

along with it and it turned into an absolute nightmare.

I tried my best, took them all to Disneyland and the Magic Mountain, but it was awkward. Any banter with the boys was impossible and all the fun that America had given me the previous year disappeared. It was hard for Betty to realise that this was a work trip, however much fun we had on the darts circuit.

Trying to balance darts and family duties wore me down. Eventually, I'd had enough and decided to pull out of the North American Open. I really wanted to defend my title but by the time the competition came around, I just couldn't be bothered with it.

I did manage to take part in the Golden Gate Classic but missed 33 darts at double one in my semi-final with Barry Davis, which must be something of a record. I certainly have never known anything quite like it. Barry had long hair dropping over his eyes and looked like Dougal from *The Magic Roundabout*. He won that leg and the match and later beat Eric Bristow in the final.

My mind wasn't on darts and for a short while the game didn't matter. The trip made me accept that my marriage was finally over.

When I first started playing darts, I never told Betty about it. I was worried that if I did, she might find another job for me to do – painting the walls or something. Darts provided me with an escape route.

We stayed together for the kids – Nicola was seven and Shane was four at that time – and we only managed that because I was so busy and hardly ever saw her. Looking back, I realise I spent the first half of our time together working away and the second half of it playing darts.

However, one happiness I got from living at home at that time came from my little old dog, Buff, a cocker spaniel who became almost as big a star as me in the world of darts. I have had dogs all my life – the old man always had cocker spaniels – but none of them was as intelligent as Buff. She was terrific. I got her one Boxing Day as a puppy, long before I was playing darts, and I would take her all over the place with me. She came to work with me, went down the pub and never left my side.

I was once told that a man will only ever have one dog that is unique. If that is true, my dog was definitely Buff. She was amazing.

She would listen to me, watch my actions and then go and do it herself, whatever the task. It was unbelievable. One day I started doing trick shots with her at exhibitions and soon she became part of my act. We began with Buff facing the dartboard. I would hide a handkerchief and she would race off to find it – just something simple to warm her up. Then we would move on to her speciality, which was to jump up and take my darts out of the board. The two of us would have the audience in stitches. I would throw my darts, and then tell Buff to fetch them. Off she would run, jump up, take the darts out of the board and bring them back to me. I used to employ her as a darts player's labourer. We teased the crowd with how high on the board she could jump to retrieve the darts but Buff was a natural and could easily handle double top.

Collecting darts was just one of that dog's many talents. She could head a football like a seal, get chocolate buttons out of a pint glass and knew the meaning of over 40 words, which is bloody good going for a dog.

After I sold my Ford Cortina, I would often borrow Kevin's Morris Minor van to do odd jobs. Buff soon worked out that if she pipped the hooter, I would come out to her. Well, she used to play some right old tunes in that van and drove the locals round the bend. Buff also learned how to unlock the van's doors, so she could come to find me if I had been gone for a while. She did that a fair bit.

She copied everything I did. I would dive into the swimming pool at home and find her swimming beside me, under the water. The vet told me it was very unusual to get a dog to put its head under the water, never mind dive in and swim. Old Buff used to struggle with her ears later on, but at least she didn't have to put up with the tunes she belted out on the van hooter.

Buff was an obedient dog and if I told her to stay she would stand and wait for me through rain, sleet or snow. I thought the world of her. She brought a lot of love – as all dogs do – but she was something else. This one was special. Buff was with me 24 hours a day until she died. Kevin buried her underneath a fountain by his garden pond and she is still there today, bless her. I still miss her.

Darts tournaments were coming around too thick and fast for me to remain down for long. I also had a new image to protect – not only was I the NOW champion but I also had a new name, Bobby George. Previously, I entered competitions under the name of Robert George. Friends knew me as Bob, but if I ever needed to write down my name for any reason, it was always Robert George. I never used Bobby and it never once occurred to me to do so.

I had never been asked for an autograph before but within seconds of Diana Dors presenting me with that giant trophy, I was besieged by fans asking me to sign all sorts of things. Johnny Wheelens, a friend of Colin Baker, saw me signing Robert George on some programmes and T-shirts. When we got outside he suggested I started signing my name as Bobby George. 'Everyone knows you as Bob and it sounds good,' he said.

I agreed with him and I have been known as Bobby George ever since. It has got a nice ring to it and it is genuinely my name, although I have Johnny to thank for pointing it out.

The name Bobby George fitted the new era of darts perfectly. Both the BBC and ITV were increasing their coverage of the sport dramatically and more exposure meant more fame and more bookings. The money was now beginning to flow in. Tournaments were being staged all over the world and the majority of them carried world-ranking points – a new points system devised by the BDO/WDF to calculate who were the best players in the world.

Later in 1979, I beat both Alan Evans and John Lowe before defeating Leighton Rees in the final to win the Butlin's Grand Masters, at Yardley, near Birmingham. A few weeks later, Leighton gained revenge when he put on his best-ever performance against me to win our quarter-final match in the Ladbrokes British Matchplay, at Great Yarmouth. He checked out on 156 to win the first set and took the other set in a leg of 15 darts.

I lost to the eventual winner Tony Brown in the semi-finals of the British Open and reached the final of the Austin Morris British Masters, where I lost to Ceri Morgan. That final was a right laugh, as any match against the Welshman was.

Ceri had an unbelievably jerky action for a start. It looked like he was throwing a hand grenade at the dartboard. It was fascinating to watch – Co Stompe's throw of a few years later seemed quite normal in comparison – but it also made it difficult to play against him without losing the plot.

Ceri picked up a brand new Austin Princess that night but couldn't drive and ended up paying out more money in driving lessons than he won in the bloody competition. I got a Mini, which I gave to Jocky Wilson with whom I was splitting at the time.

We also had a ridiculous event called the British Pentathlon, which John Lowe won. I went along to make up the numbers but it had no appeal to me whatsoever. The format was like darts' version of *Superstars* without any cycling, shooting or swimming. Any one of those three sports would have made the event more interesting. I remember it being one long, hard, boring slog.

Anything seemed to go in those days but the organisation of some events left a lot to be desired and the BDO sometimes struggled to keep up with its own high standards. For instance, Colin Baker and I were robbed of a place in the final of the British Open pairs by poor officialdom. Whether it was due to BDO official Sam Hawkins' eyesight or hearing, I am not too sure, but in a best-of-three-legs 501 affair, the small matter of who throws first is very important.

Sam tossed the coin ahead of our match with Alan Glazier and Peter Chapman, and Colin called heads. The coin landed heads but Sam gave Alan and Peter the throw. Colin complained but it was no use and Sam was having none of it. We lost the match by two legs to one, each leg going with the throw.

I had never been one for playing too many darts events outside Great Britain but in 1979 I did enter a few of the Scandinavian tournaments and they were great fun to take part in.

Unfortunately, I lost to John Lowe in the final of the Danish Open in a bizarre game of darts – I kept missing the same double time and time again. I was well on top, leading 2–0 in a best-of-five-legs match and needed double 11 to win, but I just couldn't hit it. John eventually came back and took the leg to stay in the match. In the next leg, I hit two maximums and again left myself double 11 for the championship, but it was the same old story and John levelled the match.

In all, I threw nine darts at one double and missed them all. John beat me 3–2 and I was gutted, as I always was when I lost to him. I had done the hard part as well by knocking out Eric Bristow in an earlier round.

My scoring had been good but I just couldn't finish. Afterwards, on the coach back to the hotel, I mentioned to John that I had hit five 180s against him in the final. I flexed my biceps and said, 'See that. I have got loads of ton eighties in here.'

'Maybe you have, pal,' he replied, 'but you haven't got many double elevens!'

He was damn right. I beat myself up about that match for weeks.

I did win the Danish Open pairs with Jocky Wilson and the trip to Scandinavia provided me with much more than darts, anyway. I met a young lady called Annette Rasmussen. Annette was good-looking – as you would expect a Danish girl to be – and often went by the name of Angel. She was a decent darts player, too. She had beaten Maureen Flowers, who was the world's top female player at the time, and often competed in tournaments at home and abroad.

Denmark was absolutely rife with birds and wherever we went there was always plenty of interest from the opposite sex. A lot of the boys went for it, including some of the married ones. It was an education for us all, but also great banter. The attitude of women was freer over there. The girls were much more easygoing and a lot more liberated than they were back home.

I met Annette in a hotel bar in Copenhagen after she had caught the eye and attention of a certain Cliff Lazarenko. Cliff went up to the bar to get some drinks and saw Annette standing alone. In his own particular way, he said to her jokingly, 'You're lovely you are. I'd give you one, darling, that's for sure.'

Not for one moment did Cliff stop to think that she could understand what he said. That was just his style. He was often the life and soul of the party but every now and again it backfired. This was such an occasion. Most Scandinavians can speak the English language better than some English people – particularly the likes of Cliff and me – and Annette was one of them. She stared into Cliff's eyes and slowly pronounced just two words, 'Oh, really?' He couldn't believe it.

I smoothed things over and in doing so chatted her up myself.

Annette and I got on very well and spent a fair amount of time together on that trip. Well, she was much more fun than the usual darts crowd and a lot prettier to look at. We stayed in touch and ended up having a long-distance love affair. She was a lovely lady and became very important to me at that time in my life, particularly as my marriage was breaking down so badly.

Being a darts player, I have obviously known a fair share of drinkers in my time and Cliff tops the list, but even though he was the biggest drinker on the circuit, the man was also a true professional. We often stayed up together until four in the morning, drinking wine and spirits, but he always made sure he was up bright and early to play darts the next day. I stuggled to keep up with him and, unfortunately, in Scandinavia full English breakfasts never appeared on the menu. A full English can kill off the worst hangover in the world but a boiled egg doesn't do the trick. Eggs were all that we got most of the time over there.

Once, in Copenhagen, Cliff was up, showered, dressed and whistling away to himself as usual. He picked up two teacups from the cupboard in our room and asked me if I fancied a cuppa. Lying in bed with the hangover from hell and the covers over my head, I was longing for a nice cup of tea. 'Oh, yes please, Cliff,' I replied. He handed me a cup and gave me one of his trademark winks. 'Good morning, Bob,' he said as he watched me take a drink . . . of neat vodka!

Cliff loved vodka. He even cleaned his teeth in the stuff. And he never had a hangover. I don't know how he did it. The early rounds of the Danish Open started at 9 a.m. so I guess he needed to get into the swing of things early on.

Paul Gosling, a decent darts player from Truro, was the only man on the circuit who could come close to Cliff in the drinking stakes, but even Paul would have to accept second place on that one. Cliff was always the last one standing. He could do 30 pints of beer with no problems at all, and could down a bottle of vodka without it making a mark on him. The only side effect that I ever saw it have on him was the odd fit of the giggles.

Australian Terry O'Dea was another big drinker. He was well known on the circuit for enjoying a beer or two and then sleeping it off in the afternoon. One day in Copenhagen, I was in my hotel room when Terry walked in, desperate for somewhere to put his head after a heavy morning on the beer. He caught one glimpse of the camp bed, stripped off and fell fast asleep on top of it.

Alan Glazier arrived shortly afterwards with a Danish business-woman and her young daughter to ask if I would like to go out with them for a drink. These two Danish birds walked into the room and almost stepped on poor Terry, who was out for the count, snoring his head off with his mouth wide-open and his privates looking like a salmon with a broken back.

The girls took it in their stride and left the room giggling away to themselves. Alan felt so embarrassed for Terry and thought we had to tell him what had happened but I wouldn't have it. 'What he doesn't know, he can't worry about, Al,' I said.

Alan's catchphrase has always been, 'Boy, you are.' He muttered those words to me all day long, shaking his head whenever he thought about poor old Terry in that state.

Both the Danish Open and Swedish Open carried world-ranking points in those days and so a fair few of us made the trip to play in those countries. Suffice to say that Stockholm was just as bad as Copenhagen when it came to beer and frolics, and oversleeping.

A few years later, I spent one night in Stockholm drinking heavily with Terry. We were rooming together and asked for an early alarm call, which we both slept through. We missed the 9 a.m. check-in for the Swedish Open by three hours. In fact, we were so late that by the time we got to the hall to register our names, the second round matches were already under way. Rather embarrassed by this, the two of us sloped off for some lunch and on our return tentatively asked if we would be able to enter the pairs. The organisers were good to us because, strictly speaking, they should have said no, but they allowed us to play and we won the tournament, beating Dave Whitcombe and Richie Gardner in the final.

Those trips to Scandinavia did us all the world of good. The play-ers really bonded when they were abroad and as well as having a good laugh, we all brushed up on our darts.

I represented Essex for the fourth year in a row in the 1979 Winmau

World Masters. This time I got to the semi-finals, defeating John Lowe on the way in a memorable quarter-final, pulling out a crucial 11-dart leg. I enjoyed that one.

I played Eric Bristow in the semi-finals and lost. Eric went on to win the tournament and I finished fourth – my best-ever performance in the event – after losing a third-place play-off against Barry Dunn.

To be honest, I didn't see any point in playing for third place. It didn't pay any more money and meant bugger all to whoever won, so what was the point of it? I told Olly Croft how I felt and the BDO obviously felt the same because the following year it was scrapped.

As the seventies drew to a close, the game was buzzing. The new decade was to be a golden era for darts. Anyone who was there at that time could feel it happening.

The Embassy world championship, approaching its third year, remained an invitation-only event, based on international recognition and world rankings. I had yet to receive an invite but by 1980, I could be ignored no longer. My first appearance at the Embassy beckoned and it was to change darts for ever.

9 Glitter and gold

The first two Embassy world championship finals were rather dull affairs with John Lowe and Leighton Rees playing each other in matches that rivalled watching paint dry as a form of entertainment. By the time the third event came around, however, darts was developing from an underground sport into one that had real national interest.

The BBC expanded its TV coverage across the whole seven days of the tournament, providing the 24 invited players with their biggest opportunity yet to put the game well and truly on the map, and make a name for themselves in the process. What happened in that first week of February 1980 at Jollees nightclub, Stoke-on-Trent, completely transformed the image of darts and made both Eric Bristow and me household names overnight.

Up until that tournament, the regular dress code for darts players was county shirts and black trousers. I had always tried to look better than that by wearing bright, tight sports shirts and sweatbands on my wrists, but the differences were too subtle to be noticeable. With my debut in the Embassy looming, and the prospect of nightly national TV coverage, I started to think about ways in which I could stand out from the crowd. Bizarrely, I came up with the idea in the Spanish holiday resort of Torremolinos, courtesy of a wretched cabaret singer who was failing badly to impersonate Elvis Presley.

It was a few weeks before the Embassy and I had flown to the Costa del Sol to take part in the inaugural Mediterranean Open. Keen to get a bit of sun, a few of the wives and girlfriends – including the Bo-Bo girls – also made the trip and one evening we all went out to a local bar to have a drink.

All of a sudden, this bloke dressed in a yellow catsuit trimmed with sequins – nothing like the King – gets up on the stage and starts to try to perform a few numbers. He was bloody terrible but the girls in our gang thought he was terrific. All they talked about for the rest of the trip was this singer who looked the business. The fact that he was awful at impersonating Elvis didn't seem to bother them at all. That got me thinking and when one of the girls joked that I should wear something similar on stage at the Embassy, my mind was made up.

If this excuse for a singer could cause such a stir in a bar with half-a-dozen tables, what could I do in front of a packed darts crowd with the TV cameras on me? The way I saw it, even if I lost, I would still be remembered for my clothes, just like this woeful Elvis impersonator had been.

Darts was in need of a gimmick, anyway. The game ached for a bit of showbiz to give it a lift and to entertain the crowd. In its own way, darts is a bit like a cabaret act but no one had ever had the bottle to do anything like I was planning to do. The timing was absolutely perfect for me to try to make an impression in this way, but I would be lying if I said it wasn't a massive gamble.

Bo-Bo girl Sandra Adams designed my outfit. She was there in Torremolinos and convinced me that she could come up with something spectacular for my moment in the sun. Sandra made me a chocolate brown shirt with a big letter B on the right collar and a big letter G on the left, to wear with matching trousers. Silver sequins decorated chest, sleeves and legs – nothing too fancy, just a touch of glitter that sparkled under the lights. When she showed me her work, her father Gordon Croucher, formerly of the King George V, immediately bet me £20 that I wouldn't go through with wearing it on TV.

'I'll wear it, all right. Don't you worry about that,' I told him.

It was quite a line-up for the Embassy that year. Eight of the 24 players were seeded and given byes into the second round, including me. Due to a decent 12 months in world-ranking events, I was seeded at number five.

All the players stayed together at Clayton Lodge, a hotel just down the road from Jollees. Bob Geldof and his Boomtown Rats were in the hotel one night and a mighty row broke out between one of the band and Terry O'Dea over a barmaid. All the darts boys backed up Terry, not that he needed our support.

The whole darts scene was like one big family back then. The hotel would serve fry-ups until way past midnight to satisfy the wants of the card-school players, who would raise the stakes to thousands of pounds each and every night.

Everyone gambled apart from Tony Brown. We nicknamed him 'Doctor Brown' on account of him always carrying a big bag around with all sorts of lotions and potions in it. Tony used loads of hair spray too. He also brought a set of dominoes with him to every tournament, just to ensure that he got a game before he went to bed. That was his game of choice and he would easily have won the title of BDO dominoes champion, if there had been such a thing.

Nicky Virachkul had been introduced to crib and was hooked. So much so that he became to crib what Tony was to dominoes and wanted to take on everyone at the game. Then again, Nicky would play anyone at anything for money.

Jocky Wilson, a seed that year, played commentator Tony Green at darts for cash and was racking up quite a prize fund. Tony could see his debt mounting and kept asking for 'double or quits' every time he lost a leg. Jocky was well up and just wanted to get his money and get to the bar, but Tony refused to pay up and kept saying, 'Double or quits.' Jocky was literally hundreds of pounds to the good when the commentator eventually won a leg, evened up the bet and went straight to bed. Jocky was furious and stomped around the bar screaming for the rest of the night. He vowed never to talk to Tony again and it was a long time before he did.

I think that was also the night when Jocky and Ceri Morgan got involved in the most incomprehensible drunken conversation I have ever heard. Now Jocky was difficult to understand at the best of times, even when he was sober, and Leighton Rees told me that he couldn't make out a word that his fellow Welshman Ceri was saying after he had had a few. Both Jocky and Ceri loved a drink, and watching the two of them talking at the bar, neither able to make sense of what the other one was saying but having a conversation anyway, was absolutely hilarious.

Jocky was priceless in those days. On another night at Stoke, he was playing Eric Bristow at pool and asked if he could clean the cue ball as it was dirty. He took his teeth out and put them on the baize as a marker before wiping the cue ball with his shirt.

The funniest sight of all that year, though, was when I took big Paul Gosling and the even bigger Cliff Lazarenko out for an Indian meal in my tiny Mini. We squeezed into the car and I drove to the restaurant unable to see a thing out of my rear window. Getting the boys out of the Mini turned into a military exercise and when we finally got inside, our food and drinks order was something else.

Cliff ordered the wine and when the waiter offered him a taste, he downed the whole bottle in one and ordered several bottles of the stuff. He could drink a place dry but would still have the cheek to ask us all if we would split the bill with him afterwards.

By the end of that night, Paul was in a bad way and we had to pull him out of the Mini and get him up to his bed. I have to admit that I had a very sore head the next morning but, as usual, Cliff was as right as rain.

Cliff and I practised a lot together that year and when we weren't squeezing into Minis or scoffing curries, we would play darts against each other until the early hours. It paid off. Cliff knocked out the reigning champion and favourite John Lowe in the first round and that threw the entire tournament wide open.

My first match was against Dave Whitcombe, an up-and-coming player who had won a lot of the holiday camp tournaments and had already represented England. It was against Dave that I was to unveil my glittering new look. BDO general secretary Olly Croft wasn't impressed. The first time Olly clapped eyes on me back stage at Jollees, he couldn't believe it.

'You can't go out like that,' he said. 'Don't you realise the pressure you'll put on yourself if you play in that shirt?'

'It doesn't bother me, Olly,' I replied. 'It isn't going to make me throw my darts any differently, and win or lose, they won't forget me, will they?'

I was determined to make an impression one way or another. As it happened, the shirt went down a storm as I won 2–0 to progress into the last eight.

Jollees was a very tight club and when I threw I felt as though I was stood in the middle of the crowd. It could have been quite intimidating but I just loved the atmosphere and milked it for all it was worth.

The biggest venue I had previously played at was the Wembley Empire Pool, where a much bigger crowd was kept a lot further away from the oche. That made a difference to the noise generated inside the hall, and probably the level of excitement inside it, too. The Empire Pool was a posh gaff compared to Jollees.

I got a few wolf whistles and blown kisses from the crowd during the match and I played up to that. It was all a bit of fun and I really enjoyed myself. Surprisingly, the players were quite quiet about my outfit, probably because I had won. If I had lost, I think I might well have been roasted like a pig on a spit.

I was to play Leighton Rees in the quarter-finals. Leighton had won the first Embassy in 1978 and was runner-up to me in the Butlin's Grand Masters just before Christmas. He was the one who had bored me so much the previous year when I sat at home watching his Embassy final defeat by John Lowe on TV. I thought it was an awful match to watch and very bad for the image of the game. That match more than any other had convinced me that I had to do something to change darts' image in some way, and quickly, if I could.

I defeated Leighton 3–1 and as I was leaving the stage, BDO official Billy Skipsey – a good friend of mine – handed me a massive candelabra, alight with a dozen or more candles. Within a day, a huge turnaround had taken place at the BDO concerning my attire, and after just two matches the powers that be were now recognising that it could be good for darts. Not only that but they were helping me build on the showmanship.

Billy and his BDO colleague Fred Harwood had borrowed the candelabra from a pub across the road from the hotel. They thought that my appearance resembled the world-famous pianist Liberace and wanted me to have some candles to go with it. Liberace was well known for his flamboyant and rather effeminate manner and style of dress, but that didn't bother me. The glitter and sequins had nothing to do with effeminacy. They were about looking good on stage and putting on a show for the crowd. If a man of my size and from my background couldn't get away with that, who could?

Of course, the way I dressed was a world away from the beer-swilling blokes with fags in their mouths and that is why I made the headlines.

It was a gimmick and it worked a treat. The candelabra has been part of my stage show ever since.

Not content with the candelabra, Billy apparently spent the rest of that week in Stoke searching for a huge piano. Thankfully, he never found one, otherwise I might have been carrying that around for the last 25 years as well!

The tournament was now really hotting up. I was due to play Cliff Lazarenko in one semi-final while Eric Bristow was to meet Tony Brown in the other. Big Cliff fancied himself a bit that year but I shut him up good and proper by winning the match 4–1, finishing on double one to book my place in the final. Despite not losing a set up until then, Eric struggled to get past Tony 4–3 in the other semi-final, but my old mate from London town reached his first Embassy final, too.

We were the best two players in the world and by far the most exciting. Eric had beaten me in the World Masters semi-final the previous year and I had beaten him in a few other tournaments, so we were pretty evenly matched. Eric was the Winmau World Masters champion and I was the *News of the World* champion. The two of us knew each other so well, both on and off the dartboard. We had been through the lot together and here we were on the biggest stage, playing each other.

We spoke on the morning of the final and agreed that this was our big chance to make a difference to the game as a whole. 'Let's put on a real show for them tonight, Bob,' Eric said.

Everything was set up for a great match. It was the final everyone wanted and the crowd was magnificent, creating an atmosphere that hadn't been experienced before at a darts match. It was more akin to a boxing match or a football match with half of the hall – or maybe even a little bit more – cheering for me and the rest cheering for Eric. The fans were singing and playfully taunting each other. It was fantastic, and that was before we got out on stage.

As we walked out into the arena, the tension for both of us was massive. It was such a big match and we both knew what was at stake. Darts was just about to hit the roof, and one of us was going to be crowned Embassy world champion live on BBC TV. We were like two gladiators entering the ring – winner takes all.

Eric took one look at my sequinned shirt with the letters B and G on each collar and asked me if the initials stood for Big Girl. It was game on, all right.

I won the toss and threw first. The first few sets were very scrappy and every one went down to the wire, each taking the full five legs. I had chances to break Eric's throw and get an early advantage but I didn't take them. I would nudge ahead and then miss my chance to sink the winning dart and he would come back and level it. It was the same story throughout the first six sets.

At the interval it was three sets each – I hadn't yet been behind in the match – and as we left the stage the crowd moved up yet another gear. One half of the hall chanted 'Bristow' and the rest of them shouted back 'Bobby George'. This soon built up into a crescendo of 'Bristow', 'Bobby George', 'Bristow', 'Bobby George'. The crowd made an incredible noise, as though we were playing the final in a stadium rather than a nightclub. Backstage it was hard to practise because the noise was deafening. It was just a mad experience, but a very special one.

Everyone who was at Jollees that night sensed something was happening to the game of darts right in front of their very eyes. There was a definite split in support and no one sat on the fence. Eric was an arrogant player and this could make him unpopular. He got booed a fair bit in that final and at one stage I had to ask the crowd to be quiet, just so he could throw.

When retrieving his darts, Eric blew cigarette smoke over the board to cloud the treble 20 bed. He also turned the board slightly to alter the angle on one occasion. Both are well-known gamesmanship ploys in darts and used to happen a lot in those days.

Billy Skipsey saw what happened but it was all part of the game then and I wasn't going to kick up a fuss about it. It is a lot different now, of course, and there is no way that Eric would get away with that sort of behaviour today.

Eric knew I liked a fast game of darts and so he purposely played slowly during the final, taking all the time in the world to throw his darts. He so badly wanted to win that title it was untrue.

The first set back on stage after the interval proved to be the crucial one. Eric broke my throw with a 12-darter and it was curtains for me. I never got into any sort of rhythm in that particular set and he beat me three legs to one. It was the only set not to go the distance and it changed the outcome of the final.

Even in the last leg of the match I didn't help myself. Left with 18, I hit a single nine and as I aimed for a single one I said to myself, 'Don't hit a 20, Bo' and bugger me, I hit a 20 and bust.

Eric needed double top to win. He never liked double top and always preferred double 16 but any player worth his salt is going to wrap it up from there. I nonchalantly put my darts in my top pocket because the game was over but I secretly prayed he would put his three darts above the wire. He didn't, the first dart went a good inch below double top but the second one hit double ten to win him the match and the world championship, 5–3.

The legs had gone: 2–3, 3–2, 2–3, 3–2, 2–3, 3–2, 3–1, 3–2. It was that tight.

As Eric took his darts from the board, he turned to me with a big, beaming smile on his face and planted a kiss on my cheek. I could have done without that. It is one thing getting beaten by Eric Bristow. It is another thing being kissed by him!

The former *Blue Peter* presenter Peter Purves fronted the BBC coverage that year and he interviewed us both on the stage afterwards. When asked what he made of my performance, Eric said, 'He'll make a good world number two.' He never accepted that anyone – not just me – was on the same level as he was. That was Eric's style, and you either loved him or hated him for it.

Eric was booed during his interview but when I went up to be given the runners-up cheque, I received a standing ovation from the crowd. That meant a lot to me and I felt that I could come back the following year and win it, just as I had done the previous year in the NOW championship.

All in all, everything worked for darts that night. The standard was good, the spectators were terrific and those two components made for such exciting televised sport. Ultimately, there could be just one winner and it was Eric.

I lost my chance to be Embassy world champion in the early sets of that final, there is no doubt about that. In each of the second, fourth and sixth sets, I could have broken Eric's throw. If I had, it would have been a different story.

A lot of people have since asked me why I put my darts in my top pocket that night. In fact, it was a habit. I used to do it when I was getting beaten but that match is the one occasion that people remember.

I enjoyed the match and the experience. Millions of people watched it on TV and millions of people now knew about me. Defeat didn't seem to matter that much. I felt much more positive than negative afterwards. Darts was very much on the up and it was hard to feel downbeat.

Above everything else, the 1980 Embassy world final changed darts. The crowd changed the atmosphere of darts and Eric and I changed the face and image of darts. The razzmatazz, the showmanship, the game that darts is today, arrived when we played each other in that final. That was the beginning of the game's heyday. Darts fans had never got involved in matches until then. Most of the crowd were dressed in suits and ties the night that I played Eric. We moved the whole game on. The difference between the 1979 and 1980 finals was massive. The previous affair looked as though it had been played in a doctor's waiting room by comparison. You really could hear a pin drop when the MC said, 'Game on'.

Eric and I made a lot of money in organised head-to-head clashes in London after that final. There was a big demand for us to take each other on in the same way as we had done in Stoke, and we were always sure of a big crowd in the capital. He once won 11 legs on the trot against me and I once checked out on 167 to beat him. They were fantastic occasions and the fans' appetite to watch us play against each other was insatiable for a while.

What helped was the fact that Eric and I were different characters with different appeals. A lot of people liked what I stood for – and how I looked – but some hated it. The same applied to Eric. That is what created such a great atmosphere in the final.

Of course, clothes can't win darts matches on their own and there was a lot of pressure on me to perform. I wanted to be known as the darts player with the glitter who got to the final and not the darts player with the glitter who went out in the first round. Some of the players and officials didn't like my look and didn't agree with what I was trying to do. The desire among some of them for me to get knocked out of the Embassy tournament was quite strong because of that, and I felt a cold chill from them throughout that week.

I really couldn't understand that attitude. Male ice dancers had worn shimmering clothes for years and nothing had ever been made of that. Maybe darts was seen as much more of a working-class game and something not to be messed with. The fact that both darts and I originated from the street made my appearance odd to some, but I think that is what made it so special – and it definitely worked, both for me and for darts.

The game was entering its own Glam Rock era, if you like, but there had never been a big plan on my part to achieve that. I was just bothered about getting noticed and being remembered, like that cabaret singer in Torremolinos. I loved my new look and, more importantly, so did the public. Little old ladies stopped me in the street to tell me how much they enjoyed watching me play darts in my sexy outfits on TV. My clothes enabled me to achieve what I set out to do. I had given myself an identity and made my name. There was no going back now. I had to stick with it – so I decided to go a step further, and added some jewellery.

If a Spanish singer was responsible for the glitter, my good friend and fellow darts player Tony Sontag was responsible for the gold. Tony always used to wear a huge sovereign ring in the early days when we played, until one day he needed some cash rather urgently and asked me if I would buy it from him.

I didn't think twice. I mainly bought the ring as a favour to help out a mate but I have to admit I liked the look of it. It was the first ring that I ever bought but it soon became one of many. That ring started off a love affair with gold jewellery that has lasted to this day.

The gold seemed a natural extension of the glitter and I fell in love with the stuff. I asked a local jeweller to make some more rings for me. The bracelets, necklaces and watches just seemed to follow until I had got this massive golden decoration on my left wrist and lower arm, all paid for by my right hand. My pride and joy is a big heavy chain necklace made from 46 separate nine-carat gold wedding rings. I never take it off.

The glitter and sequins immediately made me look different from the rest of the players and the gold finished off the look. Nowadays, all darts players are decked from head to toe in jewellery and a few of them go for glittered shirts as well.

I had always felt different from the other players anyhow. Unlike the rest of them, I hadn't been playing county darts for years on end and while that was also true of Eric, he had dedicated his life to the game from a very young age in a way I had never done. Darts hadn't mattered to me until I was over 30 and a few people still had a problem with that. I was treated differently and so I decided to dress differently.

Obviously, I stood out from the crowd but that was the idea. I think that is why I became so well supported in tournaments, especially those that were televised. The interest would have been short-lived, though, if my top scores had been 26. It was the combination of the darts, the dress and the fun factor that made it entertaining and popular with the punters, and the look has been with me for over 25 years.

The image made me a personality but it didn't come cheap. One shirt alone could cost £100 to make, and £100 was a lot of money back in 1980. Suddenly, I couldn't leave my house without putting on a glitzy top. Poor old Sandra Adams was working overtime on creating new designs for me but it was now expected that I would wear the glitter and if I didn't, I would feel underdressed and understated. It would be like a handyman going to work without his bag of tools.

I soon had a wardrobe of more than a dozen sequinned shirts and trousers. The fans couldn't get enough of them but some of the players were beginning to talk about my clothes bringing the game into disrepute, which was absolute nonsense. My look had turned darts into a showbiz event. Before every tournament the talk was now not about who was going to win but what I was going to wear. It was incredible. Even Olly Croft now accepted that the combination of glitter and gold made darts look great on TV.

It definitely got people on the box talking and I was soon asked to appear as a guest on the *Russell Harty* show. However, all my good work almost came unstuck. Russell had no interest in darts and no interest in learning anything about it. I think he had made up his mind from the off that we were all overpaid and overweight, and referred to us as 'lads heavily primed with pints of lager'. As he introduced me to the audience, he added, 'No matter how much fagging and boozing they do, they can still perform their alarmingly accurate thing.' What did that say about respect?

He made no effort to meet me beforehand to discuss either the game or the show. Why he even agreed to interview me, I don't know. His ignorance of darts was there for all the viewers to see and the result could have been disastrous for the game.

As soon as I walked on to the set, I noticed that four pints of lager had been carefully laid out on a table by the dartboard. Russell looked me up and down, as if to say 'You're a big boy, aren't you?' He said as much to my face. Maybe it was his style, but it got my back up right away.

'Yeah, but I'm not full of lager or nothing,' I replied. I weighed over 16 stone with not an ounce of fat on me. I had only just finally retired from floor-laying a few months earlier.

Part of the act was for me to show him how to play darts. The whole thing was scripted and full of double-entendres, written to get a cheap laugh and seemingly embarrass me. He kept mispronouncing the word 'oche' as 'hockey', and raising his eyebrows to the camera as he said it. 'Oh, my end's come off,' he said when he tried to throw a dart. It was all very camp. I felt sick and wanted the studio floor to swallow me up.

I found the whole affair demeaning and frustrating. I was absolutely fuming but somehow I kept my composure and respectability. God knows what would have happened to us all in the game had I lost it that night. The host was rude to me but at least he knew my name. Tony Green, who was also on the show that night, was treated even worse. Tony was furious afterwards. He had flown in from Amsterdam to appear on the programme and was very disappointed with how the game was portrayed. Olly Croft couldn't believe it, either.

That programme was a real eye-opener, showing us how some members of the outside world viewed darts. It did the game no favours at all. Darts commentator Sid Waddell was an assistant producer on the show, and he later told me that the intention was to have a serious look at the character of the game and that Russell's style had been an attempt to create a bit of atmosphere and banter. I don't think anyone working on the show necessarily meant any harm by it but the plan seriously backfired. It was a big mistake for me to go on that programme.

The only good thing about it was that I met singer Gilbert O'Sullivan. Gilbert was a big star in the seventies and had number one hits with 'Claire' and 'Get Down'. Gilbert and his mum were both genuine darts fans and we got on like a house on fire backstage. I became good friends with him as a result. That aside, the night was a total disaster and the fallout within darts was to go on for weeks.

Darts World magazine readers wrote in to support me. The fans had watched the programme and had seen me doing my best in difficult and unforeseen circumstances, but John Lowe wasn't so sympathetic. He did his bit in the newspapers, criticising me for bringing down the game of darts. He claimed the show should have been rehearsed and that I should have been aware of everything in it. John didn't criticise anyone other than me. Apparently, I held the game 'up to ridicule' by appearing on TV in a sequinned shirt. I did nothing wrong on that programme. I thought about every word I said and I was very careful not to be rude, which wasn't easy in the circumstances.

However, the TV invitations kept coming my way. A little while later, I received a telephone call to appear on Rod Hull's children's programme *Emu's World*. I found Rod to be a really nice, friendly guy and very good with children, but it won't surprise you to learn that I didn't find Emu friendly at all. Rod worked that act so well. Emu was nothing more than a simple puppet but Rod turned it into a real, living bird.

The programme was filmed at a holiday camp in North Wales. This time I was invited to take part in a rehearsal and Rod came up with an idea for me to throw darts at Emu. Of course, Emu never said a word but he didn't have to. That was the brilliance of the act. Emu's menacing look was so fierce that the bird never needed to make a sound. Rod told Emu that I was going to throw a dart through his open beak and into the bull. Well, old Emu didn't go a lot on that one. He turned his face to me, curled his top lip and gave me one of those trademark snarls.

Eventually, after Rod had told Emu that I was a good darts player and could be trusted, I was allowed to throw. All the children were staring at me and then staring at Emu, who was up by the board. The drum roll started up and I threw the dart. It landed right in Emu's beak. The children screamed but I couldn't help laughing. Emu wasn't impressed and he soon got his own back.

During a chat with Rod, Emu put me on the floor, just as he had done so famously with Michael Parkinson on his TV chat show a few years earlier. The *Parkinson* incident made Rod Hull and Emu. Rod could get away with almost anything with that bird on his arm after that.

When it was my turn, Rod sat me on a chair and got Emu to stroke my hair. Seconds later, Emu had grabbed hold of a couple of locks and I was on my back. It was hilarious and I just couldn't stop laughing. Rod and Emu was classic comedy. It was simple, but it worked very well.

Rod was a little eccentric but in a nice way, and he made that eccentricity work for him in his performance. I suppose Emu did become his one and only act but he was so damned good at it that he didn't require another. You could never mention the name of Rod Hull without putting Emu on the end.

My profile was now rising by the week. The glitter had turned me into a star but after my second TV appearance in less than a month, John Lowe had finally had enough. Not content with complaining to the BDO about my American cowboy hat or being quoted in the national press about my appearance on the *Russell Harty* show, he now wanted to ban glitter and sequins from darts tournaments. He planned to form the World Professional Darts Players Association, which was appropriately quite a mouthful. Topping John's agenda was the image of the game. He held strong views on dress code and wanted all sequinned shirts banned from darts because he felt apparently they made the game look like a circus and the players look like clowns. I felt that this was directed at me personally and only found out about it by reading an article in a national newspaper as all of us flew over to

Copenhagen to play in the Danish Open. John was quoted as saying, 'Legislation is likely to be introduced which could, for example, out-law the sequinned shirts used by Bobby George.'

It was the closest I got to coming to blows with John. Ten years earlier I might have handled it in a different way entirely but I decided to go about it in another way. I walked down the aisle of the aeroplane to where he was sitting and asked him if the newspaper article was correct.

'Yes, pal, it's correct,' he told me.

'Well, how's about your union also bans wigs and false teeth then?' I asked.

The whole thing eventually passed over and there wasn't any sort of organisation such as the proposed WPDPA for a few more years. That was just as well because also high on the hit list back then was the supposed problem of 'Over-exposure of the game on TV', which, in hindsight, is even more laughable.

I had to take it all in my stride. I was my own man and saw myself as a paid entertainer. Why should I change that just to keep John and others happy, because they felt darts should be played in a different way?

John used to talk about the reaction he would get if he ever wore a shirt like mine at a working-men's club in Derbyshire. Can you imagine that? I haven't got a clue what the reaction would be but the sight alone would be a giggle!

Our different styles always added an extra bit of needle when we played each other and that was definitely the case when we met in the NOW championship a few months later.

For the third year in succession, I had won through all the regional rounds, beating Neville Fountain, Ray Headitch and Steve Talbot on the way, and had qualified to play at Wembley in May. I was now bidding to become the first man since Tommy Barrett in 1965 to defend the title successfully.

West Ham United, my local football team, reached the FA Cup final that year and, despite being in the old Second Division, they beat Arsenal 1–0 to win the trophy at the famous Twin Towers just up the road. Wembley was full of claret and blue, both at Wembley Stadium for the football and at the Wembley Empire Pool a few weeks later for the darts. Being a Cockney boy and playing in my own final at Wembley, I decided to stick another one up John by wearing a West Ham football shirt with a silver FA Cup on the front and back. It looked the business.

I had beaten Colin Kenneys in the first round to set up a last-eight clash against my old rival, but my preparation away from the dartboard was not mirrored by my performance on it. I played really badly. John needed 22 darts – which is a disgrace – to win the first leg and then won the match 2–0. I was gutted.

While John was beaming in front of the TV cameras, I picked up a giant pair of Mickey Mouse ears, placed them on his balding head and congratulated him on being the new 'Mickey Mouse champion'. After all, if I was a Mickey Mouse player and he had just beaten me in the tournament that I had won the previous year, what else did that make him?

Nicky Virachkul had brought the ears over from America in recognition of John's comments about me only winning low-profile Mickey Mouse tournaments in the States. I took the ears to Wembley with the sole intention of presenting them to John live on TV in an effort to end all the nonsense.

'The difference is, John,' I told him, smiling for the cameras, 'Mickey Mouse is known all over the world and loved by many people, but John Lowe ain't.'

'Who looks the clown now, pal?' I asked him. John laughed along but I doubt he liked it one little bit.

It was a satisfying moment for me, although it further publicised the rivalry between the two of us.

My defeat meant that I had lost my NOW title but the fans at Wembley were great. I threw my West Ham shirt into the crowd – well, it was on TV – and they tore it to bits. Everyone seemed to want a piece of it and only a few years ago a lady came up to me at a darts exhibition and told me that she still had a thread of my West Ham shirt from 1980.

The summer brought another trip to the USA, this time without Betty and the kids. I travelled with Eric Bristow, Leighton Rees and Tony Sontag, among others, and we teamed up to enter some four-man events, with Tony and I playing pairs while Eric and Leighton did the same. As usual, any prize money would be split four ways. Eric and Leighton won the Santa Monica Open pairs in the very first week to put us in the money straight away, that was until Eric came off stage and said that he was no longer splitting his winnings with me.

Maybe I should have seen it coming but I didn't and that sudden outburst came as a total shock to me. Eric was a changed man. The Embassy win seemed to change him and our friendship went downhill fast afterwards. Arrogance was one thing Eric always had in abundance but deep down he was a decent bloke. Maybe the glory went to his head and he began to believe his own hype.

Off the oche, another development in Eric's life at the time was his deepening relationship with Maureen Flowers. They were besotted with each other and became virtually inseparable. Maureen was a very good darts player and for a while, when darts was in its heyday, the two of them became the game's own version of Richard Burton and Elizabeth Taylor. They were always in the newspapers and got the sport a lot of coverage.

Eric and Maureen were a very strong couple. They won the Santa Monica Open mixed pairs together with Eric playing on just the bull and 25 throughout the event. Like him or loathe him, you had to admire his talent.

I played Maureen in the semi-finals of the singles and when she took the first leg off me, all I could hear was Eric shouting out, 'Come on, Mo, stuff him.' I couldn't face the fall-out of losing to Maureen – especially with her being Eric's girlfriend – and set about making sure I wasn't going to be the biggest scalp that she had ever taken in darts. I got my act together and got through a close match.

Eric was already in the final and obviously quite fancied playing his girlfriend in it. Well, now he was playing me and, of course, we weren't splitting our winnings so it really was game on.

Within seconds of the start of the final all I could hear was Maureen shouting out, 'Come on, E, stuff him.' The two of them were like Pinky and Perky. It was unbelievable.

Well, I stuffed Eric that day and when I was handed a fistful of dollars I threw them up in the air. We were no longer splitting, just as

Eric had decreed. The singles paid big money so he had well and truly screwed up this time. I also won the North American Open pairs with Tony Sontag. The Santa Monica Open win was sweet. It was a big title and got me a little bit of revenge for my defeat in the Embassy.

Eric was never one to be gracious in defeat, but every now and again he went too far in my opinion, like the way in which he treated me at the end of our Embassy final for instance. The Santa Monica Open was just another example of that when he didn't shake my hand at the end.

The two of us went back a long way and we had both been thrown into the limelight at the very same time after that Embassy final six months before. That match was a tight affair and either of us could have won it, but Eric did. As far as he was concerned, he was now famous for his talent and I was famous just for being a showman. He always had a mouth on him but it seemed to get bigger with his success. It helped him. He played better darts because of it and it seemed to give him the mental edge over some players.

The final straw for me was when he labelled Jocky Wilson 'a fat pig' in an interview, which was out of order and totally unnecessary. It wasn't like Eric was an oil painting, either. The Winter Olympics could have used that nose for a ski slope!

Tony Sontag had become my best friend on the circuit and during that trip to America the two of us had some good laughs together. That wasn't hard with Tony. He was one of those blokes who laughed all day long and never knew when to stop.

I had my one and only experience with drugs on that trip. We were in a pub in Los Angeles when Tony offered me a roll-up at the bar. It had a bit of a scent to it but, presuming it was just tobacco, I had a few smokes and thought nothing more of it. I didn't go a lot on the taste and soon returned to the comfort of my pint. Everything was fine until a few minutes later when I went to the toilet and almost passed out. I was suddenly unable to find my feet. I felt weak and numb and had to negotiate the few steps down into the bar area as though I was walking out on to the edge of a cliff. I was all over the place and it lasted for about half-an-hour. It was only when I caught sight of Tony grinning at me like the Cheshire Cat that it dawned on me that he had given me a joint.

The words 'bad trip' don't come close to doing it justice. That was one of the worst experiences I ever had on a night out. I was powerless and totally out of it. It was scary. God only knows what I had been smoking.

All in all, Tony was good to play darts with but he could be murder at times. We won a lot of pairs events in the States, which was some achievement given that my partner would lark about so much that I often had tears running down my face when I threw during a match. Tony has the ability to make me laugh in an instant, and often that instant would be when I was throwing for a winning double.

His antics affected our opponents, particularly the home-grown players, much more than they affected us, though. I got us to the final of the North American Open pairs single-handedly. I was responsible for all our victories and just about carried Tony along with me. Before the final, I told him it was about time he pulled his finger out. I was winning our matches on my own and he was just making me laugh. Often, we were lucky to get through but there was now serious money at stake and I wanted us to win it.

We decided to change the routine of me throwing first in each leg and suddenly Tony was a changed man. He was on fire. I threw just three darts in every leg and he sunk the winning double each time on the way to us winning the title. At the end of the match, people were coming up to us saying how lucky I was to have such a good partner and that we were essentially a 'one-man team'. I looked over to Tony, who didn't know where to put himself because he was laughing so much.

Tony always had a habit of stealing my thunder. The following week, I kicked off our exhibition at the Long Bar in Antelope Valley with a personal best 19-dart finish at 1001. The pub was in the middle of the Nevada desert and full of real-life cowboys, who gave me a standing ovation. They were all on their feet, throwing their hats in the air, which made for a fantastic sight. 'Yee hah, Bobby,' they cheered as they gave me high fives, 'Right on, man,' and all that game. I was the biggest darts hero they had ever seen – for all of five minutes.

Tony got up to play his leg of 1001 and started off with a ton eighty before spotting a fly on the wall, right next to the dartboard. He stopped, pointed out the fly to the crowd and then pinned it with a perfect dart, right in the middle of its body. All the hats went up in the air again and this time so did Tony. He was carried shoulder high by the locals. They loved him. He posed for photographs with the dead fly and his killer dart. No one cared about my 19-darter.

A few days later, Tony's humour backfired and it almost proved fatal. The two of us had enjoyed more than a few morning beers in a Las Vegas pub and when we went outside for some fresh air we were literally taken aback by the power of the midday sun. The alcohol went straight to our heads. We walked back to our digs and Tony decided to jump in the pool fully clothed to cool off. Like an idiot, I followed him. As soon as we hit the water, we both started giggling and I couldn't bring myself to stop. I began to swallow water and went under. I was drowning. I have always been a good swimmer but the beer and the giggles had got to me big time and I lost all control of my body. Luckily, Tony saw that I was in danger and dragged me out of the pool. He also had the wisdom to dry out the cash I had in my pockets in the sun! It is quite frightening to think that something so silly could have easily cost me my life. I most certainly never did anything like that again.

Tony was later very lucky to survive himself when he suffered a bad car crash near to Lake Tahoe. His life was saved by a doctor, who was, fortunately, driving along the same stretch of road at the same time. Tony's injuries were so severe that for a long time afterwards if ever he scratched his head, it bled. He also experienced bad nightmares for years as a result of the crash.

In his absence, I managed to get to the final of another four-man team event on that tour, which was quite an achievement given that only three of our team turned up for it. Keith Deller, who was away from home for the first time, was getting into all sorts of scrapes and we almost paid the price for that when he left Colin Baker, Dave Lee and me in the lurch by failing to appear for the team competition. We were allowed to play without him, but only after we agreed to sacrifice our throw at every fourth turn. Incredibly, we still got all the way to the final where our luck eventually ran out and we lost.

I went looking for Keith afterwards and almost crowned him, but he was a young boy having the time of his life on his first trip abroad and I couldn't be too hard on him. Keith never looked his age, and he wasn't old enough to drink over there anyway, so no one ever served him, which was just as well because he never had any money to buy a round.

I used to joke with Keith to go and play on the swings and drink some milk and that is how he got the nickname of the 'Milky Bar Kid' – even though I always called him 'Boy' myself. I don't suppose he ever drank milk, either. Do me a favour – he was a darts player when all's said and done, even if he was super slim. The name just stuck.

Keith was very young back then. I took him under my wing and introduced him to all sorts of things on that trip to the States. The boy had a real talent for darts. I was playing in another four-man-team event with him and we required 158 to win the match on his throw. He looked at me and asked what he should do. I said to him, 'Just go 54, 54, bull, boy.' He did it and didn't even blink. It was clear then that he could play.

Keith was the youngest one of the bunch and attracted a fair bit of attention from the ladies on that trip, but his chat-up lines were dreadful. One girl, who clearly fancied him rotten, looked over to me bewildered as he told her about his love of beans on toast! I had to give the boy a few tips after that.

There was always a lot of interest from girls in the States – much more than back home or even in Scandinavia – and it could be pretty wild at times. Tony Sontag and I were two of the better-looking players on the circuit and got the most attention, but all of the boys had the opportunity to get involved in that scene if they wanted it. We were all earning a fair bit of money, playing in front of big crowds. Fame and power seemed an aphrodisiac to some women and a few of them jumped from one player to the next.

Most of the birds who followed us around on several tours to the States weren't much to look at but they were there if we fancied it, or more to the point, if we fancied them. The danger was that after a few pints even the ugly ones could start to look pretty. The phrase 'any port in a storm' springs to mind and a few of the players did dabble. The fact that we all spoke the same language broke down any sort of barrier and made picking up such women easy.

Sex was everywhere when we toured the States. We had prostitutes hanging around us, players picking up nasty infections and girls getting pregnant. It was like one big lads' holiday every summer, only we weren't lads any more. The majority of the players were well into their thirties and married with children. Sometimes, kind-hearted families put us up free of charge during those trips and one or two of the boys even tried to get it on with the wives while the husbands were out.

I think the fact that so much went off out there was due to the forward attitude of the women, who confidently approached the players by going straight for the trouser department. They didn't have any problem in telling you what they wanted. The approach from American girls was totally different from what I knew in back home. Even the classy ones would come up and ask for a drink or a dance or even a bit more.

One lady – dressed in a cowgirl outfit – approached me at a darts function and asked me to dance. I obliged and within minutes she had got her hands below my hips. I had a few rolled-up dollars in my pockets that night and when she got to them, she kissed me on the cheek and whispered, 'Wow, handsome, is that all you?'

British girls weren't as bad as that. They would grab at my sequins and jewellery but they were nowhere near as forward as the ones in the States. The worst it would get back home was when girls would hang out at hotels and try to get into the players' rooms, knocking on our doors in the middle of the night and offering their services.

Once, when I was rooming with Jocky Wilson, I woke up to find a young woman laid beside me in bed. When I opened my eyes she asked me for an autograph. I had never set eyes on her before and didn't know how she had got into the room until I looked over towards my snoring room-mate and it dawned on me that he must have let her in. I told her where to go. It wasn't my scene and it wasn't my style.

A lot was made of me being some sort of womaniser in those days – probably because I was the boy with the looks – but it wasn't true. In fact, I was quite shy and generally uninterested. It was good for the ego, though. The whole darts scene got to the stage where certain players could pull a girl just on account of their name, and Bobby George was one of those names.

The year ended on a happy note for me when victory over Billy Lennard added a second successive Butlin's Grand Masters title to my growing collection. All the best players in the world took part, including John Lowe, whom I thrashed 5–0 on my way to the final.

I played several matches for England in 1980, was runner-up in the Embassy, reached the finals of the NOW championship and World Masters, and won the Butlin's Grand Masters and the Santa Monica Open in the States. It had been another good year and I was now ranked number two in the world, one place behind Eric Bristow.

I also won the annual BDO Sports Personality award, but I wasn't sure if that was good news or not. On the one hand, I had been deemed the biggest personality in the game that year, ahead of Eric and co., but on the other hand, previous winners included BDO officials Olly Croft and Dave Alderman. So I wasn't exactly sure what sort of personality you had to be to win it anyway. Still, after all the trouble that I'd had in the game, it was nice to get some positive recognition for my efforts.

It had been another massive year for darts and there were now so many different characters in the game that every fan could have their own favourite. That mixture helped the game and it also helped the players. Less than a dozen of us had been in the right place at the right time but we were now household names and had really struck gold. TV coverage was at an all-time high and big-money tournaments were coming out of our Mickey Mouse ears.

10 A brush with death

Despite being ranked number two in the world, the BDO surprised me yet again by naming me number four seed for the 1981 Embassy world championship behind Eric Bristow, Tony Brown and John Lowe. That meant I was due to play Eric in the semi-finals. Whatever happened, there could be no repeat of the 1980 final, but I was in good form, winning various events leading up to the tournament, and I felt capable of making up for the previous year's disappointment, just as I had when I lifted the *News of the World* championship trophy two years earlier.

The BDO brought the tournament forward a month and switched it to the first week of the New Year, which has been its regular place on the sporting calendar ever since.

My first match, against Alistair Forrester, was to be the scene of things to come in darts as neither of us took either a pint of beer or a packet of fags on to the stage. We didn't realise it until we got up there. It was more by chance than anything, but it was the first time it had ever happened. Looking back now, that seems incredible and it is a good example of how things were in the game at that time.

I beat Alistair and then defeated Tony Clark to set up a quarter-final clash with Cliff Lazarenko. I had beaten Cliff in the semi-finals the previous year but Cliff was well up for it this time and he beat me 3–2. Eric thrashed Cliff in the semis and retained his title by beating John Lowe 5–3 in the final. He was now the undisputed world number one and king of darts.

Meanwhile, I was getting involved in all sorts of spin-offs from the game. A few weeks earlier, I had got chatting to two musicians, Tony Leggett and Alan Parker, in a club in Burnley. Whether it was the beer talking or the Christmas cheer I am not too sure, but by the end of the night the pair had convinced me that I had the looks of a pop star and we had decided to write a song about darts for a crack. They came up with the melody and I helped them with the lyrics. That is how the record '180' was born.

A few weeks later, Tony Sontag, Jocky Wilson, Olly Croft and his wife Lorna, MC Freddie Williams and his wife Pat and I recorded it with singer Vince Williams at Smile Studios in Manchester.

The song begins with three arrows hitting the board and Freddie calling out '180', but the darts on the record aren't genuine. Not one of us remembered to take a dartboard to the recording studio so I had to hit my knuckles hard against a cork wall to achieve a similar sound.

The flip side of the single was 'Bobby's Theme', which was sung by yours truly. It's actually more accurate to say that it was spoken by yours truly as I'm hardly singing at all.

Both songs became very popular within the game of darts and at that year's Embassy all the players – including those who had declined to sing on the record – got up on stage and did a special performance of '180'. I put the money up to record the song and the BDO sold it through their offices and at various tournaments.

It sold quite well but wasn't available in record stores so unfortunately there was never any chance of us getting into the pop charts, which was a shame as I would have been in my element appearing on 'Top of the Pops'. I know Jocky would have loved that, too. The nearest Jocky ever came to appearing on the programme was a few years later when a giant photograph of him accompanied Dexy's Midnight Runners' performance of 'Jackie Wilson Said' by mistake!

'Bobby's Theme' is still a popular song and has been played on the radio a few times over the years. It gets a spin at the Lakeside every so often and on one recent occasion BBC presenter John Inverdale made me stand up on the stage and hum along to it in front of a packed audience, which was quite embarrassing!

One good thing that came out of my defeat early on in the 1981 Embassy was that it opened another door for me. With Eric playing John in the final, I was asked if I fancied joining Tony Green and Sid Waddell in the BBC commentary box as a summariser. As it turned out, I ended up playing doctor to Sid, who was quite unwell for most of the match and very nervous of making a mistake in his commentary as a result of that.

I enjoyed myself, especially when I came out with little nicknames for the players that Sid polished off in his own unique style. Sid was very talented and came up with plenty of his own creations but I like to think that I got him started with my own contributions that year, such as 'Stoneface John' and 'Cocky Jocky on the Oche'.

I also used to call Jocky 'Bumblebee' to his face because not only did he look like one but he never accepted that he was beaten either. If you look at the ratio of a bumblebee's wings to its body, there is no way that it should be able to fly, but it does. Do you know why? Because it doesn't know it can't! That summed up Jocky – the little man never thought he could lose.

Jocky was developing into some player and along with Eric, John and me, he became one of the top four names in darts. He beat me in the final of the Bullseye trophy that year at Camber Sands, a tournament shown on the BBC and not to be confused with the game show that was just about to start over on the other side.

Bullseye launched on ITV on Monday nights in the spring of 1981 and ran until 1995. It took darts to a new level and in its pomp would get viewing figures higher than some of the soaps. Over 15 million watched it at one time. It was that popular. I was involved in its concept but didn't manage to get a full-time job on the programme as Tony Green did. He really made his name on the show.

The two of us were doing an exhibition together in the north of England when Tony told me that he was going to Central Studios in Birmingham the next day to do a pilot for a new TV game show. I went along with him and found myself putting in my penny's worth to Andrew Wood – who devised the show along with Norman Vaughan – about what I thought would and wouldn't work. The pilot was a success, *Bullseye* was commissioned and Tony got a job out of it that made him for life.

Comedian Jim Bowen was the host. Jim was a nice bloke, a jovial father-figure type who always got his lines wrong. He would have to do about 20 takes to get his words right and often didn't hear half of what the guests said to him. He would regularly embarrass himself –

and the guests – by saying, 'Super, smashing, great,' in response to being told that some poor sod's wife had run off with the milkman! But it all helped to make *Bullseye* such a hit.

Jim was a very funny bloke. I question how keen he was on darts but he made a lot of money out of the game. He performed his role very well and was perfect for the show. He also worked wonders for Tony's career and really played him into the programme, telling contestants to 'Listen to Tony' and all that jazz if they needed advice. Some of the more intelligent contestants – those who answered the quiz questions – were dangerously bad darts players and Tony would be stood so close to the board that I sometimes tuned in just to see if someone threw a dart in his beak, like I did with old Emu! Tony put his heart and soul into roaring out such catchphrases as 'Bully's special prize' and it paid dividends for him.

When *Bullseye* made a comeback in 2006 – 25 years after that first pilot – on satellite TV, the producers made sure that Tony was again on the show, which was a wise move by them and really nice for him. The format of the show remains the same and the part when a darts player has to score 301 with nine darts gets no easier. I know because I have already been on the new programme and failed. If you achieve that total, your score is doubled and turned into pounds for charity.

I went on the original show a few times and the score was so hard to achieve. Professional darts players should find it easy, whether it is on TV or in their own front room, but what made it so difficult on *Bullseye* was the set. There was no raised oche and the board was a good two inches higher than it should have been due to the wheels underneath it, which were used to turn the board. That is why so few of us managed to do it. You also had to come on cold and it was difficult to make the score in those circumstances. A few well-known stars ended up looking right mugs on the show, and I include myself in that, but it was another winning ingredient for the programme and became as big a joke as the top prize of a speedboat, which was paraded at the end whatever the outcome. Hopefully the new *Bullseye* show will be a hit. There is no doubt that the old one was a huge vehicle for players to get even more exposure on TV.

In the early eighties, anticipation of what I was going to wear at tournaments reached fever pitch. My shirts were such a big deal that I was using a proper dressmaker to keep me ahead of the game, so that I could change my look regularly. I used to get through 20 outfits in a few months. The shirts were very warm to wear on stage, and the sequins made them difficult to wash. In fact, they would often be ruined after just a few washes. Anyway, there was an unspoken expectancy that I would wear a new design every week. No sooner had the shirts left my back than they were off to various charity functions.

My favourite outfit from that era was my Mexican look – an all-black get-up with silver sequins on the shirt and 'Bobby' written in diamante around the bottoms of my flared trousers. I looked beautiful, even if I say so myself.

The TV cameras would show more shots of my outfits than my darts. I was like the David Beckham of darts. You have to remember that I was a fit bloke – look at the pictures. I honestly believe that, given the industry that sport has now become, I could have got modelling work through darts. I was blessed with a well-toned body and good looks. Unfortunately, I was also 20 years ahead of my time.

If I felt as though I was a pop star, on my next trip to the USA I got my chance to sing with one. Leo Sayer was a keen darts fan and came along to a darts tournament in Las Vegas to cheer the British boys on during his American tour. He invited Eric Bristow and me to one of his shows and we sat in a dressing room famously used by the King himself, the one and only Elvis Presley, during his Las Vegas era.

Some of Elvis' old shirts from his concerts were hanging up on the wall. A lot has been made of him being very big in the later years of his life but I can tell you here and now that he was nowhere near the size of a darts player! I tried a few on for size and they were far too small for me.

Leo invited Eric and me up on stage with him in front of thousands of his fans. Eric stayed in his seat but I got up there, lifted Leo on to my shoulders and he sang a song from there. Leo was a fantastic bloke and very talented.

Getting up on stage was obviously the thing to do in Las Vegas. Diana Ross also invited me to join her in the spotlight at a concert in the city when I was sat – glitter and all – in the front row VIP area.

She didn't have a clue who I was and her first words to me when I got up there were to ask if I was German!

I returned home in the summer of 1981 at the top of my game and eager to represent my country. Thankfully, earlier disappointments were now behind me and I was a regular in the England team. I felt that I had served a very long apprenticeship but I was grateful that I had finally been recognised by the selectors as one of the top players in the country. International recognition plays a massive part of any sportsman's life. In darts, you can't play in either the World Cup or the European Cup unless you do so for your country but, crucially, you have to be chosen to do so.

Internationally, England has always been the team to beat in darts. In the early 1980s we totally dominated the world game although, funnily enough, 1981 was the only year during my playing days that England didn't win the home international championship outright. We shared it with Wales, on St David's Day, appropriately enough. The Wales boys were cock-a-hoop, acting like they had won the World Cup. It was such a rare occurrence for England not to win that sharing the title was an achievement for any other nation and the Welsh duly celebrated as only they could.

Wales had good players – Alan Evans, Leighton Rees, Ceri Morgan and Peter Locke – who were very passionate about playing for their country. I often struggled against them. My personal record against Wales was four wins out of 11, which isn't too clever, but I think that Wales produces the best darts players in the world. Considering its size, the talent that has come out of that country is staggering. I have always been impressed at exhibitions with the standard of darts from the ordinary man in the street. The Welsh love their darts. There is no question about that.

Wales always proved to be difficult opponents, but no other home nation posed a problem for me. My 25 international appearances show 100 per cent personal records against Scotland, Northern Ireland and the Republic of Ireland. I played nine times against the Scots and won every one, much to the annoyance of Alistair Petrie, the man who almost signed me to play for them.

My highlight against the auld enemy was a man-of-the-match display in a 12–3 trouncing up in Sunderland, which confirmed my inclusion in the England squad for the 1981 World Cup in New Zealand. That meant so much to me. After all the heartache I was finally in the four-man England World Cup team, with Eric Bristow, John Lowe and Tony Brown, and New Zealand sounded such a wonderful place that I couldn't wait to get over there. I never made the trip, though. Serious illness was to prevent me from travelling, but the disappointment was a small price to pay as I very nearly lost my life.

I hadn't felt well leading up to that September's Unipart British darts championship in Stockton-on-Tees and a few days before the tournament, I fell ill while visiting my sister Heather at her house. A doctor checked me out and said that my symptoms of constant sweating and no appetite indicated that I probably had a bug, which should clear up in a day or two. So I went up to Stockton to play in the tournament, where I roomed with Jocky Wilson in the Crest Hotel. Little did he know it, but Jocky was about to save my life.

My first-round win against Billy Mateer was achieved despite me suffering from severe stomach pain throughout the match. I was at nothing like my best. I really felt that something was seriously wrong with me and I said so to a few of the boys. My stomach was bloated and I constantly wanted to be sick but just couldn't bring anything up.

That night my condition worsened. I was coughing, sweating and retching so much that Jocky woke up. He put the light on and told me that my face was completely white. Jocky called a doctor, but when he arrived I was again told there was nothing to worry about and given more tablets for stomach pain. By the next morning I was a lot worse. Jocky was now very worried about me. He went down to reception and informed the BDO that I was in a serious state. Alan Glazier's girlfriend and manager, Andrea Hanson, was a former nurse. She came up to my room and was alarmed that I looked so white and that she could hardly feel a pulse. I remember her commenting that it was as though no blood was pumping around my body.

Andrea immediately called for an ambulance and I was rushed to Hemington hospital in Cleveland where it was discovered that I had a ruptured spleen and severe internal bleeding. I required urgent treatment.

My spleen had swollen to 20 times its normal size and eventually burst. I was actually bleeding to death when I arrived at the hospital. I was very, very lucky. The blood was rapidly leaving my spleen and entering my stomach. The surgeon later told me that I had been less than an hour away from death. Apparently, when I was opened up in theatre there was so much pressure from the blood that it hit the lighting on the ceiling! Blood had splattered everywhere.

The surgeon didn't know what was wrong and couldn't afford to mess about. So he didn't bother to check the spark plug and went straight for the whole engine. Afterwards, I wasn't a pretty sight. He had had to cut into my stomach muscles and their appearance was distorted. My six-pack now goes the wrong way with a nine-inch scar from my rib cage to below my belly button. It still isn't pretty but it was necessary to keep me alive. The fact that I am here today is thanks to the surgeon, the quick thinking of Andrea and the justified concern of Jocky Wilson. Jocky later told me that his first thought during the night was to give me some brandy. His decision not to possibly saved my life, too. It could easily have killed me.

I remained in hospital for over a month and my weight plummeted from 18 stone 6lb to just 11 stone. I was told that my size and general fitness made the difference between me living and dying.

An old RAF hospital, the place was in the process of being closed down. Patients were being moved to a new hospital up the road every day but, due to the seriousness of my condition, I had to remain there. I was actually the last one to leave.

Most of the players came to visit me while the tournament was on. Jocky was there throughout and Leighton Rees and John Lowe both popped in to say hello, which was good of them. Disappointingly, Eric Bristow never visited me in hospital. Always the joker, he did remark that my illness was just for publicity and that my recovery had cost him money, because he had bought a wreath for my funeral and wasn't able to get his money back when I pulled through.

Doug McCarthy, a local player, was a true gentleman and visited me every single day I was in that hospital until the day I was finally released. That meant a lot to me. When all the players left Stockton I was stranded up there, 250 miles from home. Doug was a real mate.

He would bring his acoustic guitar along and play some songs to cheer me up.

Stuart Stamp, an old mate from my times with Chubby Brown, and his brother popped in every day, too, along with Archie Knox. Another regular visitor was the Middlesbrough and Northern Ireland footballer Terry Cochrane, who was a keen fan of darts. They all played a part in keeping me sane through a very difficult time. Thanks boys!

When I was discharged from hospital I was advised to take a break from darts for at least six months and have a complete rest. My publican friend Gabriel Nolan generously offered to drive up to the North East to pick me up in his comfortable and spacious Jag, but no sooner had we hit the road than we ran out of fuel. Gabriel had to walk to the nearest pumping station to fill up a metal can with petrol and when he got back to the car he couldn't get the bloody lid off. After watching him struggle for a while, I'd had enough. Hardly able to move due to severe pain, I got hold of the can myself and angrily ripped its lid off. 'I ain't that fucking ill,' I told him. We were soon back on the road and heading towards London.

My world ranking dipped during my time in hospital and not playing in the World Cup was going to affect it even more. I thought that if I didn't try to rectify things, I would be on the darts scrapheap. Rankings mattered a lot and six months out of the game would definitely mean me losing my place in the top eight if not the top 16. I needed to play darts and so I ignored medical advice and quickly returned to play in tournaments. Looking back, it was a ridiculous thing to do. I still had stitches in my stomach and was just not fit enough, or strong enough, to return to the game.

The player who reappeared on the circuit was unrecognisable from the one who had left it a few months earlier. I was gaunt and so much lighter in my build that my throwing action was all over the place. I hadn't foreseen how badly the illness would affect my game. I was buzzing in the early part of the year but I never really recovered that form. In fact, it was a long, slow process to get back to being able to play darts at all.

My enjoyment of life suffered. Unable to drink alcohol because of the medication I was on, I had to remain off all beer and spirits for a few years and drank only lemonade and later milk during tournaments. Can you imagine what I looked like playing darts in those days? I became a connoisseur of lemonade and by drinking all the different types of it across the country, I could tell a particular brand by taking just one sip. R. Whites won the Bobby George lemonade challenge. It had the best bubbles and the finest fizz, and I lived off the stuff for two years! It is the best lemonade in the world.

During my sober period I once came out of a pub in Liverpool, drove off in my Rolls-Royce and was stopped by the police. I had done nothing wrong and so it must have been for no other reason than the fact that I was leaving a pub and getting into a car. The copper knocked on my window.

'Have you been drinking tonight?' he asked me.

'Yeah,' I replied.

'How many pints have you had?'

'About fifteen.'

'Fifteen? Come with me. I'm going to breathalyse you.'

With that he took me into the back of his car and got me to blow into this bag. Of course, nothing showed up.

'You'll have to do it again,' he told me.

'OK,' I said.

So I blew into the bag once more and again nothing showed up.

'What have you been drinking tonight?' the copper asked me.

'Lemonade,' I said.

'You didn't tell me that,' he said, annoyed.

'You didn't ask,' I told him.

He had wasted his time but the assumption that I was over the limit was all his and no doubt due to my profession, the pub and the fact that I was driving a Roller.

I always drove a Rolls-Royce in those days. Since boyhood, I had dreamed of owning one. I used to talk about it with my friend Barry Lee when we were at Gearies Secondary School together. Barry loved cars more than I did, so much so that he went on to make a living out of them. He was a very talented driver from a young age – the envy of all his mates – and it was no surprise to me when he later became Hot Rod world champion.

Mr Davis, our headmaster, washed his hands of both us at school. He gave neither of us a chance of doing anything with our lives. So when I bumped into Barry and discovered that not only did we both have Rollers – mine was dark blue and his was dark brown – but Mr Davis was still at our old school, there was only one thing for us to do. We drove into the school car park and put our motors either side of Mr Davis' old Morris 1000. He took it on the chin. Neither of us had been very bright at school, and it was just nice to show him that we had achieved something after all.

The Rolls-Royce has always been the car to have in my opinion, and contrary to what some people may think, it can also be one of the cheapest to run. If you look after a Rolls-Royce, it can last you until you are 80 years old. No word of a lie. Just look at Olly Croft. He has always driven a Roller and people assume he is loaded, but he isn't. He just loves that type of motor.

A Rolls-Royce looks the part, whether it is a new one or an old one. It is a fabulous piece of engineering, comfortable and classy. I owned five different Rollers during the best part of ten years. They were my special treat to myself.

The first major tournament I played in following my illness was the 1982 Embassy world championship. My look was tight and white. Then again, I didn't have much choice, given that I was six stone lighter than I had been just four months earlier. The white shirt and skin-tight pants look was simplistic compared to previous designs, and had been created by Rita Valliss after Sandra Adams left the area. Rita did a very good job, considering that she had to work around my bloated stomach and a corset that I had to wear in order for me to be able even to throw a dart at the board.

The Embassy had been expanded to 32 players and so there were no byes in the opening round, which must have disappointed Eric Bristow because he crashed out 2–0 to Steve Brennan, of Northern Ireland, in the very first match. The Crafty Cockney was outclassed that day as Steve put on a great performance to cause the biggest ever shock in the event and blow the tournament wide open before it had even properly got started.

Suddenly, everyone thought they could win it. It was just my luck that the year the world number one went out in the first round was the year I wasn't really fit enough to play. In addition to that, Eric was in the top half of the draw while I was in the bottom half and seeded to meet John Lowe in the semi-finals. I hadn't been scheduled to meet Eric until the final anyway.

I had been keen to draw an overseas player in the first round and get the easiest start possible but I was drawn against Alan Glazier instead. It was a big relief to get past him 2–0. Keith Deller was on hand to support me throughout. The cheeky youngster would sneak into Jollees through the fire exit and at night he slept on my hotel room floor.

Of course, the darts boys would never allow anything like an illness to stop their pranks on the road, and so when Sid Waddell put a call out for me at the hotel the next day, saying that the police wanted to speak to me urgently regarding some stolen gold rings, I assumed it was a wind-up to celebrate my comeback, and acted accordingly. The fact that I wore over £5000 worth of over-sized rings on my left hand made me a target for such punishment on the circuit. Shortly afterwards, I got another call, this time from the hotel's front desk, asking me to meet two policemen downstairs at reception. I fully expected them to be in fancy dress, especially as Sid had been involved, but this was no joke. These boys were genuine policemen.

The police had received a call from a member of the public claiming that the rings I had worn against Alan had been stolen in a house robbery in 1976.

'Well, I did do a few bank jobs around this way back then,' I joked.

This was no laughing matter, though. This was a proper inquiry and I ended up having to make a statement. I tried to make a joke out of the situation by appearing on TV and inviting the man who had called the police to pop down to Jollees to see the rings for himself, and buy me a pint for the inconvenience. No one showed up.

The second round pitched me against Doug McCarthy, the man who had kept me company and sane in that Middlesbrough hospital during my illness. It was a tight match. I didn't play well and needed eight attempts to hit my favourite double 14 in one leg. Doug was left with double top to beat me but I saved the match with a 161 checkout and went on to win, 2–1. That checkout was the most replayed shot of the week on TV that year. It was a fantastic moment as I looked up and clasped my hands as if to say, 'Thank God.'

It did a lot for my self-confidence, knowing that I could still pull off a shot like that in such circumstances. Eric rang me up in my hotel room that night and opened with the words, 'Is that Houdini?' He couldn't believe I was still in the competition.

But the big story of the second round came in the match between Alan Evans and Jocky Wilson, sparked by an act of gamesmanship, as most rows in darts are. The players had a rivalry going back a long way and whenever they played each other, especially in Scotland versus Wales matches, it was a tense affair.

One version of events had Alan trying to wind up Jocky. Another had Jocky trying to wind up Alan. It depended on which story you believed. What is for certain is that the argument resulted in the two of them coming to blows. It was silly really but quite funny to watch because both of them were so small. The needle definitely made for a good game of darts that night, which Jocky won, 2–1.

Alan was all right – I once shared a bed with him in his old man's pub in Merthyr Tydfil after an exhibition night – but, just like Jocky, he could never quite handle his drink. He could get quite fiery once the beer took hold of him. Alan often wrote letters of complaint to the BDO. That never got him anywhere because Olly Croft didn't go much on confrontation. Otherwise, Alan had a good sense of humour. I once arranged to meet him in London and he turned up over an hour early with tales of speeding past John Lowe on the M4. 'John was doing a good hundred himself,' he said, 'but I was doing 180.' He delivered that line so deadpan that it still makes me chuckle, even now.

By the quarter-final stage of the 1982 Embassy, I was beginning to fancy my chances of winning the title. My next match was against my old money race pal from the States, Nicky Virachkul. Nicky had caused a shock by beating Cliff Lazarenko in the previous round and was determined to take his time against me, so much so that the match lasted 77 minutes and we played just five sets. I won it, 4–1.

I switched from lemonade to milk that day and downed ten pints of the stuff. Well, if it was good enough for baby elephants, it was good enough for me. But the bottom line was that I just wasn't fit. I tired during the match and, despite winning it quite comfortably, I knew that the length of the contest had taken its toll on me.

However, I was still in the tournament and, on paper at least, I had a chance. If I needed to go up a gear, though, I knew I was going to struggle, and with John Lowe in the semis and either Jocky or Stefan Lord in the final, there was going to be no easy ride.

The one thing my win had ensured was that an Englishman was going to be in the final. There was a fair bit of aggro between the English and the Americans that year, and after Eric had gone out, the Yanks claimed that our domination was slipping.

The 1982 Embassy was by far the best performance the USA ever achieved in an event in England. Both Nicky and Dave Miller made the last eight and both of them were mouthing off. We needed to put them in their place. Americans are very competitive when it comes to darts – it is win or bust – and they saw this as a chance to turn the tide, but their hopes were short-lived. Jocky thrashed Dave and my victory over Nicky meant I would fight out an all-English semi-final against John.

It turned out to be one match too far for me and, despite taking the first set, I couldn't get my game going and was well beaten, 4–1. I didn't feel anything near my best so, for me, getting to the last four was a good performance. It represented triumph over adversity, but that tournament taught me a big lesson – the public don't sympathise with illness when it comes to entertainment. Once I was up on that stage, the crowd expected me to put on a show for them, regardless of my condition.

Meanwhile, my old room-mate was faring a lot better. Jocky took one leg with just ten darts as he crushed Stefan Lord, 4–0, in his semi-final. In fact, he reached the final having dropped just one set, against Alan Evans, in the whole tournament. By then, Jocky was running so low on shirts that he had had to borrow one of mine to play in. He beat John 5–3 in the final and was a worthy Embassy world champion.

I roomed with Jocky for a fair few years and we were very good mates. His real name was John Thomas Wilson, and I made a point of calling him that whenever I could.

Jocky was a polite man and had good manners, but he loved a drink and that was often his downfall. It could turn him into a different person. He would drink a fair amount of vodka and polish off about five pints of lager before he went out to play darts. That fired him up and when he was fired up, he could turn on a sixpence.

Jocky didn't really eat that much, although he could devour a Chinese meal, but he always enjoyed a drink, whatever the circumstances. We had our one and only row over drink. Jocky sometimes played in exhibitions when he had already drunk quite a few, which I thought was out of order, and when this started affecting my earning power during some darts nights in Los Angeles, I decided to have words with him. He didn't like it one bit, swore at me and stormed off.

The next day the two of us were due to travel to Las Vegas for an exhibition but Jocky missed the bus and I had to make the trip on my own. Incredibly, Jocky hitchhiked his way across the desert to join me. He covered 400 miles in two days and turned up at the Sahara Hotel in Las Vegas looking like a drowned tortoise. Apparently, he had drunk vodka on the road at night to keep warm.

Jocky was a decent bloke and a good friend to me. He was blessed with a natural personality that you couldn't help warming to and was pure comedy to be around. On another trip to the States, I discovered that I hadn't got any toothpaste with me. Now, I can't function without cleaning my teeth. It is the first thing I do every morning. If my teeth are clean, I feel clean.

I asked Jocky if I could borrow his toothpaste and he answered, half-asleep, in his Scottish brogue, which I had no chance of understanding. The next thing he jumped out of bed and started rummaging through his suitcase, looking for some toothpaste to lend me. Suddenly, he stopped in his tracks, looked up and said, 'Why am I sat here looking for toothpaste for you, Bob? I haven't got any fucking teeth!'

His suitcase was another story. He always used to have a sizeable one, despite it never having anything in it. I discovered this once in America when I carried it up to our room and couldn't believe how light it was. I asked him what he had got in the case and was amazed when he told me, 'Just some pants and socks. It looks so much better when you check into a hotel with a big suitcase though, Bob, especially in the States.'

As well as a drink, Jocky loved a fag and a laugh but he was never one to chase the birds. He got his kicks out of darts and sea-fishing instead.

I came up with plenty of nicknames for him. As well as 'Bumblebee' and 'Cocky Jocky on the Oche', I also called him 'Spike' because his confident walk and lack of teeth reminded me of the bulldog from the *Tom and Jerry* cartoon. Jocky's toothless grin was his trademark. He never cleaned his teeth when he was a boy, lived on sweets and was scared of dentists. This all added up to him losing his teeth when he was still in his twenties from periodontal disease, but it also gave the man an image in darts. I helped Jocky with the way he looked on stage. I got him to wear jewellery – a chain around his neck and a couple of rings – and helped him to develop his self-confidence.

We earned a lot of money on the exhibition circuit together, both at home and abroad, including a ground-breaking trip to the Middle East in 1982 with former NOW champion Billy Lennard. We went to Abu Dhabi, Dubai, Bahrain and Kuwait, had a right laugh and earned good money. It was a great experience. I found that certain areas were quite westernised and that a lot of sheikhs loved darts. The scenery in some of those places was simply stunning – essentially desert but it didn't look like it. So many trees have been planted that soon there will be forests. The cities, especially Abu Dhabi and Dubai, shimmered with glass skyscrapers, and had magnificent beaches. It felt like paradise, especially as we enjoyed a curry every night. I was amazed that people didn't eat with knives and forks, using their hands instead, but I loved the food, the way in which it was cooked and all the spices. It was the business.

British Airways flew the three of us to the Middle East, and handed us Bermuda shorts for the trip. Billy and I tried ours on for size before we left Heathrow airport but Jocky put his straight into his suitcase. When he put them on to lounge beside the hotel pool in Dubai, they were so big for him that he looked like he was wearing a skirt. He was so desperate to go home with a sun tan that he couldn't care less what he looked like. He never bothered with sun cream either and so he spread out in the midday sun and burned himself to a cinder, in his over-sized Bermuda shorts.

Billy burned himself as well on the first day and decided to wear a handkerchief on his sore head for the rest of the trip. He looked like he was in bloody Margate or somewhere. I don't know quite what the locals made of the three of us walking around the place.

On that trip, I told Jocky that for religious reasons only men with a full set of teeth could be served alcohol. Incredibly, he believed me and for two whole days stayed away from the bar.

The reason we were there was darts and we would happily show off our talents to the sheikhs by going out on double doubles. Jocky's favourite was two double fives when he needed 20. They loved to see that and couldn't get enough of it.

Jocky has now retired from darts and moved back up to Fife to live. I can honestly say that he is the one man I really miss from that golden era.

My semi-final appearance at the 1982 Embassy was later recognised by the BDO when I was chosen alongside Eric Bristow and John Lowe to represent England in the three-man Nations Cup event at Wembley, which we won, beating Sweden in the final. This was some consolation for me after missing the World Cup the previous year.

Things got even better when I was selected to play for England in the European Cup at Southend shortly afterwards. The European Cup is second only to the World Cup in international darts. I had been very disappointed to be overlooked in 1980 when I stood at number two in the world rankings, and so it was pleasing to join Eric, Cliff Lazarenko and Dave Whitcombe in the England team.

I put my Welsh jinx to one side by winning both my legs against Peter Locke and Tony Ridler to help us to victory in the four-man team event, but we lost to Sweden in the pairs. Decent performances from all four of us in the singles secured the European Cup and won me a place in the European singles final against Eric.

Before the match, Eric picked up a big number 2 from the old-fashioned scoreboard and stuck it on my back. He just couldn't resist telling everyone which one of us he thought was second best, even when we were playing in the same bloody team. This wasn't about playing for England, though – it was about the two of us. Eric had beaten me in the final of the Embassy and I had beaten him in the final of the Santa Monica Open. His rude comments about that match still rankled with me. The European singles definitely mattered. Make no mistake about that. I was determined to beat him and I did. It was a great victory for me and I made sure that I gave Eric a kiss afterwards, just like he had done to me in the world final two years earlier.

I was absolutely thrilled to win the title, but I was never allowed to defend it and that was a huge disappointment. Just like the World Cup, playing in the European Cup is by invitation only, and it hurt me badly two years later when I wasn't selected to play in the event and therefore couldn't defend my singles crown.

I actually never played in the tournament again and so, given that I have never been beaten in the competition by anyone, I regard myself as the undisputed European singles champion.

The following year, darts reached its absolute peak when, in the first week of 1983, unseeded Keith Deller checked out on 138 to beat Eric Bristow in the final of the Embassy world championship. That moment, watched by over ten million viewers on TV, was front as well as back-page news, a far cry from nowadays when the game struggles to get even a few column inches in the newspapers.

Keith was magnificent. His final with Eric had everything. By contrast, that year's tournament was the first time I found myself beginning to fall out of love with the game. I was still ranked fourth in the world, despite my illness and consequent absence from certain tournaments, but I was handed a very tough opener against England international Tony Brown in the first round. I was the seeded player but Tony had been an Embassy semi-finalist in 1979, 1980 and 1982 – three of the previous four years – and was a very dangerous player.

Tony played well and won – he ended up getting to the semi-finals again that year – but he needed a scorer who couldn't subtract to help him get past me. All these years on, it sounds like sour grapes on my part to mention this, but you would expect organisers of a world darts championship to employ officials who can count. Of course, everyone can make mistakes but the bloke who called my game with Tony was something else that day. He really was.

It was a big game for Tony. He had slipped down the world rankings and was keen to get back. He was a good player and we both knew that whoever won the match had a good chance to progress in the tournament.

Tony took the first set and I won the first leg of the second set. We were evenly matched when MC Freddie Williams made a mistake in the second leg of the second set. Tony had left himself 50 but Freddie called 40. Any darts player knows that there is a world of difference between being left 50 and being left 40. Tony made hard work of it anyway by throwing 5, 3 and then double 16, but it wasn't right and I queried the call. I was met by a shake of the head from Freddie. I looked over to Tony but couldn't make eye contact. I tried to forget about it and get on with the game but it niggled at me. I felt sure that Tony must have known what he had left himself – every darts player knows what he has left himself – so I couldn't understand why he hadn't corrected Freddie.

Then, in the next leg, it happened again. Tony left himself 104 but Freddie shouted out 102. The only difference this time was that my opponent queried the call and it was amended. Again, any darts player knows that there is a huge difference between requiring 104 and 102. The higher score is a two-dart finish and an easier out-shot. Tony managed to spot that error. I was now all over the place. I missed doubles and soon enough Tony had beaten me.

Friends who watched the match on TV later confirmed to me that on both occasions the computer on the bottom of the screen showed the correct score and the MC twice miscounted.

I am not blaming Tony. Bigger sins have been committed playing darts and maybe he was unaware of the mistake, but it upset me a lot. Things like that do. Looking back, I am angry with myself for not making a bigger fuss at the time. Today, I would ask for the leg to be replayed but I was naïve and stupid back then. There is no doubt that it had a big impact on the outcome of the match, the championship and, ultimately, my future.

The problem with miscounting still exists and I can't understand why the BDO hasn't invested in video technology to stamp it out in the big championships. It may slow down the game but surely it is better to get it right. I can't believe we still have to rely on chalkers when we could be using computers. A player knows in his head what he has left and shouldn't really need the caller to tell him. When it is called incorrectly, it can be upsetting and can also prove to be costly, as it did for me in that match with Tony Brown.

That year was another case of what might have been for me. Tony cruised past outsider Jerry Umberger and Stefan Lord to reach the semi-finals, where he lost 5–1 to Eric Bristow. The draw seemed mapped out for one of us to progress.

Eric had a decent draw, too, and played two qualifiers, Peter Masson and Dave Lee, in the first two rounds, although Peter was one dart away from beating him. Meanwhile, Keith Deller was ripping apart the top half of the draw. After I went out, I stayed on to support him. The year before he had come up to Stoke to support me, so the least I could do was to repay the compliment.

To a lot of darts fans, Keith came from nowhere but he was very well known on the circuit. His mum had a dartboard on the back of the kitchen door – both his parents loved darts – and he would practise as she cooked meals. He was darts mad, that boy.

Keith had to qualify to play in the Embassy and then beat Nicky Virachkul and Les Capewell to get into the last eight. From that moment on, he really made a name for himself. He comfortably beat John Lowe 4–2 in the quarter-finals and then defeated Jocky Wilson 5–3 in the semi-finals, but he was still the rank outsider when he played Eric in the final. There might only have been four years between them in age, but there was a massive gulf in experience. Eric was world number one and already had two world titles to his name. It was classic David and Goliath stuff – the pretty and innocent young qualifier up against the best player in the world.

There was nothing between them but the match will always be remembered for its finish. At five sets all and with Keith leading 3–2, Eric was left to score 50 with one dart to level the match. If he missed it, Keith would throw for the championship, needing 138. Famously, Eric hit a single 18 to leave his favourite double 16 next time around, and Keith punished him by checking out to become world champion.

That moment has since gone down in darts folklore. Eric has been described as laying down the gauntlet to the young pretender, as if to say, 'Finish that, then,' and getting caught out, but I am not so sure about that. At the time, I couldn't believe Eric would be so foolish as to purposely leave Keith a shot out, and over 20 years later, I remain unconvinced that he did. I believe that Eric went for the bull, the nerves got to him and he threw a wayward dart that landed in 18 – it almost hit the treble bed – and it just so happened that left 32. Knowing Eric as I do, I can't see why he wouldn't have thrown for the bull. He was never stupid, not when it came to playing darts at that level.

Keith had been consistently checking out on big scores all through the tournament and no player in his right mind would have taken such a chance. It was too much of a risk at such an important stage in a world final. If Eric had wanted to shake up Keith, there was surely no better way than hitting the bull. Levelling the match like that would have upped the stakes a lot more than leaving himself double 16 and his opponent an out-shot for the championship.

Eric was more than capable of finishing on the bull under such pressure – we all know that – and if he failed, he would still have had three darts to save the leg should Keith not have finished.

Even though it has now gone down as fact in the darts history books, I just don't believe that Eric went for that shot on purpose. Of course, only Eric knows the truth. I have asked him about it many times but never get a straight answer. He just likes to keep us all guessing.

MC Freddie Williams later told me that when Keith won that match he left his darts in the board and, according to the rulebook, a result should stand only if the winning darts have been retrieved. The BDO and WDF spent a lot of time coming up with some very strange rules.

Keith became an overnight star and was suddenly all over the newspapers and TV. He had boyish good looks and even appeared as a Page Seven pin-up, with a bottle of milk in one hand and a dolly bird in the other. I had a chuckle to myself about the milk connection. The press boys genuinely thought that it was Keith's favourite drink when, in fact, a bottle of lager would have been much more appropriate. That boy loved his beer.

Darts never got any bigger than this. No one in the game could have asked for more than an unseeded and good-looking young boy checking out on 138 to beat the one and only Eric Bristow in a world final watched by millions on TV. The style of Keith's victory, as well as the climax, made it special. We love an underdog in this country and everything fitted the bill perfectly that night.

Unfortunately, but perhaps unsurprisingly for such a young player, the attention went to Keith's head a bit and he started to behave like he thought he was better than the rest of us. He distanced himself from a lot of the players and became a bit star-struck by it all. A few months after his Embassy win, I played him in an exhibition match and he criticised me for driving a Rolls-Royce, wearing jewellery and all sorts. That was out of order. After a while his ego came back down to a reasonable size and the boy became likeable again. Everyone was better off for that, not least, Keith.

Keith's win was fantastic for darts but he struggled to get anywhere near that level of success again. His best performance was a last eight place at the Embassy a few years later but he had his day in the sun, that is for sure.

Keith was seriously ill with a brain tumour a few years ago. Thankfully, he fully recovered and is back on the darts circuit. He is also a regular visitor to my home and we have become very good friends again. Keith is now approaching 50 but still looks like a boy to me. He always will.

While Keith was enjoying his moment in the limelight, I was getting ever more frustrated with poor officialdom at the BDO, which was costing me money and world-ranking points, and was gradually wearing me down.

The 1983 Unipart British Masters was where I chose to unveil my new look, featuring Mickey Mouse sketched in gold – in homage to John Lowe and his infamous comments about me – on the back of my shirt. I also had a shirt with the words 'I'm so perfect, it frightens me!' on the back and I wore it for my first-round win over John Cosnett.

One of the press boys asked me afterwards, 'How would you feel if you'd lost wearing that shirt?' I replied, 'Well, it says nothing about my darts.'

Apart from the larking around, that event in Redcar pushed me closer to considering my future in competitive darts. One reason was the money, or lack of it, and another was the poor quality of refereeing. After beating John on a tie-break and then Leighton Rees, I came up against Dave Whitcombe in the quarter-finals.

Dave had developed into a very good player – he was to make the Embassy final in both 1984 and 1986 – and was seeded three for the event. He was on fire when I played him and threw an 11-darter in a performance that I just had no answer to. But the match was affected by more miscounting, this time courtesy of MC Jack Price. I tried to have a word with Jack afterwards but he refused to apologise for his mistake.

A few months later, Jack miscounted again in a match involving Cliff Lazarenko. Cliff complained and refused to play his next match if Jack was to be the MC. The BDO relented and appointed another official.

Money was becoming a major issue, too. Darts was in its heyday but there were no longer just four or five of us competing for the top prizes. We were also TV stars, individual entertainers in our own right. This had a lot to do with the nature of the TV coverage. Big close-ups of our faces meant that we were better known than many other sports stars. People recognised us easily and got to know the names, particularly the ones that stood out, as mine did. This meant that we could venture out on our own and make good money from darts away from the TV tournaments.

I learned all that early on through my sponsorship deals, and Courage brewery took it a step further by pushing me to work in pubs and clubs in preference to entering tournaments. It made sense. So many players were entering competitions, both at home and abroad, that winning prize money and precious world-ranking points was getting harder. There was plenty of dough to be made on the outside through exhibition work.

For the first five or six years in the game, I had entered every tournament going but I realised that I wasn't going to be able to survive in the competitive game for ever. Deep in my heart I knew that the game was moving on. The players were getting younger and would continue to do so. Travelling is very much a young man's game and there is a lot of travelling in darts. For me to make a living in that way for another 20 years was a huge ask, whether the game retained its popularity or not. I recognised that I needed to build something extra within the game, a strategy that would work for me whether I was the reigning world champion or never played in the world championship ever again.

Working for Courage was brilliant. I was asked to push myself forward and it was good advice. I earned a lot of money and put on great shows for the punters. Exhibitions were the future of darts and I got in there first. Like the tournaments, the exhibition honey pot could only cater for so many teddy bears.

I enjoyed the work. It was far better than playing in tournaments and being let down by poor MCs and bad gamesmanship from certain players, although I continued to play some events on the circuit. Darts was also starting to become bitter and twisted. The camaraderie was almost gone. In the early days, all the British players would cheer for each other in tournaments, but that had changed. Your own countrymen wanted you out because the stakes were getting higher – the prize money was bigger and the prestige was greater.

Then, without warning, the number of tournaments on TV began to dry up and the whole scene got worse. With less exposure, there became just enough room for one or two stars in the game, and it all began to get rather nasty.

The family atmosphere that once existed, particularly on those early trips to America when we were all in it together, evaporated. Acts of comradeship became very rare and I was astonished some time later when young Kevin Spiolek offered to split with me when we met in the county finals of the British championship. I didn't know the boy at all but his first words to me were, 'Are we going to split?' This was now so uncommon that I asked him what he meant.

'Whoever wins today, splits his eventual winnings with the other one,' he said.

I considered that Kevin probably thought he was going to lose, otherwise the idea made no sense, but I agreed to it, and he beat me.

Kevin got all the way to the semi-finals but I never gave our conversation another thought. I didn't know him and a lot of players said things like that but didn't keep their word – even in the good old days – but not this one. A few weeks later, I received a cheque in the post from Kevin for half his prize money. For that gesture alone he deserves a mention in my book!

Kevin was a true diamond, but that behaviour was no longer the norm. The game had become dog eat dog.

I had already decided that exhibitions were the way forward for me. Putting on a show always meant as much to me as winning, anyway. Once the winning mentality takes over, the fun goes out of any game and that is exactly what happened in darts, but it turned up in exhibition darts. Playing pubs and clubs was always enjoyable, the venues would be packed, the beer was free and the players got a kick out of feeling like a pop star for the night.

I love exhibitions. Well, I suppose I am an exhibitionist. You are paid to put on a show and entertain the crowd. It is the perfect job for me. I was the first player to put on a proper, professional show with electronic scoreboard, my own MC and scorer. My shows were a lot more professional than some of the tournaments that I played in and I packed out some large venues. When you come on stage all dressed up, you need a proper hall with a decent sized stage, and people who are prepared to participate, to pull it off.

Darts exhibitions have always been about the people, those who watch and those who come up to challenge you. Mostly, they have a story to tell and I have met some real characters from all walks of life through my exhibition work. I regularly write about them in my column in *Darts World* magazine.

The main reason why my exhibitions have been so popular is that I put the time and effort into making them fun. Some players just turn up with a set of darts and a frown. What good is that? Some of them even sell signed photographs! That is a shocking way to treat darts fans. What sort of image does that give the game? Those players finish up being the losers in the long run, because they won't get booked again. That is for sure.

Plenty of decent players turn up at exhibitions to challenge you, especially in Wales, and sometimes you lose the odd leg, but the important thing is not to lose too many. There can be a bit of pressure because everyone wants to beat you and a few bad legs can quickly turn the night into an embarrassment. Generally, I play fun darts at exhibitions and only ever play seriously if money is at stake, or someone makes me angry.

Of course, some of the punters are real no-hopers. I remember once in Wolverhampton playing a guy who was absolutely hopeless. He was left on 420 when I required a double to win. Suddenly, an old lady shouted out, 'Go on Bernard, you've got him rattled.' The whole place fell about laughing.

As already mentioned, darts exhibitions are a great way to raise money for charity – that is how they began – but not everyone in the public eye is generous with their time. I was once invited to a charity night at the Winter Gardens in Blackpool with some big names from the world of showbiz and was appalled when it later transpired that some of these so-called gents and ladies were charging fees. Talk about defeating the object! I employed my own driver to get me there, paid for my own petrol and gave my time free of charge. I was absolutely disgusted with those who didn't do the same. Even in the name of charity, some of them wouldn't do anything for nothing. It was a real eye-opener for me, but sickening as well. I am sure the members of the public who came along that night and paid good money would have felt sick, too, if they had known about it.

I am only showbiz to a degree. I have been asked to appear in pantomime – oh yes, I have! – but I couldn't cope with that game and have always politely declined. For panto I think you have to be on the same wavelength as the rest of the cast and I don't think it would be too much fun for someone like me. I am an entertainer but I am not a luvvie. Don't get me wrong. A lot of actors are decent people, just different from me, and some have become good friends of mine through darts. Robert Powell, who first made his name in the film *Jesus of Nazareth*, was a good mate for many years and loved darts. We played pairs together and whenever he missed a double I made a point of shouting out 'Jesus' for a giggle. We did a lot of charity work together and he never asked for a penny. The decent ones never did.

Dennis Waterman often came along to help out at exhibition nights with Robert, as did The Monkees drummer and singer Micky Dolenz. Together, the four of us formed the 'All Stars' and did many charity darts nights, raising a lot of money in the process. We had some good laughs.

Meanwhile, back at the ranch, as darts coverage dipped on TV and more players pulled out of tournaments to concentrate on the exhibition circuit, the BDO and WDF faced another problem over the sensitive issues of alcohol and cigarettes.

I rarely drank to excess when playing darts. Occasionally, I would have a few pints – probably up to as many as 20 at exhibitions – but that was a pretty rare occurrence. I never smoked on stage, either. I wasn't against it – each to his own – but I did have a view on opponents who blew smoke over the dartboard to affect my game.

The BBC comedy programme *Not the Nine O'Clock News* did a famous sketch about darts and drinking, which I thought was very clever and very funny. It was also an indication of how big the game had become, but it all backfired. Darts was criticised and scrutinised, and eventually victimised. Within the game, that sketch was blamed for being the catalyst that turned darts into a laughing stock. I never agreed with that view. The game is played in the pub. We should be proud of our roots, but everything got out of hand. The BDO and the WDF – both of which should have stood firm, in my view – crumbled under the pressure and beer and fags were banned from televised darts tournaments. To my knowledge, not one TV organisation, venue or sponsor put pressure on the darts chiefs to change the rules and alter the game's image. They just did it.

It made no difference at all to the fading interest in the game and the expected cash injection from governments around the globe that the WDF had hoped for wasn't forthcoming. Interest in darts began to fall after the 1983 world championship – as so often happens when you hit any high – and I think the BDO and WDF put two and two together and made five. They thought that if beer and fags were banned, everything in the garden would be rosy again, but that didn't turn out to be the case.

Darts is a pub game and while you can take darts out of the pub, you can't take the pub out of darts. That is where the game belongs. If you were to design the perfect British pub, you would always put a dartboard on the wall. Maybe the BDO and WDF hoped that one day we would all end up playing the game in bow ties and waistcoats like snooker players. Do me a favour!

11 Life begins at forty

The year 1984 wasn't only a big one for George Orwell, it was also the year that changed my life.

I went out in the first round of the Embassy again, losing to Malcolm Davies, and had not won a major trophy since the European singles two years before. The arse was beginning to fall out of darts and the row over beer and fags had speeded up the game's decline. I was making money through my exhibition work but the buzz of competitions was quickly fading. With less to focus on, the unhappiness of my life at home started to become a bigger problem for me.

Betty and I had lived separate lives for several years but I had been too busy with my darts to notice or care. I'd had a few girlfriends on the circuit but nothing serious apart from Annette Rasmussen, in Denmark. That relationship failed because of the distance and the fact that I was still married. I didn't feel that the time was right to walk out on my wife and kids and, as much as I cared for Annette, I guess my feelings weren't strong enough.

That all changed when I met the love of my life at a Licensed Victuallers' function at the Connaught Rooms in London on – of all dates – 14 February, Valentine's Day, 1984. Mackinlay's whisky were replacing Courage brewery in the chair. The girl in question was Maria Del Carmen Tanti – although everyone knew her as Marie – and she was working for Mackinlay's. It was her job to hand out the whisky and it was my duty to throw the darts, on behalf of Courage. I think you call that fate.

Marie was in her early twenties at the time and very sexy. My heart felt like it had been hit by a juggernaut. Suddenly, I believed in love at first sight. Mick Kelly, the new landlord of the King George V in Ilford, was with me that night and as soon as I clapped eyes on this girl I told him that I was going to marry her. I had never even thought that before in my life, let alone said it, but I was that sure. This one was just perfect for me.

I was never one to chase the girls and I needed a few whiskies before, jokingly, asking Marie to marry me and inviting her to come to America with me that summer. I played every card in the book but I was honest with her. I told her I was in a rotten marriage and that I was ready to get out, but she was hard work. 'That's what they all say,' she said. Marie seemed unconvinced by my sincerity and told me there was no way she would ever marry an old man like me. How wrong was she?

Marie's colleagues at Mackinlay's tried to warn me off, telling me that she had a reputation as a very good girl and that I would be lucky even to get a date with her.

I managed to leave the venue with her work number – she kept her home number firmly under wraps – but because I was so busy with darts, I was only able to arrange to see her on exhibition nights. Our first date was, in fact, at a darts night at the New Inn pub, next door to Brentford FC's ground, and Marie turned up with a friend! We got on well, though, and after that first night Marie started to come along to see me on her own.

I was so busy with exhibitions that all our meetings surrounded my darts and I never really took her out as such. She would watch me play darts and then we would go for something to eat. That is how our relationship began. There was none of the other, either. I didn't even get to have a reef around! Marie insisted that we kept our relationship platonic and we remained friends for a while.

However, she did agree to come to the States with me. Her main reason for saying yes was that she had never been across the pond. Anyway, it is fair to say her presence caused a bit of a stir. I had always kept myself to myself where the fairer sex was concerned and I wasn't really known by the other darts players as one for the ladies on the road.

Nicky Virachkul was immediately impressed. He took one look at Marie in her swimsuit and asked me how old she was. 'Wow,' he said in that drawn out American accent of his. 'Any chance of finding one for me, man?'

The players were fine but a lot of the wives and girlfriends weren't. Marie was, by some distance, the youngest and most beautiful of them all. She was simply class. I couldn't believe my luck.

That particular tour of America did me the world of good. Trips to the States were usually fun – apart from that one summer I spent with Betty – and this was one of the best, mainly due to Marie.

As usual, we stayed with some great people, including Joe and Carole Klinginsmith, who owned Chris' Club in Vallejo, near to San Francisco; Bob and Sybil Malcolm, who lived down the coast in Los Angeles; and my good friends Mike and Lynda Boyd, in Las Vegas. I am still in touch with Mike and Lynda today.

Having Marie by my side certainly had a positive impact on my darts. I won the mixed triples in the Golden Gate Classic and got to the final of the North American Open at the Sahara Hotel in Las Vegas, where I met Eric Bristow. The NAO was the first major trophy I won in my career, back in 1978, but there was no repeat success. I played well and had two darts at double 18 for the title but missed them both.

However, it was just great to have some support – something that I had learned to do without in darts – in the shape of Marie and, despite losing, it felt good to play in the final once again.

This was the summer when Los Angeles hosted the Olympic Games and while they were taking place, Marie and I ventured out to the beach in nearby Santa Monica one day to relax in the sunshine with some ice-cold beers. All of a sudden, two policemen – straight off the TV show *Chips* – rode on to the beach on motorbikes and asked me if I could see a whale. I hadn't a clue what they were on about and wasn't aware that whales frequented the water around those parts. Obviously, it was a big deal if the police were searching for it, so we had a good look out to sea. The policemen didn't seem too impressed with that and pointed to a sign with a big whale on it, stating that it was an offence to consume alcohol on the beach.

They booked me and I had to go along to the police station to produce my documents. Luckily, I was let off by the captain, who couldn't believe how the *Chips* guys had acted, particularly as there were thousands of foreigners in and around the place for the Olympics.

I really enjoyed that trip to the States and when we returned home it got even better when Marie told me what I had known from day one, that the two of us were meant for each other.

The time was right to get out of my marriage. Betty must have been thinking along similar lines because she was the one who started divorce proceedings.

I kept my relationship with Marie out of it, mainly because I didn't want her to get caught up in something she wasn't really involved in. It was clear to me that I had met my true love. Family and friends had faded into the background as darts took over my life but I didn't want that any more. I had finally found what I wanted and it mattered more to me than darts.

Apart from that relatively successful trip to America, my form hadn't been the best. In all honesty, I hadn't felt right since my illness three years earlier. I knew I still had the talent but maybe not so much the flare. Tournaments came and went uneventfully until it was time for the Embassy again.

With Marie's encouragement, I was fired up again for the 1985 world championship, even when I saw that I had drawn up-and-coming Mike Gregory in the first round. Mike had been a quarter-finalist the previous year and was seeded three. He was very much the favourite in our match and was just one leg away from beating me. I lost the first set and was 2–0 down in the second set but I fought my way back by winning six legs in succession to beat him 2–1.

The two of us had some real ding-dong battles over the years – particularly in that tournament – and we always provided some fantastic entertainment when we played against each other. Mike was to become another of those great players never to win the Embassy title.

After getting past that test, Northern Ireland's Fred McMullen should have been easy meat, but it didn't turn out that way. Fred was a worse counter than I had ever been. The boy couldn't count coconuts and had to ask me for out-shots throughout the match. Silly bollocks here would tell him what to hit and he would hit it, saying 'Cheers, Bob,' as he checked out. It was unbelievable really, but also quite off-putting, to play against him. I was stupid, my concentration slipped and he defeated me 3–1.

Fred was a former boxer – he looked like someone had driven over his face with a steamroller – and a nice guy, but he should never have been in the quarter-finals of the world championship. Cliff Lazarenko thrashed him 4–0 in his next match.

That pattern of beating the best players and then losing to the weaker ones has affected me throughout my career. Marie couldn't believe how well I played against Mike only to throw it all away against Fred, but she would soon get used to it as a regular occurrence. It had always been the same. The difference now was that I was with someone who cared about such things.

Later that year, Marie again joined me for the annual sojourn in the States and we enjoyed a great time. It was becoming ever clearer to both of us that we would soon be together for keeps.

I even got on with John Lowe on that trip. We had agreed to split for the first time in our lives, so we had to be civil with each other. Cliff Lazarenko was a big friend of John's and sometimes split with him. When Cliff asked me if I fancied joining in with them on that tour, I agreed.

I played quite well in the North American Open and got to the semi-finals where two narrowly missed six-darters proved costly and I was beaten. John, on the other hand, managed to get all the way to the final and, with me cheering him on, lifted the bloody trophy. I was in my element. 'Come on, my hero,' I shouted out during the match.

Eric couldn't believe what he was hearing and later called me an 'arsehole' for acting in that way, but I had the bees to think about, and John – to his credit – was winning them for me.

John had all his winnings stuffed in his top pocket and so I got all the money out and we sat down at a table and I did the old Peter Sellers trick of counting out the money – 'one for you and two for me' and 'two for you and three for me'. I kept going for a giggle and he never spotted it. He just kept nodding and all he said was, 'Is that right, pal?' I said, 'Yes, it's right.' Of course, I came clean in the end because my pile of dollars was so much taller than his.

John had never won in the States before and walked around all night with the giant North American Open trophy under his arm and a beaming smile. After years of knocking it as a Mickey Mouse tournament, he now seemed happy to accept it was a prize worth winning.

He won the title with a 78 out-shot and was persuaded by Cliff to celebrate his win by ordering 78 white Russians from the bar. The round cost John over $200 and later Cliff had to drag him by his feet through the hotel lobby to his room.

John was good fun that year. He lightened up a bit with me and we got on. I think that is all he needed to do where I was concerned, but sadly it was a rare occurrence.

Marie had made a massive impact on my life in a very short time and turned me into a much happier person. That American tour recharged my batteries and made me realise that darts could still be fun, but my dismal run in the Embassy continued. In 1986, the first time the tournament was held at the new venue of the Lakeside Country Club in Frimley Green, I went out in the first round again, this time to Bob Anderson.

That match remains the one and only time since 1980 that I played darts dressed in civvies. My car was broken into the night before and all my shirts were stolen. There was no glitter or gold in my performance, either, but that might have had something to do with the severe pain I was feeling in my back and legs – a problem undoubtedly caused by years of floor-laying. By the mid 1980s, it was affecting me whenever I played darts. Before my match against Bob, the pain was so bad that Marie had to come over to the hotel just to put my socks on for me.

Bob knew all about my condition. Once, during the Butlin's Grand Masters tournament in Birmingham when I was rooming with him, I was so poorly that I could hardly get out of bed to use the toilet. I was virtually bedridden and starving, so I asked if he would kindly pick up a Chinese takeaway for me. I waited until midnight for him to come back to the room, only for him to tell me that he had forgotten all about it.

Bob was on the verge of the big time back then. We played pairs together for a while and he was a very good player. I knew everything there was to know about him. We roomed together in Denmark when he beat me in the Danish Open semi-finals on his way to winning the competition. That was his big breakthrough, and as well as winning the trophy he was presented with a medal. He was so proud of that medal that he went to bed with it around his neck.

In the middle of the night I was awoken by the sound of what I thought was Bob talking in his sleep, but when I looked over to his bed it was empty. Then I saw him – stood in front of the mirror with nothing on but a pair of bright red underpants and his treasured medal around his neck, saying, 'You're on your way now, Bob. Oh yes, you are.' I couldn't believe what was going on in front of my very own eyes.

Later, he bought a cowboy shirt and a cowboy hat and even tried to develop an American accent as he changed his image into the 'Limestone Cowboy'. One time, when he was quite famous, he turned up at Heathrow airport for a BDO flight dressed in an orange shirt with white trousers, bright red shoes, sunglasses and a baseball cap. I asked him why he had changed his image to look like Coco the Clown and he told me, 'I'm incognito, so no one can recognise me.'

It all clicked for Bob after he beat me at the Lakeside. He went on to win the first of three successive Winmau World Masters titles that year and was crowned Embassy world champion in 1988.

All I can remember of our match at Frimley Green was Bob going out on bull, double 16 on five separate occasions. I would miss double top and he would check out on 82, I would miss double 18 and he would do it again. I had never been on the receiving end of anything like it before but credit to him, he played well and beat me at my own game with his own unorthodox finishes.

Bob got to the semi-finals that year, where he lost to Dave Whitcombe. Eric Bristow won his fifth and final Embassy title by thrashing Dave 6–0 in the final.

I was now rooming with Terry O'Dea, a man who really could charm the birds from the trees, and he had become friendly with one of the Embassy promotion girls at the Lakeside. I was smoking a fair bit back then and encouraged Terry to spend as much time as he could with his lady friend, just so he could keep me in cigarettes. By the end of the week, we had about 500 packets of fags stacked up in our hotel room. The sponsors should have taken a photograph of us.

Terry was a scream and for many years after we went our separate ways, I regularly received postcards from Perth, Australia, with the word 'Bollocks' scrawled across them. It was Terry's way of staying in touch.

By now, my exhibitions were earning me a good living but I needed another major trophy to keep my name in lights. My world ranking was down to tenth but with Marie's support and encouragement I decided to put my heart and soul into regaining the *News of the World* championship title after seven long years.

I was often reminded by the locals at the Old Maypole that I had won the NOW championship for a pub in nearby Ilford. That was true enough. I entered the competition under the Maypole's banner every year, but the year that I won it, 1979, was the year I missed the pub's registration date and had to go down the road and play for the King George V.

Despite the growth in popularity of the Embassy, I still believed that the NOW championship was the one to win. Most of the top players felt the same. Three legs, 501, 8ft from the board, no seeding and open to anyone who wanted to have a go – every game was a final in itself.

Getting through the pub stage was the easy bit, the area finals were a lot harder – Keith Deller and Dave Whitcombe were both involved – but I managed it and so, for the fifth time, I took my place in the grand finals at Wembley.

A technicians dispute meant no TV coverage, but it was something else that really gave me the needle. My back was causing me more problems and almost every time I played darts I suffered some form of pain when I leaned forward. I was told that an operation would have a 50-50 chance of success and it was suggested that I tried acupuncture instead. I dismissed that notion from my mind until a few days before the NOW championship finals, when I was in such agony that I decided to give it a go. An acupuncturist in north London stuck a load of needles into my body and, strange as it may sound, it did the trick and alleviated the pain.

The championship still had an odd number of area finalists and among the 13 that year were Richie Gardner, Mike Gregory, Brian

Hardy, Chris Johns, Jack McKenna, Ronnie Sharp, American Rick Ney and Canadian Bob Sinnaeve. Mike was the favourite.

There was no light above the practice board and so I sent out my driver Ray Brooks to find a light bulb from another room just so the finalists could throw. There was plenty of lager, though, and we all helped ourselves to a few cans each. We had a drink and a laugh together and got into a good mood for a day of darts. The alcohol further numbed my back pain and I really enjoyed the lads' company. It was just like the early days, but I was in my forties and felt like a grandfather to most of them.

Thirteen finalists meant that, as usual, three players got byes into the quarter-finals. This was always the way with the NOW championship and the luck of the draw went a long way towards winning it. Richie Gardner, who was playing in his first grand finals, told me that he hoped he didn't get a bye because the player he would then meet in the quarter-finals would have already played and won a match. That is how daft some darts players are. I told him I would happily take a bye, so if he got one he could give it to me. In the end, we both got byes and went straight through to the last eight.

Brian Hardy was the other player to get a bye and we met in the quarter-finals. He won the first leg and had a shot for the match in the second leg but busted. I cleaned up to save the leg and went through against the darts, 2–1.

Richie beat Chris Johns and now we were to play each other in the semi-finals. The Londoner played well but I missed nothing, winning both legs in 15 darts. Richie brought the best out of me. I won the match on the bull to set up a clash with Rick Ney in the final. Afterwards, Richie said to me, 'It took me ten months to get here and three minutes to get beaten.' That sums up the event.

I knew Rick well from my trips to America. He was a good professional and had reached his first NOW final after four appearances in the grand finals. For some reason, he was booed throughout our match by a section of the crowd, from the moment he walked on stage to the moment he walked off it. It was terrible for him.

By contrast, when I was introduced the whole place went berserk. I have always been fortunate to attract that level of support, especially when I play in London. It turned out to be an easy 2–0 win for me. Rick had just one dart at a double throughout the match.

Within moments of winning, an official from the NDA warned me that I wasn't going to get away with nicking the dartboard again, as I had done in 1979. 'You did that to us once and you're not going to do it again,' he told me, but when we turned around together, the dartboard had already disappeared from the stage. Incredibly, this one found its way into my car boot as well. Both of them are now hanging on my games room wall at home.

Getting hold of the boards was only part of the process. The 1979 board was made out of elm but, post Dutch elm disease, the 1986 board was made out of poplar, which is a much softer wood. I needed to soak both of them in water and dry out the cracks before immersing them in resin to preserve the quality. I left both boards like that for over ten years and then got my friend Harry Kicks, who makes dartboards for a living, to sand all the resin off, rewire the boards and hand them back to me in mint condition. They are my most treasured mementoes from my darts career.

Both *News of the World* Championship wins gave me equal pleasure. The first one put my name on the map and the second one re-established me as one of the top players in the game, but while my 1979 win was watched by millions on TV, the 1986 triumph was blacked out by that industrial dispute and no TV footage exists.

However, given the problems with my back and my age, my second win was a sweet victory for me. It meant a lot to Marie too, because it was the first major tournament I had won since I met her.

Marie was made up with my success but she was still officially the other woman in my life, even though my divorce had now come through, and had to sit with the Welsh supporters in the crowd because my mother-in-law, showing a rare interest in my darts career, turned up to watch me play at Wembley.

When I won the NOW title in 1979 actress Diana Dors had made the presentation. When I won it in 1986, top Page Three model Maria Whittaker did the honours. My dear old mum was well into her eighties and from that day on thought that Marie was Maria Whittaker, confusing my girlfriend with a topless model. She thought Marie was a nice girl but didn't quite understand why she had to take her clothes off for a living. I would go over to see Mum and she would have a copy of a newspaper featuring a topless Maria in her hand and shake her head at me.

'Tell your girlfriend to stop taking her clothes off, Robert,' she would say. I never did get around to telling Mum the truth about Marie not being Maria. I met Maria again a few years later when Cliff Lazarenko, Mike Gregory, Jocky Wilson and I did a photo shoot with her. She was always good fun but I was too embarrassed to tell her the story of how my mum thought she was my girlfriend.

Winning the NOW title reminded me how nice it was to lift a trophy again – I had almost forgotten what it felt like – and I was made up that I had returned to winning ways in that particular tournament. I gave the top prize of a holiday in the Caribbean to NDA official Jim Dowsett, and split my winnings with Rick, who was a good guy and a worthy finalist.

The press made out that this gesture was to say sorry for the hostile reception Rick received from the crowd but it was nothing of the sort. I had faced enough boos in my career – especially in America – to know that you just had to play through it.

Rick had a good tournament. He had knocked out Mike Gregory, who ended up in tears as a result. The NOW championship meant a lot to players and I remember Mike telling me it was the one trophy that gave you instant respect all over the world. Mike was heartbroken that day but he won the championship the following year, so the story had a happy ending, or at least his did. The NOW championship was scrapped a few years later and the world's original and best darts competition is now sadly no more.

I enjoyed a very good record in the competition. I won it twice, got to the grand finals five times and qualified for the area finals on 14 separate occasions, which must be some sort of record. All true darts champions won the NOW event but the BDO never properly recognised it because it wasn't one of their tournaments. Instead, the BDO put its considerable weight behind establishing the Embassy, but the NOW championship lasted for over 60 years and should never be forgotten. I was one of the few players who won the title twice and so I will never forget it. It will always have a very special place in my heart.

My two wins sandwiched the glory days of darts, from 1979 to 1986. It was quite a time in the sport and quite a gap to have between victories, but interest in darts on TV was now well on the decline, and fewer tournaments meant much less prize money. I was playing an increasing number of exhibitions for a growing number of sponsors. Courage, in particular, had been putting pressure on me to concentrate on exhibitions for some time. Winning an Open here or there was not making any difference to them. I was driving over 150,000 miles per year and getting so much work on the exhibition circuit that I was entering fewer and fewer tournaments. My world ranking slipped as a result and so did my interest in tournaments, particularly when the TV companies stopped showing the majority of them. It was a downward spiral. On the other hand, I was recognised as a champion in pubs and clubs up and down the country and loved being paid to be a professional entertainer.

Courage also sponsored snooker player Steve Davis at that time. Steve hailed from nearby Romford and we did a fair bit of promotional work together. He dominated his sport throughout the 1980s and was a quiet and very professional man.

Snooker and darts have a lot in common. Both sports come from the army. Darts originated with the bowmen in the fields while snooker was popular among army officers. Darts players and snooker players got on well. Each had respect for the other's profession. They couldn't throw maximums and we couldn't pot maximums, but players from the two sports don't appear to mix any more. The big difference today is prize money and while that kept growing consistently in snooker over the years, it virtually ground to a halt in darts.

I received tremendous support from Dave Clarke, Michael Jackson, Susan Roberts and the team at Courage. They even made sure that I was given a curry every night on the road, but then that was stipulated in my contract! Michael was a great bloke. He once came along to a venue and saw me putting the stage together by myself. He was so shocked that he immediately arranged to pay people to do it for me. I have never assembled a stage since then.

Courage paid very well. By the mid 1980s, I was on an annual six-figure retainer with an extra £650 thrown in for every show I did for them. Lovely jubbly!

At that time, Mick Miller was acting as my agent. His big problem was reading maps and he once booked me to appear in Liverpool, then Norwich and then Manchester on successive nights. 'They're really close, Bob, just two or three inches apart on the map,' he told me. He was murder. I eventually insisted on getting a plane to fly me around the country whenever I could.

I had a purpose-built trailer with all my gear and stage equipment – including a dozen glitter shirts and electronic scoreboard – and it followed me around on tour. Once, I did an exhibition with MC Martin Fitzmaurice at The Greet Inn in Tyseley, Birmingham, and afterwards we walked out into the car park to find that the trailer had disappeared. Luckily, I had taken the NOW trophy inside the pub to show off to the punters at the exhibition. Everything else I owned was stolen in the raid.

That was not the only close shave that the two of us had with the old trophy. The Fat Man somehow managed to snap off the head of the statuette while we were sat in a traffic jam. It was lying in bits on the back seat of my car. We took the trophy to a back-street repair shop in the city where Martin told the guy behind the counter to look after it because it was the most prestigious silverware in darts and most likely the most expensive item he had ever had in his possession.

The young lad looked at the Fat Man, then looked at me and shook his head. 'I wouldn't agree with you on that, mate,' he said. 'I've got the Ryder Cup in the back.' He then showed us one of the top trophies in world golf, complete with a bent lid.

After my divorce from Betty had been finalised, I was granted care and control of the children. I was finally free to marry Marie, the love of my life. My next problem was my former mother-in-law.

Betty and I had moved in with her mother in the early days of our marriage after the old girl had got herself into debt following the death of her husband. She was set to lose her house and so we moved in. I paid off all her debts and the mortgage. I even put her name on the deeds, just so she had some security in case anything happened to me.

My relationship with the old girl was fine until the day she found out about Marie, and then everything changed. She didn't agree with the relationship and made things difficult for us as a result. I had paid off all her debts and looked after her financially, even when I had no obligation to do so, but now she was against me. In the end the divorce was easy but the settlement was messy.

The life I was leaving behind was nothing compared to the new one that I was building with Marie. I was a single man again but all I wanted was to get married and on 21 March 1987, Marie and I tied the knot at Barkingside registry office. We held the reception back at the house, much to the disgust of my former mother-in-law. Marie and I actually lived in that house with the old girl and Nicola and Shane for a while but it soon became awkward and, eventually, impossible.

The final straw came when Marie – who was eight months pregnant with our first child at the time – decided that she had had enough abuse and moved out to live with our friends Joe and Mavis Matthews, at their home in Hainault.

It was during a darts exhibition in Plymouth in December 1987 that I got the call to say that Marie had given birth to a baby boy. My driver Tom Brown drove me straight to the hospital and when we arrived the nurse said, 'It's husband only, please.' Tom replied, 'Well, he's the husband but I'm the father.' She laughed so much that she let us both in to see Marie and the baby, which was nice of her.

We named our baby Robert, for the simple reason that when he got older I could open all the love letters from his girlfriends!

Due to the tangled mess that surrounded the house that we had shared with my former mother-in-law, Robert had to spend the first three months of his life with Marie and her parents, Salvador and Camelia. Marie's parents were a great help to us at that difficult time.

By now, Marie, Robert and I were living in a flat in Romford. I gave Nicola and Shane the option of moving in with us but they decided to stay at home with their mother. For many years afterwards I didn't have much to do with either of them, and that was very difficult for me.

I am pleased to say that I do now have a relationship with both of them again and am a grandfather to three children, but it took many years to rebuild those particular bridges.

Marie and I wanted to make a new start away from London. We found a piece of land next to the River Colne in Halstead, Essex, and I began to build a house on it. The land had the potential to be a dream home and the fresh water at the bottom of the garden made such a difference to me. There wasn't any particular reason to choose Halstead. It was just the best land available at that price, and it also happened to be just an hour away from my roots.

Every morning I was up with the milkman and Marie would pack me off to the building site with some sandwiches and a flask. I would return at midnight and used to look forward to having a bath with my newborn son. With Marie pushing me every step of the way, I was making a real go of this different life, and the work did wonders for my waistline. I was shifting bricks, timber and bags of cement and was soon down to 14 stone again, the lightest I had been since my illness back in 1981. The daily routine of up to 20 pints of beer and a late night curry was knocked on the head, which also helped. For the first time in years I could keep the light on in the bedroom!

We eventually moved into our new home and almost immediately I knew that I never wanted to live in London again. I could spend time fishing at the bottom of the garden. There were all types of fish in that river and it was a lovely way to relax. Fishing has been a life-long passion for me, and the peace and tranquillity it provides is a million miles away from the darts circuit. It helps me get away from all of that.

Over the first few months, I would regularly get up in the middle of the night and walk down to the river to see all the fish swimming about before going back to bed. Once, in the early hours of a New Year's Day, I broke the ice and fished like an Eskimo. I didn't need a party or even a beer to celebrate the moment, just a fishing rod and Marie by my side.

My favourite TV programmes have always been about nature and wildlife with history close behind. I like to be educated when I watch TV, and love to sit in my palace with my wife and a pint, watching the box. Marie always taped *Wildlife on One* for me when I was away playing darts in our early days together. I would come home to cheese, biscuits and the video. Looking back, she must have been in love with me.

I have always felt that the Victorians invented class, and indoors I tried to copy that in the furnishings with dark antique furniture, made of mahogany.

That house was a real labour of love and I had to pull out of darts exhibitions left, right and centre to build it, which affected me financially. By now, competitive darts had hit the wall. I played on for a while but my heart was no longer in it. The results were meaningless and so I decided to retire for good and bring the curtain down on my competitive career after the 1988 Embassy world championship, but I didn't even manage to do that. My world ranking was so low that I had to qualify for the Embassy and I lost in the play-offs to a young Swedish boy called Magnus Caris.

The fact that I needed to qualify for the Embassy tells its own story. I had played in so few tournaments that my world ranking had eventually slipped down to its lowest point since I turned professional and was insufficient to get me an invite. It was a kick in the balls but understandable.

The qualifiers took place in Earl's Court, and were a completely new experience for me. I may have been out of match practice but I was still the big-shot player and the one everyone wanted to beat. The qualifiers had started at two in the afternoon and by midnight only Magnus and I were left playing darts, when I lost in a sudden-death tic-break. Everyone who remained in the hall was watching us. One of the waiters came up to me at the end and said it was the best darts match he had ever seen. I hope he saw the one Magnus and I played a few years later as well.

Magnus told me that when he was a young boy he used to write to me, asking for my canes and flights and I used to post them to him in Sweden. Apparently, we had been pen friends of a sort for a while.

So, after eight successive appearances in the Embassy, I wasn't going to the Lakeside for the 1988 finals. I had put my wife, my baby boy and my new home before my darts and this was the price I had to pay – it was inevitable, really.

It hit me hard, but not that hard. I thought about my life and earning a living, and within hours of losing that match to Magnus, I made the decision to quit. I didn't need the hassle of it all. Darts tournaments no longer mattered to me. There was nothing for me to prove any more. From now on, exhibitions would pay my way. My sponsors were delighted.

Exhibitions still gave me the buzz that tournaments couldn't. I wasn't bothered about entering competitions because the enjoyment factor was nil. Maybe so much was going on in other areas of my life that I needed to give something the sack in order to fit everything else in, and tournaments fitted the bill.

I no longer needed the TV fame either. I was a born-again husband and the happiest I had ever been in my life. It was all down to Marie. All I ever wanted was a partner to share my life but I never found that until I found Marie. She is the business. I might have the body of a man but I have the brain of a six-year-old boy sometimes and I need looking after.

I really don't think men have a clue about life until they are well into middle age. No man should get married until he has properly grown up. Women seem to mature a lot quicker and I think that a woman of 25 is usually a lot older in the head than any man of a similar age.

Young men know bollocks in all honesty and that was most certainly true of me. The difference between being a dad in my twenties and being a dad in my forties was massive. Back in the 1970s, all I could think about was earning a pound note but now I could concentrate on the important things in life. There was much more love in me and much more time for me to give it. I know that I am very lucky to have been given a second chance.

After we moved to Halstead, we sometimes used to eat at Friends, a Chinese restaurant on the town's High Street. When the drains got blocked up with fat, its owner Alan Mann came over to ask me to rod them for him. Alan was a fantastic cook but he wasn't too hot at building work and a few days later he asked me to help him with some refurbishment plans. I did some drawings for him and he presented them to the Council. The plans were passed and when he came to see me to say thank you and ask how much I wanted in payment, I told him that all I wanted was for him to teach me how to cook.

The best way to learn anything is to be shown first hand by a professional, whether it is rodding drains or cooking chicken chow mein – and I had always loved Chinese food. All darts players eat Chinese and Indian food. We have a taste for it because those restaurants are always the last ones to close when we are out on the road.

I spent weeks in the kitchen with Alan and his chef, Mr Lo, and they showed me the tricks of the trade, such as how to cut the food and make spicy and non-spicy dishes with different recipes. All Chinese chefs have their own recipes. I love garlic and use it a lot on my dishes.

Rice is the hardest thing to cook. It is very easy to make a mistake. You need to get the starch out of it and then boil it up until it's fluffy. The first Chinese dish I mastered was rice because Mr Lo told me that I would be lost without it. I had learned to cook Indian food in similar circumstances years beforehand – after doing some building and plastering work – but that was far easier to master than Chinese cooking.

If I could have my way, I would eat Chinese food every day of the week but I have special orders to settle for it just three or four times. Now I have my own kitchen to cook in, that is easy.

Whenever I am away from home, I go looking for a Chinese restaurant. One time, when I was up in Glasgow for an exhibition, I ordered king prawn curry with egg fried rice and watched in disbelief as the chef stood at the front of the restaurant in an open kitchen preparing it for me. He put eggs, salt and a bit of soy sauce in a dish to make the rice and then handed it to me within seconds. Well, that isn't egg fried rice. That is just posh boiled rice and I told him as much, with bells on.

'You want to cook, then you cook,' he shouted back.

'All right,' I said, and I got behind his stand and cooked my own meal with garlic and all the trimmings. The restaurant owner was flabbergasted and gave me the meal for free. That's the way to do it!

Two years after Robert was born – almost to the day – Marie gave birth to our second child, another boy. We called him Richard. Our family was complete. I was determined to give both boys the love and attention I was unable to give my first two children.

Both Robert and Richard could be little buggers and they soon picked up on my traits, including the industrial language I have used at home since I was a kid.

'What's for dinner, Dad?' Robert asked me when he was about four. 'I'm fucking starving!'

I have always had my own bar at home and both of my boys got used to pulling themselves a pint whenever they were thirsty. Robert, in particular, was drinking beer from a very young age, but he didn't go a lot on Hofmeister. Neither of them did and it was all to do with 'George the Bear'.

Courage, who promoted Hofmeister lager, featured a huge bear in their advertising campaign, and my sister Heather's ex-husband, Roger, often wore a 'George the Bear' costume at my exhibitions to promote the brand. I kept it in the house and the boys were scared of it. I had thought they liked it from the TV but one night after I told them I had brought George home, I found Robert standing motionless at the bottom of the stairs at bedtime.

'What's up with you?' I asked him.

'The bear. He's up there, Dad,' he said.

Robert was scared stiff and made me promise that I would immediately get the bear out of the house. So I went upstairs, packed the costume away, put it in the wardrobe and went back downstairs.

'All clear now, the bear's gone,' I told him.

The next day, both boys were pinging me with questions left, right and centre about the bear. Where did he come from? Where did he live? Was he a friendly or a nasty bear? Their imaginations were running wild. We had a river at the bottom of the garden that was as deep as 8ft in places, and the current was quite fast, so it was dangerous for the boys to play near it. I warned them about the dangers but they wouldn't listen. I made wrought-iron railings to keep them away but they just climbed over them. I had been trying to think of a deterrent, so I told them that the bear lived down by the river and that it was a gentle creature until anyone trespassed on its land and then it could get very nasty. The story I fed them was that George the Bear had spotted Robert down by the river and had gone upstairs to tell him off. Both of the boys were absolutely terrified.

George the Bear's head had a mark on its nose and I told them that was where I had punched it in a fight down by the river one night. I played the part well. I sometimes even dressed up in the costume and walked around the garden late at night, with Robert and Richard staring at me from behind the curtains. It was a scream.

They got braver as they got older, though, and it wasn't long before they started going down to the bottom of the garden as far as the railings to look for the bear. It was only a matter of time before they began to work it all out. They started to ask more searching questions – 'What's the bear doing upstairs when he lives by the river, Dad?' and 'How do you know the bear so well, Dad?' Robert finally hit the jackpot. 'You're the bear, aren't you, Dad?'

They had never seen the bear and me in the same place at the same time, and children are far from daft, so I got my mate Dean to dress up as the bear and knock on the front door. We were just about to sit down for dinner one night when there was a knock and I asked Robert to answer it. He opened the door and ran off screaming as soon as he saw the bear. That fixed that for another few months. I think my boys believed that George the Bear existed for longer than they believed in Santa Claus.

They found that George came in useful sometimes, though. Robert and Richard loved chocolate when they were children. They would pinch the sweets hanging off the Christmas tree and act totally innocent. One year I got up in the morning to find both boys sat on the floor with chocolate smeared around their mouths and wrappers all over the place.

'I see all the chocolates have gone off the tree. Who's eaten them?' I asked.

'It was the bear, Dad,' Robert answered. 'He came inside and stole them all.' You had to admire my son's cheek.

Robert could lie for fun when he had to. There was a big grandfather clock in the house and he used to love to get inside it. One day he brought the whole thing crashing down to the floor. I ran into the room, fearing the worst and found him standing next to a smashed up grandfather clock.

'What happened?' I shouted.

'Batman knocked it over, Dad,' Robert replied.

'Fucking Batman. I'll give you batman, you lying bastard. Where is he then?' I boomed and chased him around the room.

Robert turned to me with a straight face and said calmly, 'He's just flown out the window.' Honestly, I could never get too angry with those two because I just had to admire their bottle and ended up laughing, whatever they got up to.

They both had a marvellous imagination. I used to watch them play in their bedroom for hours with nothing but a few toys, and listened to fantastic stories coming out of their mouths. It was a fabulous time for me, watching my boys grow up. Life is what you make it and I made sure that I spent time with my new family, something I wasn't able to do first time around when darts just took over my life.

Sadly, Robert and Richard never really got to know my dear old mum. She died in 1990, when they were toddlers, at the age of 86, after being bedridden for years. The old man looked after her throughout her later years in his own domineering way. He fed her on vitamin tablets and one day gave her so many that she had to be rushed into hospital. She recovered from that scare but later became quite poorly with shingles and was taken back into hospital. That is where she stayed until just before she died. I think she was grateful for that. Being in hospital towards the end allowed her to spend some time with the family without the old man controlling her. It gave her some peace at the end of her life. The old man refused to put a headstone on her grave and, just as with his first wife, he never went to the cemetery.

Around this period, I was spending a lot of time entertaining the British troops all over the globe from Europe to the Falklands and later the Gulf, just as the first war broke out. It was a tremendous experience and something that I feel proud to have done.

I went over to East Germany a few times, too, before the Berlin Wall came down. It was fascinating. I was given proper documentation so I could cross Checkpoint Charlie without needing to get my passport stamped. I felt like one of the soldiers. The Russian army manned the entrance to the East and they seemed quite friendly with the Brits. Guns would be pointed at you while your papers were checked and then you could proceed to the next barrier. It was quite intimidating. I was looked up and down, from head to toe. It was like playing a game but I couldn't afford to mess about. I tried to play the part but often got it wrong and the British lads would whisper to me, 'Salute them, don't wave at them!'

East Berlin was a very bleak place. Everything was painted grey and the exhaust fumes from the antiquated vehicles were disgusting. I was pleased to be there for the British troops but always happy to get out. There were no police as such and so you just had to watch yourself and watch out for the soldiers.

The cost of living was a joke. I could order steak, champagne and a cigar for about three quid. A pint of lager worked out at nine pence. It was Mickey Mouse money, a world away from what I was used to and a world away from life on the other side of the wall. The West Berliners had nice clothes, classy restaurants and BMWs. The contrast shocked me and I found it hard to accept. As I was out there to play darts, I was dressed in all my glitter and gold most of the time. I was very aware of it in East Berlin and felt humbled. Whatever those people thought of me driving around in a sponsored Ford Sierra with my name emblazoned across the door in bright colours, I will never know.

Within reason I was able to walk around as I pleased and one day I was even allowed to visit Rudolf Hess' cell in Spandau prison, which was a great privilege and well beyond what I expected as an entertainer of the troops.

The British boys were absolutely fantastic. They loved darts and called me 'Sir' all the time. Even when I told them not to, they would reply, 'Understood, Sir.' I had a brilliant time. The army used all sorts of code words. 'Rocking Horse' prepared them for action. At one exhibition I got the MC to call out 'Rocking Horse' instead of 'Game On' and all the boys ran outside. It was a good crack and they enjoyed the joke.

Lofty Newman, my driver, came to East Berlin with me and he went down a storm. Lofty was a true character and I nicknamed him 'King of Cock-ups' because something always went wrong when I was with him, but he was a very funny man and had his uses. He smoked like a train and one night when we got lost, we found our way back to base by following Lofty's discarded fag packets all the way home.

Lofty once drove me to Liverpool for an exhibition and pulled up behind a skip. There I was sitting in a car with my name emblazoned on its side, nodding and smiling to all the passers-by while my driver delved deep inside this bloody skip. He eventually appeared with an old brass lamp, looking like an extra in Aladdin. 'Never pass a skip without having a butcher's indoors, Bob,' he said. A few weeks later he had cleaned up the lamp and flogged it for £125. What a man! There was never a dull moment when Lofty was around, but sadly he's dead now.

When I visited the Falklands with MC Phil Jones, it took ages for us to get there. We flew to the beautiful, volcanic Ascension Island in the middle of the South Atlantic Ocean and waited for the opportunity to proceed south west. The weather conditions were so bad that we were hanging around for well over a day. We put up a board and passed our time playing darts.

The Falkland Islands cover a deceptively large area. I was expecting one small group of islands but there were hundreds. A lot of them are still covered in mines and it could be a dangerous place if you ever got lost. There were signs all over, warning people to 'Stay on the rocks'. We went out for a five-mile walk one day with the soldiers and I mistakenly stepped off the path halfway along. I was terrified. I literally froze on the spot. The place was so quiet and peaceful but little things like that reminded you of where you were and what went off there not that long ago.

The marshland also looked treacherous and made me realise how fit and strong the British soldiers must have been to win a war on it. I have never known wind like that at Penguin Point, either. It was a case of one step forward and two steps back. True to its name, penguins were everywhere and were in their element.

I saw an albatross at Penguin Point. This massive bird has the biggest wingspan of all, but I didn't realise just how big that is until I saw one in flight with my own eyes. I was fascinated and never lost sight of it as it flew away.

The national sport of the Falklands is darts – one of the few sports that can be played there – and the interest in the game is incredible. Some Falkland Islanders once took part in the world play-offs, which surprised a few BDO people but not me. However, it is one thing to visit British troops in an area that was once a war zone and quite another to visit them in an active war zone. I found that out for myself in 1991 in the Gulf.

When the opportunity arose, I desperately wanted to go but I was warned about the dangers and was told there was no guarantee that I would be able to get out of the Gulf at any given time or – if the worst came to the worst – at all. It was a frightening prospect but I had faith and wasn't deterred. I did make a will, though, and gave it to my friend Kenny Harris, just in case anything happened to me. I didn't tell Marie – she was already petrified.

Perhaps I was brave to go but I never thought about it in that way. I just wanted to do my bit for my country, however small that was in the scheme of things. Having entertained the troops for many years, I felt it almost a duty to carry on when they probably needed a bit of distraction more than ever. Even though I was nothing more than a darts player sent out to entertain them, those soldiers gave me so much respect it was untrue.

I was based on a ship off the coast of Bahrain but, although I had been told all about Scud missiles and received tuition in what to do in case of an emergency, I really had no idea of what I was letting myself in for. We have all seen pictures of wars on TV and in news-papers but nothing can ever prepare you for the real thing. The sights, the smells, the taste and the fear were something else. All my senses were working overtime. I had never experienced anything like it before.

I was fitted out with a plastic suit and gas mask, which I found un-comfortable. Breathing was quite difficult, never mind walking, running or fighting. I was sweating up just standing still.

I can clearly remember when the oil wells were set alight at the end of the war. Everything was covered in black dust from the ground to the sky. It was terrible. How the troops managed to put out those fires, I will never know. It was a sobering experience to meet such brave young men in the front line of action.

12 Broken dreams

Eric Bristow remained the big name in darts, although despite reaching three more Embassy world finals, he was never able to add to his tally of five wins. John Lowe and Jocky Wilson were also still around, and these three were soon joined by two new kids on the block, Dennis Priestley and Phil Taylor. Dennis and Phil went on to monopolise the game in the early 1990s.

Darts was looking to the future and any new player who emerged on the scene seemed to come equipped with a ready-made nickname. Dennis was, unsurprisingly, known as 'The Menace' while Phil was on his way to establishing himself as 'The Power', an apt title for a man who was to dominate the game in the way he did.

Phil looked up to Eric and the two were good friends but that didn't stop the young pretender slaying his hero 6–1 in the 1990 Embassy world final. Dennis went one better the following year by thrashing Eric 6–0. Then in 1992, the best final of all, Phil somehow defeated Mike Gregory. Mike had six darts for the title and was never behind in the final set of that match until The Power hit the winning dart in a final-leg tie-break.

To the outside world, darts appeared to be in decent health but the prowess of both Dennis and Phil was papering over some serious cracks in the game. Basically, most of the top players were unhappy with how the BDO was running darts and they wanted a change. They set up their own organisation, the World Darts Council, and everyone who was anyone signed up.

It was quite a list. Established players such as Eric Bristow, John Lowe, Jocky Wilson, Bob Anderson, Keith Deller and Cliff Lazarenko were joined by the new brigade, including Dennis Priestley, Phil Taylor, Mike Gregory, Peter Evison, Rod Harrington, Jamie Harvey, Kevin Spiolek and Alan Warriner. These were big names and the only top players who didn't sign up were Dave Whitcombe and Leighton Rees, who both had pubs, and yours truly. I was busy with exhibitions, houses and my young children.

The WDC represented a sizeable body of opinion but the BDO stood firm and there was a stand-off. This was the backdrop to the game of darts when a letter arrived on my doorstep from BDO general secretary Olly Croft, in the autumn of 1992. Olly had remained a friend and stayed in touch during my absence from competitive darts. After the house in Halstead was eventually finished, he would regularly ring up for a chat and often joked about me returning to the game.

This time he was serious. He had written the letter on behalf of the sponsors, Imperial Tobacco, inviting me to come out of retirement to take part in the qualification play-offs for the 1993 world championship.

It was getting on for five years to the day that I had last played competitively, my defeat against Magnus Caris coming in the final round of the 1988 Embassy qualifiers. The qualifiers are hard, especially for a big-name player from the past trying to muscle his way through against young talent. I thought about it and my gut feeling was to say no – that was until the wife got involved.

Marie had been saying for a little while that one day she hoped I would make a return to competitive darts, just so Robert and Richard could see me in action. Marie had first got the idea in her head when she gathered together all my trophies from my golden era in the game and displayed them throughout the house. Richard, in particular, would watch darts on TV with me and say that he wanted me to be the best player in the world. My wife has always been a persuasive girl and her two boys are quite similar. So, I allowed the heart to rule the head and changed my mind.

When MC Phil Jones heard about this, he picked up the phone straightaway to invite me to play county darts for London in preparation for the qualifiers. That didn't go down too well with some of the London players, who were unhappy that I went straight into the A team, but as I told a few of them, 'I have never played for a B team in my life and I ain't starting now.' I found that the fire was still in my belly. I practised hard for the qualifiers and got through, beating up-and-coming player Dave Askew in the final round.

Going back to the Lakeside after all those years was strange, but all of the players gave me a warm welcome and I soon felt as though I had never been away. The only one I had stayed in touch with was Eric Bristow. I had even gone to his wedding in the late 1980s. I mentioned this to him on the night and he told the barman that I shouldn't be charged for drinks but all the other guests should be. He was still unbelievable at times.

Tension was in the air at the Lakeside because of the stand-off between the BDO and the WDC, but since I didn't have all the facts to hand, I wasn't really sure whose side I was on. I told the boys I was there playing for the Bobby Darts Organisation that week.

I have always been someone who plays darts, not someone who wants to run darts. I leave that side of things to other people, but that wasn't good enough for some of the WDC members, who felt that if I wasn't with them, then I was against them. The WDC never asked me to sign for them, yet some members of the organisation regarded me as a BDO supporter. In fact, I was more of a BDO sympathiser. It was a terrible time for Olly Croft and I really felt for him as a friend. He may not do everything right but he is a good man and has devoted his life to darts.

I tried hard not to get involved in the politics and concentrated all my energies into giving the tournament a much-needed breather from the issue that was choking it.

There was one other bone of contention that year. The WDC wanted former world champions to be invited to play by right, but the BDO wanted all players to qualify via world-ranking points, the county system and the qualifiers, which I had come through.

By this time, both Eric and Jocky were struggling with their form and the BDO relented under pressure and granted both of them wild cards for the tournament. I love the thought of wild cards – God knows, I have badgered Olly enough over the years – but the BDO system firmly says no and I felt it was wrong to give way on this occasion, however delicate the situation was with the established players and the WDC.

Deep down, every player at the Lakeside felt that 1993 would mark the final year that we would all be together in this way. It might not have been official news at that time, but everyone knew that it was going to be the case very soon. The rivalry was very bitter and both sides were desperate for one of their members to lift what was probably going to be the last unified world title.

Everyone was there. It was a real who's who of darts and a great privilege to be part of it. The WDC players were joined by the best of the new BDO crop, including Dutchman Raymond Barneveld. I was just desperate not to embarrass myself and had even practised on Christmas Day in preparation for the tournament, which really is saying something for me.

Marie and the boys were pushing me all the way. They wanted me to win one game to give them something to cheer about and remember. I was really focused and my averages of 29 to 30 were encouraging. I felt that if I could keep up that standard, at least I wouldn't make a fool of myself on TV. That was my main goal and I wasn't looking any further than that going into the tournament. I was extremely rusty when it came to competitive darts and I wasn't going to heap more pressure on myself by making rash promises.

From what I could tell, the standard was similar to what I had left behind in 1987. The overseas players had made big improvements but the play-offs suggested that I might be OK. My first-round match pitched me against the number seven seed Keith Sullivan, and any hopes I had of a quiet return were dashed when the BBC decided to show the game live. The schedule was turned around and our match was switched to the afternoon.

I wore a new spangled gold shirt for the occasion. Eric took one look at it and said, 'Welcome back, Bob, that'll get you a few more exhibitions.' He was spot on. Despite everything I had said beforehand, here I was inadvertently putting more pressure on myself to win, but the stakes were so high I couldn't help it.

I knew nothing about my opponent. I had heard he was Australian and had a fair bit of experience, but that was about it. He was also the seed and I was the qualifier but few people saw it like that. Although the bookmakers made me the underdog, most of the fans expected me to win.

Everyone got a seat for this one. I made a nervous start and Keith had darts for the first set but I snatched it from him, and when that dart was greeted with a massive roar from the crowd and cries of 'Bobby', I knew that I was on my way. It was like I had never been away.

I relaxed and played my own game, waltzing through the second set before throwing away the third set in a lapse of concentration. I wasted eight darts to win the match. I was sat on tops and Keith was way back on 326, but he took the set to get back to 2–1 and sow some demons of doubt in my head.

Concentration remained my biggest obstacle in darts. I lost many matches that I should have won due to being miles away in my own little world when I should have been in there for the kill. Maybe it's something to do with the entertainer in me.

I have always done things the hard way in darts. If faced with a mountain to climb, I would probably climb it with no problems at all and then fall over a little gate at the top! It is hard to explain but when matches should be difficult they are easy for me, and when matches should be easy they turn out to be difficult. The examples I could give are endless because I have had that problem throughout my career. The fact is I am easier to beat when I am in front, and I am a far more dangerous player when coming from behind. It frustrates me to hell.

Only twice have I remained totally focused throughout a tournament, both times in the finals of the *News of the World* championship, which were so short that I didn't have a choice. I was rewarded with two much-treasured world titles.

However, being so far in front in that leg against Keith and throwing it away taught me a timely lesson. I hadn't experienced anything like that in my five years away. I got my act together and won the match 3–1. It was a big relief to get through and coming back to win the fourth set fired me up.

Being back on the TV was great as well, of course, but the new gold shirt caused me no end of problems. It was so tight, heavy and hot under the spotlights that I sweated like a pig throughout the match. I swore never to wear it again and swapped the spangled gold number for a much safer black option. It is so easy to sweat on stage with all the nerves, tension and heat of the spotlights beaming down on you. Some players sweat more than others and I seem to be one of the worst for it.

One part of competitive darts that I had really missed was the post-match TV interview. I went backstage to chat with the BBC presenter Dougie Donnelly and told him, 'Elvis ain't dead, after all.' In truth, I felt more like Shakin' Stevens but it was great to be back all the same.

Darts coverage on TV had definitely changed. There were now more features, interviews and analysis and it seemed absolutely made for me. The next day, Dougie sat me down by a piano in the Lakeside hotel and interviewed me for that night's programme. Almost over-night, I was re-established as a top darts player. Back on TV and back in the public bloodstream, Bobby George was a name once again.

TV presentation wasn't the only change. The dartboards were dif-ferent, too. The Embassy now used Winmau blade boards and every double and treble bed was wider due to new wiring. For someone returning to the game, it was a doddle to play on. The old-style board was much more difficult to play on and made for better players. Back in the 1970s, I designed the 'Champion's Choice' board – a smaller version of the normal clock dartboard – and that improved my game enormously. I was quids in with this new model.

I was enjoying myself so much that I completely forgot that the whole WDC thing was going on behind the scenes, but I think that the political undercurrent affected a lot of performances in the early stages of that tournament. A rather posh-looking and bespectacled Jocky Wilson went out in the first round and, perhaps more tellingly, Eric Bristow, Dennis Priestley and Phil Taylor didn't make it into the quarter-finals either.

Dennis' defeat surprised me. I practised with him ahead of the second-round matches and he completely blew me away. In our first leg he threw two 180s, then 60, treble 15 and missed double 18 by a whisker for a nine-darter. He went out on his next throw. In the second, third and fourth legs it was the same routine – 180, 180, 60, treble 15 and two darts at double 18. In the fifth leg he went one bet-ter and finally recorded a nine-darter. It was unbelievable. We played five legs of darts and he carded one nine-darter and four identical ten-darters. He won five legs in 49 darts against me! My mate Kenny Harris scored the game and kept the sheets as souvenirs. It was the best darts performance I had ever seen in my life and remains so to this day.

I was as sure as I could be that Dennis would win the tournament. He had to, playing like that. Who could possibly stop him? So, I went into the main hall and placed a sizeable wager on him doing just that, and then watched in total disbelief as he crashed out 3–1 to Steve Beaton within the hour.

My second-round opponent was Martin Phillips, of Wales, but the 3–0 scoreline I recorded doesn't tell the true story of the match because he took five legs off me. Martin is a diamond of a bloke. His nickname is 'Napoleon' and he is a very good left-handed player. He made polite remarks throughout our match. 'Well done, Bob,' he said, and, 'Good darts, Bob.' I lost a flight at one stage and couldn't find it anywhere, so Martin gave me one of his. I had never known anything like it. He is a true gentleman, and that is a rare gift in darts these days.

Incredibly, I was now through to the Embassy quarter-finals for the first time in 11 years. After the match I went over to kiss Marie. My wife had persuaded me to give it another crack and I wanted to thank her for what was turning into a wonderful experience for both of us. Marie was in the audience to watch my matches. She was the first wife to sit with the spectators, simply because she didn't want to stay in the players' bar and watch me on TV. Of course, the TV cameras picked her up and she was all over the match coverage. It wasn't long before all the other wives and girlfriends were out there doing the same. That sort of thing has since gone down in Lakeside folklore and Marie started it. Eric referred to us as the 'Bobby and Marie road show'.

Another thing that the TV cameras picked up on were my little catchphrases. At the end of one interview with Dougie, I said, 'May the darts be with you,' and this clip was replayed so much that fans even started writing it on banners inside the hall.

As the quarter-finals approached, for the first time I sensed a real BDO v. WDC rivalry. Bob Anderson, Mike Gregory, John Lowe, Kevin Spiolek and Alan Warriner, all signed-up members of the new organisation, were still in the tournament but they weren't a happy lot. The BDO refused to allow them to wear WDC logos on their shirts and this added more fuel to the fire. The three non-WDC players were Australian national champion Wayne Weening, Steve Beaton and me. The press were in no doubt that the likeliest scenario was that four WDC players would contest the semi-finals of an event that was the pride and joy of the BDO.

I was just enjoying the crack. I was set to play Mike Gregory in the quarter-finals and with no Dennis Priestley or Phil Taylor, the number two seed had been confirmed as the clear favourite to make amends for his disappointment the previous year. It didn't bother me at all that Mike was the tournament favourite. I had been the underdog in each of my matches so far and, despite the fancied players dropping like flies, I knew that if I was to win the championship I still had to beat some top names.

Mike was a brilliant player on his day but one thing he could never handle was a crowd and I knew that. On the night of our match, the fans were absolutely magnificent. Support had grown steadily for me during the week and I got a real sense of the fans starting to believe that I could come back from five years in the wilderness and win the biggest prize in darts. I wasn't getting carried away – every game is a final in itself in a darts tournament – but there was no question that the crowd believed in me and, importantly, I now believed in myself.

Support in sport is a two-way thing but not everyone understands that. I make sure that I always put on a show for that reason, and I am usually supported in return. The Lakeside crowd, in particular, are very knowledgeable and appreciate your efforts, even when things aren't going so well for you on the oche. If I was to stand any chance against Mike, I needed to get the crowd behind me from the start. So I turned the clock back 13 years and walked on with a candelabra. The crowd went wild and it all just took off. The more they got behind me, the more I put into it. The buzz pushed me to such a high level that it felt just like that 1980 world final again, only better, because this time I was playing to my full ability. It was some atmosphere – not unlike that match against Eric Bristow. With all the WDC players supporting Mike and all the BDO officials and players backing me, I once again felt like a gladiator in ancient Rome.

Despite breaking Mike's throw in the very first leg, I lost the opening set 3–2. Then something quite peculiar happened. Mike asked MC Martin Fitzmaurice to make a request on his behalf to the audience that they remained quiet during play. Well, of course, this was like waving a red rag to a bull and, noticing that he was rattled, the crowd played on it even more. I thought it was bollocks. The crowd were for me not against him and to make a complaint in this way – particularly when he was winning – was stupidity on his part.

The crowd got even louder and when Mike asked Martin to quieten them down again, I put my tongue out at him in disgust. The crowd loved that and it was soon utter mayhem in the hall. It was great to be back.

Mike was on top early on but he was now playing into my hands. When the 'Bobby' chants started up after I took a leg in the second set, he complained to Martin for a third time about the noise. He had darts for a two-set lead but couldn't take them. I looked over to Marie in the crowd and realised it was now or never for me. Mike had been all over me like a rash. It was time to find a different gear.

I hit my first maximum of the contest and was so pumped up that when Mike was at the oche throwing for the set, I kept muttering to myself, 'Get out of the way, you fat bastard.'

Mike required 141 and missed, I levelled the match with a 76 checkout and when my final dart hit double top, I jumped about a foot in the air. So did the crowd.

Now I felt I had got a chance. I was in the zone and couldn't wait to throw my darts. I was so focused that I couldn't hear the crowd, but I did notice Mike staring down at the floor and we were at the start of only the third set in a best-of-seven set encounter.

I was throwing so well that even if a dart fell below the treble bed, I knew I had got the confidence to throw over the dart and into the red bit – and I was taking my doubles at the first time of asking. A sweet double 16, right in the centre of the bed, gave me the third set against the darts. The crowd went bananas. I sensed that where there was once hope among them, there was now real belief that I could win.

My concentration was crucial. I needed to make sure that I didn't give Mike – a world-class player at the top of his game – an inch. I had to grit my teeth and fight. I couldn't afford to lapse in any way and had to remain focused throughout if I was going to beat him.

The final leg of the fourth set was crucial. If I took it, I would lead 3–1 in sets and if Mike got it, the match would be tied at 2–2. One leg was worth two sets – it was as simple as that – and I was the one with the throw, which was a huge advantage. I aimed for a 12-dart leg, knowing that Mike would then need a nine-darter to win it. Given that there has only ever been one of those in the history of the Embassy, I felt that 12 darts should be sufficient for me to move into a 3–1 lead.

This was my big opportunity. I remained calm and started off with two tons and then recorded a maximum to leave 121 for the set, my favourite unorthodox finish. I went out on the bull and sent the crowd barmy.

I didn't just jump, I threw myself up in the air in jubilation, delighted that at the moment when I needed it in a pressure situation, I was able to throw perfect darts. That 12-dart leg gave me a two-set lead and all I had to do now was to keep my head. The match wasn't over but Mike required all three remaining sets to beat me.

Mike played well throughout the match but whenever he did something special and turned to the crowd, he was met by silence and that was tough for him. The crowd refused to help him one little bit and I knew that the match was mine to lose rather than his to win. I really didn't think that he could beat me from two sets behind but I wasn't sure because he was such a fine player.

He never gave up and some relentless scoring put him back in the match at 3–2. I had the throw in the sixth set and that was vital. The nerves began to get to me and I scraped through the first leg on double one before making up a 275-point deficit in the second leg to lead 2–0.

That leg more than any other did Mike. He held a handsome lead and threw twice for double top but put the darts either side of the double bed to leave 20. I then hit a maximum, putting some pressure on. Mike had darts for double ten and hit a single ten. He then needed double five and hit a single five. He couldn't finish and aimed for a single one to leave four but hit treble one to leave two.

As he walked back from the board he was shaking his head and staring at the floor. I hit double 18 at my first attempt to move just one leg away from victory. I finished the match off with a 66 checkout on double top and again leapt up in the air in celebration. The crowd were on their feet and Marie was close to tears.

It was an unbelievable victory for me, and a fantastic feeling to perform so well on such a stage in a match of such importance against a player of the calibre of Mike Gregory. That match probably ranks as my best-ever performance in darts and I have got the picture of my winning celebration on my wall at home. I walked off the stage and gave a thrilled Marie her standard snog before blowing a kiss to Bob Wilson, my all-time favourite BBC cameraman who is sadly no longer with us. I finished off by blowing kisses to that fantastic crowd, all those people who had got me through it. As Mike trudged off the stage, they were too busy singing 'Ole, ole, ole, ole, Bobby, Bobby' to notice.

I was in shock. I didn't know whether to be happy at being back in the limelight or to be sad at having been away from it for so long. I thought I should just enjoy the moment. That whole night was marvellous and it still brings a lump to my throat whenever I think about it.

My only aim when I travelled to the Lakeside that week had been not to embarrass myself and to put on a bit of a show for the fans. Not for one moment did I consider I might win the tournament, but here I was in the last four, having just knocked out the favourite with the performance of my life. Now I had to admit to myself that I stood a chance of finally winning the Embassy world title.

My doubles percentage against Mike was awesome and I hit virtually every shot I went for. Double 16 was my double that night and I seemed to hit it every leg. There is no doubt that my excellent finishing won it for me.

That match was something else, which was down to both Mike and me, and it should be recognised as one of the best ever in the history of the Embassy world championship, but due to the WDC business, the 1993 championship was quickly swept under the carpet.

I was suddenly even bigger news. No one had expected me to do anything apart from turn up but now that I was a potential world champion the whole media bandwagon was starting up again. Marie and I were invited to do interviews together left, right and centre and this was very exciting for her because she had missed out on all that the first time around. She had persuaded me to go back to competitive darts and now she was living the dream.

Marie made the moment very special for me. The look on her face after I won that quarter-final meant more to me than anything I won in the 1970s and 1980s. There was no one to share those wins with simply because no one was interested. No one ever cared for me like Marie did, and so the least I could do was dedicate that win to her.

Cards were arriving at the Lakeside from members of the public every day, wishing me luck in my quest for a most unlikely title success. My odds had been slashed from 14–1 to 7–2 as I faced my old adversary John Lowe for a place in the world final. As long as I could retain my form, I was confident that I would have far too much for John and that I would get through to the final. I was playing too well to lose to him.

Unfortunately, once again I produced an abject performance that came nowhere near my true potential on a dartboard. I gave John too many chances, my finishing was woeful and he punished me. I had done the hard bit by beating Mike but I had nothing to show for it in the end. John went on to win a world title that could easily have been mine. For me, it was another opportunity spurned. No disrespect to Steve Beaton or Alan Warriner, the other two semi-finalists, but I think both John and I felt that our match was the final. It was our final, put it that way.

John is a slow and precise thrower. He will speed up and slow down his game to upset your rhythm whereas Mike is a fast player, like me, and much easier to play against. John did slow me down and as much as I tried to gee myself up against him by muttering, 'Get out of the way, you ugly bastard,' this time it didn't work. Also, John always has a decent fan base of his own – not as big as mine, of course, but large enough to be heard.

For all his confidence, John tried a bit of gamesmanship on me during that semi-final – he flicked the flights of his darts to make a

The Embassy final of 1980.
Eric beat me 5–3, but it was the
game that changed darts for ever.

◁ *Top* In my West Ham United shirt (after The Hammers won the FA Cup in 1980) I present John Lowe with the Mickey Mouse ears (Charles R. Cramp).

◁ *Middle* The North American Open, 1980 – the four-man team event is played by three of us as Keith 'the Milky Bar Kid' Deller goes missing.

◁ *Bottom* Revenge for my defeat at Jollees – beating Eric in the 1980 Santa Monica Open.

▷ The slim-line Bobby George, following a ruptured spleen and a diet of milk and lemonade, February 1982 (PA).

▽ On England duty with Eric, relaxing off the oche.

▽
M
ar

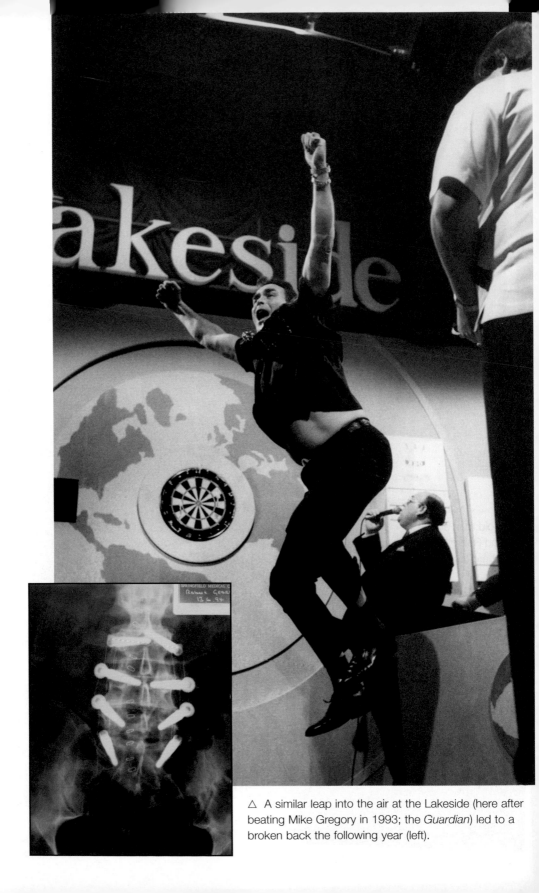

△ A similar leap into the air at the Lakeside (here after beating Mike Gregory in 1993; the *Guardian*) led to a broken back the following year (left).

△ The house that Bob built (Tom Jenkins).

◁ A chip off the old block: back on the county circuit, playing for Suffolk with Richard.

▽ Robert is good with his hands.

◁ I really enjoy working for the BBC, pictured here with Mark Pougatch and Ray Stubbs. The late Peter Dyke, of World Promotions, is on my left.

The dream lives on . . . in the last 16 of the Winmau World Masters (2005; Hans Willink).

I just can't let go . . . the buzz of the crowd . . . you can't buy that . . . (Hans Willink)

noise when I threw. He isn't the only one who does that, though, and while it surprised me, I am not going to use that as an excuse for my defeat.

Our rivalry was as intense as ever that night. John hit his trademark bull finish in one leg with his first dart of three and his little 'Toby Jug' face was a picture, as if to say to me, 'That'll stop you jumping up and down.'

It was such a shame to throw away all my good work in that semi-final, and against John of all people. I had gone from playing the best match of my life to playing one of the worst. The next morning when it all sunk in, I was absolutely devastated. The truth is that I was in nowhere near the form necessary to reach a world final but I still regard 1993 as the year when I should have got my name on the Embassy trophy. It was all set up for me and I blew it.

After months of wrangling between the BDO and the WDC, the inevitable happened and there was a split in professional darts. The WDC players decided that they would be better off on their own, running their own show with its own sponsors and televised events, which were subsequently picked up by Sky, and they resigned from the BDO.

The upshot for the BDO was that as well as facing competition from a rival organisation, it was left, overnight, with virtually no known names in its ranks. I wouldn't have signed up with the WDC even if I had been invited to join. The BDO system was in place when I started out and I have always been happy with it. Of course, the main difference for me was that I concentrated on exhibition work, and so the running of tournaments didn't really affect me.

I guess that I was always on the side of the BDO but I was never anti-WDC as such. At the end of the day, every player has to try to make a living out of the game. I know that more than anyone. Each man controls his own destiny. That doesn't necessarily make him right, but it doesn't necessarily make him wrong, either.

The main disappointment for me, and most darts fans, is that we now have a crazy situation with two world champions. That is a shame but it was inevitable, given the circumstances. Since 1994 both the BDO and WDC (later called the PDC) have hosted separate world championships, which often overlap in the first few days of the New Year. That is only part of it, though. The bitterness that ensued over the split was terrible and still exists today in some quarters.

All the breakaway players came through the BDO system, and the officials, including Olly Croft, Dave Alderman and Sam Hawkins, were badly hurt when the WDC was set up. They reacted swiftly, and perhaps a little harshly, by banning any player who so much as attended a WDC function from all BDO competitions. I thought this was over the top but the BDO felt strongly that the WDC players had acted in an improper way, and closed the door on them all. The whole thing became very hostile.

I essentially remained loyal to the BDO, but apart from an invitation to return to play in the 1994 Embassy – semi-finalists qualified by right – I didn't really get involved. The BDO has 64 counties in its membership and each one of them has a vote. It is a democratic organisation and everyone has a say. I am a BDO member and I don't agree with everything that is done, but what is agreed is agreed, otherwise what's the point?

I have always believed that the BDO system is there to give players such as me an opportunity to succeed in darts. It isn't up to the BDO to provide a living for me, it doesn't organise my exhibitions and I wouldn't expect it to. That isn't its role.

The timing of the whole issue was very interesting. Players such as Eric Bristow and Jocky Wilson were approaching the end of their playing days. No doubt they could see that a lack of exposure on TV would seriously affect bookings for appearances and subsequently the bees and honey. For Phil Taylor and his generation it was a very different story. They had long careers in front of them, and Phil became a vital cog in the WDC machine. All the WDC players were united and believed in their cause. I think that had to be the case if they were ever going to make any form of success of it.

I didn't have a problem with any of the WDC players over the split, because I have always believed that every man should answer only to himself, but I can't pretend it was a nice time for any of us. Eric tried to persuade me to play him head-to-head in a darts challenge, which he said would be shown on satellite television, but his invitation was politely declined. As far as I was concerned, the politics of all this had moved on to another level and I wanted to keep clear of the whole mess.

With the big names gone, the BDO looked to its county system to provide the stars of tomorrow and, of course, it still had one remaining light from the golden era! With my competitive spirit reawakened, and the NOW championship no more, the Embassy became the big tournament for me to win. My performance in 1993 guaranteed me a place the following January, and did wonders for my exhibition work, which really took off as a result. The impact was immediate and the work never stopped throughout the year.

The 1994 Embassy world championship was always going to be difficult but we all just had to stick together – players, officials, everyone – and work hard to make it a success. Peter Dyke and John Exon, of World Promotions, worked tirelessly on the sponsorship side and Olly Croft brought Robert Holmes in to mastermind public relations. Robert remains an important member of the BDO crew today and he has become a good friend over the years. Keith Mackenzie of the BBC also played an important role at the time. The Lakeside owner Bob Potter continued to give his full support to the championships, and he placed total faith in Rob Goodwin, whose lighting show brought some much-needed razzmatazz to the event and changed the atmosphere inside the hall.

This was a big moment for the BDO. The boys who turned up for the 1994 finals were all capable players but none of them had a profile – I knew about six of them – and I realised that I was going to have to play as big a role as anyone during the week. I had received hundreds of telephone calls and letters asking me to confirm my attendance. It felt a bit like the changing of the guard but I thought that if I could put on another good performance and keep interest in the tournament alive, some of the newer players would have time to establish themselves and take it forward into the future. Although I didn't let it bother me, and tried not to think too much about it, there was an unspoken acceptance around the place that a lot was riding on my shoulders.

I concentrated on having another great opportunity to win the title. Just four of us – Steve Beaton, Kevin Kenny, Ronnie Sharp and me –

had got to the quarter-finals at the Embassy before, and I was the only one to have played in a world final. Martin Adams, Colin Monk, Kevin Painter and Roland Scholten were all making their debuts, as was an unknown Canadian called John Part. Having said that, I wasn't in the top ten in the betting, despite my performance the previous year – 25–1 were my odds going into the tournament.

The atmosphere was totally different from the previous year and the fact that two Embassy champions of the early 1990s were playing in the WDC world final less than 100 miles away in Purfleet made for an unfortunate backdrop to the entire week. The Embassy was still on the BBC, though, and the whole week would again be shown on terrestrial television. We just needed something to get it on its way.

I had done the glitter and the gold. Now I needed a bit more and I hit on the idea of walking out on stage dressed in a cape while carrying the candles. With no John Lowe to wind up, I also replaced Mickey Mouse on the back of my shirt with Mr Punch. I plumped for Mr Punch because he is the original cartoon character – Mickey Mouse isn't even 100 years old yet – and I had always been fascinated by Punch and Judy shows as a child.

Sayings work in darts, just like they do in films, and so I added the line 'That's the way to do it' underneath Mr Punch's face. I always loved that saying and used it a lot at my exhibitions. Mr Punch was my new look. He was much naughtier than Mickey Mouse, but just as nice.

The Punch motif on my shirt was unique. A friend of mine, Russell Newman – son of my old driver, Lofty – drew it for me and had him facing the wrong way. I received a nice letter from the Punch Society, thanking me for the publicity but informing me of the mistake. Apparently, Mr Punch always faces to the right – apart from when he's on my back that is, and then he faces to the left!

However, the biggest change in style that year came from the BDO. International flags were featured in the walk-ons, and Martin Fitzmaurice – a firm BDO supporter – introduced his 'Let's play darts' call to kick off proceedings before every match. I went one better than just a flag and used pop music for my walk-on, too. It was a no-brainer really but I was still the first darts player to do it at the Lakeside. I walked out to the Glam Rock anthem 'I'm the Leader of the Gang (I am!)'. It was an obvious thing to do. All the other players followed suit and soon had walk-on tunes of their own.

The over-riding reason why I stood out from all the other players, though, was my age. At 48 years old I was up against some guys in their early twenties. Nevertheless, my defeat by John Lowe the previous year still rankled and so I decided to take the unusual step of working with a psychologist in my attempt to finally win the Embassy.

Linda Batten had been a top darts player in her day and was now qualified in matters of the mind. I was doing some plastering work for Linda and her husband Tom prior to the tournament and mentioned my problem with concentration levels during big matches, which had reared its head again in my match against Keith Sullivan the previous year. Linda suggested giving me a few tips if I felt that I needed them and I took her up on the offer.

She believed that I had enough talent to win any tournament if I could just get my head right. She gave me some words to say during matches and tips on how to focus mentally when my mind decided to wander.

'Don't worry about the glitter and the candles,' she told me. 'Just concentrate on your darts.'

Unfortunately, that is just not my way, and despite Linda coming down to the Lakeside to offer her support, by the end of the week I had to accept that perhaps I am more about glitter and gold than winning darts matches. Maybe that is why I enjoy my exhibitions so much.

At one stage Linda even suggested that I should stop smiling when I played because she was convinced that playing to the crowd cost me matches. I couldn't do that. I am what I am and I can't change. Eventually, we decided that sports psychology wasn't for me and binned the idea.

My first-round draw against Australian Russell Stewart was a difficult one. He was seeded and had the experience of playing in eight previous Embassy tournaments. Our match was selected to kick off the tournament. There was no defending champion and so it was chosen for live TV coverage on New Year's Day. I took this opportunity to introduce my cape and candles to the world, but my big entrance almost went tits up, literally. I stepped on the cape as I walked up the steps to the stage and nearly tripped over, candles and all. It was a close call and ever since then Marie has walked behind me holding the cape.

I always find first-round matches the hardest in any tournament and this was to prove no exception, but this time it was due to poor lighting over the dartboard. Both Russell and I were complaining about it as early as the first leg. Bad light can be a problem in darts and it has consistently been a problem at the Lakeside, where there is often a lot of light around the board but not enough on it.

All Russell and I could see when we threw were shadows. It wasn't clever but it was the same for both of us and we just had to get on with it. Players shouldn't really have to throw in such conditions, particularly in a world championship. We laughed our way through it. I said to Russell that I couldn't see what I was hitting and he said that he couldn't, either. It was ridiculous.

I beat him 3–0 in an otherwise uneventful match, played out in front of an uneventful crowd that seemed in the midst of nursing New Year hangovers. Russell was one of seven seeds to crash out in the opening round – only Roland Scholten remained – and this was another potential nightmare for the BDO.

My second-round opponent was the same as the previous year, Martin Phillips, a very consistent ton player and one of the nicest blokes around. Martin blew my candles out for me when we got up on stage and congratulated me when I checked out on my favourite unorthodox finish of 121, which meant a lot as he was one of the few people that seemed to understand that it was a proper out-shot.

The result was the same as the year before – although Martin won a set this time – and once again, I was into the quarter-finals. There were now no seeds left and the bookmakers didn't know whether to shit, shave or shampoo in terms of finding a favourite for the championship. All the attention was suddenly on me again. The interview requests were piling up, but all I really wanted to do was relax and go fishing. When Dougie Donnelly requested an interview ahead of my quarter-final match, I suggested combining the two and we went fishing at nearby Willow Park.

I love to fish, it helps me switch off and I much prefer it to practising or sitting at a bar drinking beer. It is a world away from the show-biz lifestyle I sometimes lead, but being able to enjoy different aspects of life is an important part of my make-up.

My new shirt went down a storm that year. I would stand with my back towards the crowd, pointing to Mr Punch and his words of wisdom, and the crowd would shout back, 'That's the way to do it, Bobby.' It was fantastic.

Mr Blobby was very big at the time – the pop record had even made Christmas number one – and plenty of Mr Blobby toys appeared in the audience, renamed Mr Bobby, although I thought they resembled Martin Fitzmaurice suffering from a bout of chicken pox more than they did me.

Somehow I kept missing the younger players left in the tournament and my next opponent was Kevin Kenny, another good, experienced, solid professional. The match turned out to be a very memorable one.

Kevin was no mug. He had made the Embassy semi-finals in both 1991 and 1992 and came from a nice big family in Liverpool, who supported him wherever he went. It was a great atmosphere in which to play darts and we both got into the groove early on. In the first leg I hit a maximum and called out, 'One, two, three,' as each dart hit its target. Then Kevin did the same, calling, 'One, two, three,' as well. It was brilliant.

In the final leg of the opening set I left myself tops, only for Martin to tell me I required 39. I thought, 'Here we go again,' and queried the call, but he was adamant that he was right. So I had to hit single 19 and double ten to take the set.

When I removed my darts, I told Martin that he had made a mistake. He had simply miscounted but it was a big moment in the match for him to make such an error and it could yet again have been very significant for me. As I have already said, darts players always know what they have left, and that is particularly true when it happens to be double top.

Kevin is one of the fastest throwers in the game but I could match him for pace. We were attempting nine-darters in every leg and were rattling through the sets with a lot of fun and laughter. The fifth and final leg of the second set was important. Depending on the outcome, I would have a 2–0 lead or we would be level at 1–1.

I had the throw but seven of the first eight legs had gone against the darts so that meant nothing. We both missed a lot of chances to win the set and the release of pressure I felt when I finally hit double four was incredible. I shouted out, 'Yes, c'mon Bo,' and leapt high into the air with my fists clenched, but when I landed I felt a sharp pain in my back. Kevin heard a click.

'Has your back just gone, Bob?' he asked me.

'I think it has, yeah,' I replied, slowly.

The pain shot down both of my legs but, with the adrenalin pumping, I continued the match, albeit somewhat gingerly. I wasn't sure what had happened and didn't know what damage might have been done. All I knew was that I stood two sets away from a place in the world semi-finals. The back could wait until later.

The pain was constant and at first I thought I might have torn a muscle. However, when my legs started to feel numb I did worry that it might be something a lot more serious. All sorts of thoughts were flashing through my mind, but I was cautious and felt in control. I never considered pulling out of the match for one moment. I just kept thinking to myself, 'Get through this and then work on a plan.'

Kevin could see that I was in a lot of pain and helped me where he could. On more than one occasion he picked up my darts for me. He is a good bloke and was a real friend to me that night, but my back problem didn't alter the fact that we were involved in a real dogfight of a match. I lost my way for a while and he squared the match at 2–2.

I'd had darts for both the third and fourth sets and could have already been in the semi-finals but instead I was kicking off what had essentially become a best-of-three-sets encounter. If this had been any other tournament in the world, I would have quit, but I couldn't bring myself to do that in an Embassy quarter-final. The pace of the game got even faster. I just wanted to get the match out of the way and get off that stage, but the darts and the speed at which we were throwing them made for great entertainment.

Pain was now searing through my lower body and I was sweating badly as a result. I had enough to do just to throw my darts but I had to keep going. In this state, I somehow took the fifth set and the first two legs of the sixth set to stand on the verge of victory. By the time I hit double eight to win the match I was physically, mentally and emotionally exhausted. I just looked up to the ceiling and thanked God.

Kevin was gracious in defeat and gave me a kiss, his raucous brothers kissed Marie and the crowd were up on their feet celebrating a second successive semi-final appearance for me. I took a deep breath and knew that I had just won the toughest match of my life.

I made light of it all in my post-match interviews. I told the press that Kevin had picked up my darts for me because he was so much younger. I didn't want to talk about my back – I didn't know what to say about it – but I was in agony when I met Marie afterwards. My first words to her were, 'I have done some serious damage to my back, doll.' She didn't even get her regulatory snog off me!

Neither of us could have imagined just how serious the damage was, but the moment I woke up the following morning and was unable to get out of bed, it hit me. With Marie travelling to and fro from Essex to look after the boys, Kenny Harris took me to the nearest hospital for a check-up. Doctor Austin Brown saw me and I explained to him that I needed a quick fix because I had got a world championship semi-final to play the next day. He looked at my X-rays and then looked at me as though I was mad.

'You can't play darts,' he said. 'You shouldn't even be able to walk. You've broken your back, Mr George.'

Basically, the bottom of my spine had cracked and it was sheer muscle that was keeping me upright. The doctor told me that I needed an operation and rest, and that any physical activity could result in permanent paralysis, in which case I would have to spend the rest of my life in a wheelchair.

That didn't help me in my quest for the Embassy world championship and my semi-final against Magnus Caris the following night. Doctor Brown reluctantly agreed to make a steel corset for my back, but told me that he couldn't give me any form of injection or medication to deal with the pain for fear that I would move in an unnatural way and cause even more damage. He was adamant that he couldn't support the notion of me playing darts. He explained the dangers to me and he couldn't do any more than that, but I was adamant that, if I could, I was going to play in the semi-final.

The corset enabled me to stand upright, and being able to stand upright enabled me to play darts, but it didn't allow for any movement, and that included being able to go to the toilet. Once the corset was in place, I was stuck in it.

It was some procedure. I was given tablets to release my bowels and instructed not to eat or drink before the match. I ignored that advice and drank some rum and Coke to take the pain way. Then I was fitted into the corset. It was cream in colour and resembled old-fashioned fancy pull-up underwear. I looked like I was set to appear in panto never mind a world darts semi-final.

Hardly anyone knew what had happened and those who did kept it to themselves. I didn't need sarcasm. I'd had enough of that in the early part of my career to last me a lifetime. Tony Green mentioned that I was suffering from a bad back in his commentary but he wasn't aware of just how serious the situation was. In fact, the whole truth only came out a few months later when Ray Stubbs and a film crew from the BBC's *Sportsnight* programme did a feature on me that included X-rays of my spine with eight titanium screws through it.

The Magnus Caris match was one of the most memorable and remarkable in the history of televised darts. It contained everything, including the greatest comeback ever seen. Magnus was playing well and had beaten Wayne Weening, Leo Laurens and Martin Adams to get into the last four.

In normal circumstances, I would have fancied my chances in a semi-final line-up that included Magnus, John Part and Ronnie Sharp, but my form wasn't as good as last year and now I faced the added problem of the injury to my back. I didn't know how I would play – or even if I could play – but at least my semi-final appearance guaranteed another invitation to the tournament the following year and that would keep the exhibitions coming in thick and fast. As for the match, it was going to be a case of suck and see for me. I didn't know what to expect from my body, but accepted that the quicker it was over, the better.

My walk on to the stage was unrecognisable from the one that darts fans knew and loved, but at least I was out there. By contrast, Magnus came out punching the air. Within minutes we were backstage again. The light over the board was so bad that both of us complained and asked for it to be fixed. The crowd weren't too happy and I understood their frustration but I wasn't in the mood to put up with more shabby treatment. The match was too important for that. I wasn't on a short fuse but I felt much more focused than usual. I was out there to do a job. I was much less the entertainer and more the workman.

I wore big black sweatbands for the match. They weren't in fashion but I had sweated buckets against Kevin and wasn't going to have a repeat performance. My stance was quite static and, if anything, I leant back on my throw rather than forward – it was just too painful to lean forward – so I needed to adjust my throw accordingly. I was careful not to move around too much or throw my darts with a lot of power. I did everything I could in order to keep the pain down to an absolute minimum.

Then Magnus started to flick the flights of his darts and I snapped. For the second successive Embassy semi-final my opponent was trying this trick. I had let it go with John Lowe but I wasn't prepared to let it go with Magnus, not with my back and all. Usually I would have tried to ignore it but I wasn't in the mood that night and told him so to his face. Suddenly, my careful mental preparation was out of the window and my aim now was to smack his arse, win the match quickly and get off my legs.

I strolled through the first two sets but there was hardly a smile on my face. I was concentrating hard on getting through the match in one piece. Then, without warning, the pain hit me hard – so hard that I couldn't even lift my arm above my head. I was done. I couldn't see how I would be able to get through a minimum of three more sets, but I had soon got through four more sets and lost every one of them. From being 2–0 up, I was 4–2 down and one set away from defeat. It all felt so impossible and so inevitable as I hobbled around the stage in agony. The doctor was right. I had been mad to even attempt to play.

Magnus took the first two legs of the seventh set and now stood just one leg away from the final. I had won just two legs from a possible 14 and couldn't wait to get off that stage, get out of that bloody corset and get into my bed. Then it came home to me that this could be the last time I ever played in this great arena. If I was going to get beaten, I should at least go down with a fight in the final leg.

I managed to get down to a finish but Magnus required 141 for the match and when he leisurely threw a treble 20 and a treble 15, I placed my darts in my top pocket. He put his final dart a millimetre past the outside wire of double 18. Magnus didn't seem at all bothered – he was at the top of his game and I was at the bottom of mine – and confidently smiled as he retrieved his darts from the board. I pulled the darts from my pocket, gritted my teeth and gave my world title dream one last try. I managed to hit single 16 and double 16 to save the match.

Magnus had the darts in the next leg and this was his real chance. I needed big scores and hit two 140s to put the pressure on. 'Fight, you tart,' I said to myself as I aimed for the big red bit. Magnus had another 141 out-shot for the match and missed. I hit tops to make it 2–2.

The pressure was beginning to turn and somehow I was throwing for the set. I took it with another double 16 and roared with relief. The crowd were up on their feet and the noise was incredible as they chanted, 'Bobby, Bobby, Bobby.' I had given myself a lifeline. It was now 4–3 in sets but a totally different game with totally different players. I limbered up at the side of the stage, doing stretches that the doctor had showed me while a once casual Magnus stared glumly at the floor.

Those three legs completely changed the complexion of the match but I was still behind. I set myself a target of winning the next leg and looked no further than that. The pain was bad but what difference was another two minutes going to make?

Magnus had three darts for the opening leg of the eighth set and missed them all. The cheers from inside the hall compounded his mood and left him in no doubt whose side the crowd were on. I took the leg and started to believe that I could actually win the match.

I took the second leg with tops and whipped the crowd up a bit more. My hair was now wet through with sweat and the pain from my back was almost unbearable but the adrenalin had kicked in once again. I was playing the match of my life against all the odds and had managed to adopt a new form of celebration in the process, which resembled pulling the reins back on a wayward horse.

Lucky double 16 won me the all-important third leg and took the contest into a ninth and deciding set after almost two hours at the oche. I had wanted to play a very quick semi-final and got the longest match of my career. I had gone through the full range of emotions and tactics. I started calmly, went into my shell as agony took hold and became the entertainer again right at the end, facing the crowd with my arms in the air and shouting, 'Come on!' They had got me through the pain barrier and I just needed them to give me one final push.

Magnus had a chance to take first blood again in the final set but his one dart at bull hit the wire. I hit double ten to move ahead in the match for the first time in over an hour and wrapped up the next leg with the same double. I was totally spent and could hardly summon up the strength to collect my darts from the board after each throw, but I was on the verge of the world final and kept telling myself that. I had to keep it going for just one more leg.

I put everything I had into that leg and got down to needing tops with one dart for the match. I took a deep breath and shouted out, 'Do it,' as I let fly with my third and final dart. Marie couldn't watch and buried her head in her hands. The dart was good. I almost collapsed with relief when I saw it hit the target. The crowd went mad and I was through to my second Embassy world final.

I hobbled over to Martin Fitzmaurice, feeling like a man of 80, and he gave me a big hug. I turned to the cheering crowd and mouthed to them, 'I love you, thank you so much.' More than in any other match in my career, the crowd won that game for me. They were unbelievable that night.

As I left the stage to rapturous applause I could hardly walk and had to hobble down the steps to reach my beloved wife. Backstage, I went into the gents with my mate John Stretch and wrung out my socks into the sink. My shirt, trousers, underpants and corset were all soaking wet. Never in my entire life had I been in such a state. It was a combination of the heat on stage, the sweat and the searing pain. I wondered if it had really been worth it.

I had read about going through the pain barrier and that experience convinced me it does happen. It was like my nervous system couldn't take any more pain, so it was a case of either getting through it or passing out. Thankfully, I got through it.

In terms of atmosphere, that semi-final easily ranks in my top three of all time alongside my matches with Eric Bristow (1980) and Mike Gregory (1993). In terms of sheer support, it would probably come out on top. I wouldn't have missed playing in it for the world. Yes, it had been worth it.

As darts comeback stories go, it is probably the best ever – the old man with the broken back winning nine successive legs to save the match, beat the young pretender and reach his first world final in 14 years. Apparently, my comeback against Magnus is one of the three most requested TV clips every year at the Lakeside, alongside Paul Lim's nine-darter and Keith Deller's 1983 world triumph. It is part of Embassy folklore.

While it provided me with one of the biggest highlights of my career, the pain robbed me of any form of post-match celebration. Instead, I was tucked up in bed early in the hope of finding some relief ahead of the world final, which was due to take place the very next day.

After a difficult night, I woke up on the morning of the final in an even worse condition than the night before. I went to see the doctor again, hoping for some miracle cure, but he just shook his head and told me it was impossible for me to punish my body like this and not suffer serious consequences. The doctor suggested I thought long and hard about playing another match. It wasn't ideal preparation for a world final. I couldn't get my mind around playing darts. All I wanted was to get rid of the pain.

Time was running out. After I had beaten Kevin I'd had two days' rest before my match with Magnus, but the schedule was such that I now had only a matter of hours to recover from my semi-final before I was due on stage against John Part. All the journalists were looking forward to the match and asking endless questions about it. I should have been in my element but I was in total agony and despair.

Apart from John Part and a few Canadians, everyone seemed to want to see me lift the one crown that I had never won. Such support lifted me but deep down I knew that I was in no state to play the match, either mentally or physically. I couldn't eat or drink and had no time to rest.

Marie drove over to the hotel in the afternoon and we discussed the situation. Her advice was to pull out but I wasn't sure. I couldn't win either way – one half of me didn't want to play and the other half felt I would always regret my decision if I didn't play. In the end, the sponsors made up my mind for me. They were desperate to have me in the final and made all sorts of promises to persuade me to give it a shot.

I also felt that I had to play in the final for the sake of the tournament. So much had been made of my return to the Lakeside during the WDC split that I considered it my responsibility to try to keep things alive for the BDO, but I was on a hiding to nothing by playing the match. John was a good player and had only dropped one set throughout the tournament. The odds were very much against me. If I played, I would most likely be the loser, and if I didn't play, the tournament would definitely be the loser, with possible implications for the entire BDO set-up. The WDC would be watching, that much was for sure. What would it look like if we couldn't even put on a final?

I had a massage, my system was cleared out again, the corset was fitted and I went over to the Lakeside for pre-match interviews. I didn't dwell on my back problems. I didn't think my fans wanted to hear any negatives. They just wanted to watch me play darts. The next thing I knew my name was being called out and I was walking out on to the stage.

While I still had confidence in my ability, I had none at all in my health. I tried to go about things in a calm and steady way but with no adrenalin to take it away, the pain was worse. My only chance was to try to make it a quick final and play as few sets as possible. I managed that but with disastrous results and was on the receiving end of a 6–0 scoreline.

John wasn't that much better than I was and I outscored him in practically every set but I couldn't finish, and as the saying goes: 'It's trebles for show and doubles for dough.' The steel corset kept me upright so that I could score big on the treble 20s but when it came to leaning in or to the side to aim for a double, I was totally buggered.

Things might have been different had I won a tight opening set but I lost it, 3–2. In the second set I hit my first maximum of the match but it was a rare occurence and after I lost the third set, 3–2, the game was up. Sid Waddell, commentating on his last Embassy, said my stance during that third set made me look like the Hunchback of Notre Dame. It was an accurate description.

I took the opening leg of the fourth set in 15 darts, which was much better, but I had privately conceded by then and was just going through the motions to get off the stage as quickly as I could. It was by far my worst experience in professional darts.

Both of us were poor. Our scoring was spasmodic at best and our finishing was absolutely terrible. It was taking me more darts to hit a double than it was taking me to get down to a double. I had 49 shots at doubles and got five of them. That is a pathetic statistic but it tells its own sad story and explains why I lost the match in the way I did. Any movement felt like I had razor blades shoved up my arse, and from the bottom of my spine all the way down my legs. So I stayed upright throughout and lost virtually every leg by allowing my opponent to catch me up and nick it. It was so frustrating.

Finishing decided that final, and John had a success rate of only 42 per cent himself, which must be the lowest ever percentage for a world champion. In hindsight, I should have left myself tops all the time, because that was the easiest double for me to hit in the circumstances, but then hindsight is a wonderful thing.

It was a disappointing final, a real non-event with not much atmosphere. There was no jumping around from me – I shouldn't have even been up there – and John was just a faceless overseas player with no support back then. That sounds harsh, but it is true. He wasn't an explosive player by any means. He just about took his chances against me, and that is all that I can really say about him. He is a much better player now and has added a lot more to his game. I think he won the Embassy too easily in 1994. He never had to raise his game above average. Magnus played much better against me than John did, but I had that little bit of luck against the Swede. Maybe that match was my final.

If I hadn't broken my back, I am confident that I would have been Embassy world champion that year. I generally outscored my opponent in the final but just couldn't finish. That was my downfall. The standard of the darts made it easily the worst Embassy final, and so I suppose losing it 6–0 probably makes me the worst of the worst. It was a sad state of affairs.

John collected the trophy to chants of 'Bobby, Bobby, Bobby' ringing out around the arena. I stood there and wondered if one day I would finally give those fans the one prize that their support for me deserved. More pressingly, I wondered what sort of damage I had caused to my back.

Marie had to leave the Lakeside straight after the presentation dinner to get back to the kids, so I was on my own. I wish I hadn't bothered with it all. I had gone from hero to zero within 24 very short hours and all the accolades were now for my opponent. I was the forgotten man. I just wanted to get out of there.

John had a fair idea of the pain I was in but he didn't mention it in his speech. I felt I had made a fool of myself by playing him

I hobbled back to my hotel room and on the way came across a lone swan by a rock at the side of the frozen lake. I rested by the rock and everything suddenly hit me. It felt like neither of us had a friend in the whole world that night. I told the swan that if I ever won the Embassy trophy, I would throw it in that lake. I was totally gutted. Here I was, hardly able to walk and without anyone to comfort me, but none of that seemed to matter. There had been a final. There was a world champion. Everyone was happy. Well, I wasn't happy. That night was the most depressing of my entire life. I didn't know if I would ever be able to play darts again and I didn't know if I ever wanted to. I felt I had served my purpose and that was that. Game over. John Part was the winner. I was just the runner-up with the bad back.

I was very angry with myself for even playing the match, because in my heart of hearts I always knew that I couldn't win it. Sid Waddell had been one of the worst for pushing me into it. 'We haven't got a final without you, Bobby,' he told me. Then he left the whole set-up to join the WDC boys on Sky. He knew how much trouble I was in, yet whenever he mentions the 1994 Embassy final in commentary even now, he always mentions the scoreline but never the reason for it or the pain I was in. Back in my hotel room that night, I got on my bed and went to punch the pillow to get rid of all my anger and frustration – and missed it three times!

There was no mention of any back problems in the match reports the following day, or any kind words about me giving it a go. Although I had played it down, I expected something about it to be recorded to explain the scoreline, but there it was, just the result in black and white for all to see, 6–0. It still makes me sound like a right pillock today, all these years later, but what were the options? What would have happened if I hadn't played?

Maybe John Part would have been handed the trophy and there wouldn't have been a final, but the match was scheduled for live TV coverage and so that wouldn't have looked very good for the BDO, particularly in the first Embassy after the WDC split.

I suppose the two losing semi-finalists could have played off for a lucky loser place in the final, but that would have been odd as well. How could either Magnus Caris or Ronnie Sharp claim to be the world champion if they had already lost a semi-final?

The whole thing would have been a mess either way. There was only one easy solution to the problem and that was for me to hobble up on to that stage. There wasn't really an alternative, but I risked humiliation and that is what I got.

Perhaps the best thing for me would have been to pull out, unbeaten, and leave the BDO with the headache, but when all's said and done, that would have been a very big decision for me to make on the eve of a world final. One thing is for sure – I have never forgotten how desperate and disillusioned I felt propped up against that rock by a frozen lake with just a swan for company, and I don't think I ever will.

13 George Hall

The only good thing to come out of the 1994 Embassy world championship was the runners-up cheque for £16,000, which went towards paying for the operation on my back. It is a good job I won that money because I had no health insurance to speak of, or any big company pay-off waiting for me. I worked for myself and if I wanted urgent treatment, I had to pay for it myself.

When I returned home after the tournament, the first thing I did was make an appointment with a back specialist. I had no choice. I couldn't ignore a diagnosis of a broken back, and anyway I was holding on to the walls just to get around the house. Years of ignoring persistent pain had finally caught up with me.

I went to see Doctor Alan Gardiner, a back surgeon at Springfield Hospital in Chelmsford. He told me he had seen me on TV and realised I had serious back problems. He confirmed I had broken my back and that I required an operation as a matter of urgency. As I left his office, Doctor Gardiner asked me, 'Where did you put your wheelchair?' I told him that I didn't have one. 'How did you get to my office, then?' he asked and I explained that I had walked. 'That's incredible, you've broken your back,' he said. 'I think we'll definitely be able to get you better, Mr George.'

All the heavy lifting over the years had caused irreparable damage to my spine but it had also developed my back muscles so much that they had effectively replaced it. Sheer muscle strength had essentially been keeping me upright for years, but it didn't make Doctor Gardiner's job any easier and the operation took over four hours. He later told me it was like sawing through bone.

He explained to me that when I jumped up in the air during that match against Kevin Kenny at the Lakeside, the muscles in my back moved and suddenly all the strength that was enabling me to stand and walk disappeared.

I consider that what Doctor Gardiner did for me was nothing short of a miracle. He took part of my spine away and inserted eight titanium screws, each two inches long, through what remained of my lower vertebrae and joined them together with nylon straps, similar to giant elastic bands.

The operation was dangerous. If any of the nerves had been affected it could have left me paralysed, but I had total confidence in Doctor Gardiner. He was a marvellous surgeon and the work he did on my back has allowed me to walk ever since, even if it did mean losing a few inches in height.

John Part was the first overseas Embassy world champion but with so little money in competitive darts at that time, he returned to his native Canada after winning the title. This meant that a lot of his exhibition work in England went the way of the 'unofficial world champion'. I was a popular runner-up and the bookings flooded in, even more than they did in the previous year, but my health came first. I had to get well and darts had to take a back seat for a while. Steve Beaton and Mike Gregory among others benefited greatly as a result of my condition.

It was a difficult time financially. My earnings were obviously severely affected and we had to live off our savings, but the matter had been taken out of my hands. I had to get fit before I could go back to work. Fate had intervened and one consequence was that, while I had time on my hands, I was able to realise a dream that was far more important to me than playing darts had ever been.

For a long time I had wanted to move Marie and the children to a house with a lot of land, possibly with its own lake, somewhere I could relax and fish. My mate Pat Long rang me one day to tell me that his wife, Vicky, had seen an advertisement in the local newspaper for a piece of land at Ardleigh, near Colchester. It sounded just what I was looking for.

Pat, who works in construction, went to have a look at it for me and reported back that the land was full of water. It was basically a massive, soggy field – caused by a blocked stream – with hundreds of trees. It sounded absolutely ideal.

'Sunny Afternoon' by The Kinks is my favourite song of all time. Back in the sixties I used to love the line, 'The taxman's taken all my dough'. It just about summed up my life back then. Now I felt a connection with other lines in the song, such as, 'Sipping at my ice-cold beer' and, of course, 'Lazing on a sunny afternoon'. It was like my life had come full circle. I could just picture myself underneath those trees on a balmy afternoon, even though it was wintertime and I hadn't yet even seen the plot of land.

My head was buzzing when I went over to see the place for myself. Hobbling around the boggy ground on walking sticks, Pat asked me if I was seriously going to go for it. 'Absolutely, mate. This is exactly what I've been looking for,' I told him. The place was overgrown with trees, brambles and stinging nettles and had become a local dumping ground for rubbish, but it had real potential and its own water supply, which was crucial. I knew that the land would be ideal for lakes. I didn't want to build a big house. I just wanted a nice house with lakes, but it didn't quite work out like that.

On further investigation, it turned out that this wasn't any old bit of land. It had once belonged to another famous bowman in the shape of William the Conqueror and had a fair bit of history to it. It is even listed in the Domesday Book. The land was bequeathed to the nobleman Geoffrey de Mandeville as a reward for his loyalty during the Norman Conquest. He later handed it over to John Martell and Martell's Hall became one of four manors in Ardleigh. Thomas Martell was the last of the male line of the family and he died in 1424. For many years there was a stone memorial in the centre aisle of Ardleigh parish church commemorating his life, before the army of Oliver Cromwell destroyed it.

The whole area has a lot of history attached to it and Colchester is the earliest recorded town in the country. The Romans settled nearby after landing at Brightlingsea. There is a Roman well on the land, and Roman pottery, dating from AD 300, was recently found in the hollowed out trunk of an old oak tree. Archaeologists have found various treasures on the land. The snout of a Ziphoid whale – which lived more than 250,000 years ago – was discovered during the last century along with the teeth of elephants and relics from the Bronze Age.

It was a great place to set up home and I already had a name for it in my head – George Hall. I bought the land and set about drawing up plans for an 18-bedroomed property over three storeys. Marie got on to the Council and as the land had no given name we were given permission to call it George Hall. To come from a tiny flat above a motor garage in the East End of London and end up in a place called George Hall made me feel extremely proud. I later put the flag of St George on the top of the house as a finishing touch.

The planning was so difficult that it gave me headaches but I was determined to succeed. It was a means to an end and the only way for me to learn was to get some books and ring up some people. Mathematics has never been my strong point, although I picked up bits and bobs during my time as a builder, and the local Council helped me a great deal with the details. It was quite a stylish design, if not a little ambitious, but I genuinely thought that the plans would get cut down, so it would probably be a wise move to go big, but the Council accepted the plans and I was lumbered with them.

It is one thing designing a house on paper with a pencil – nothing more than a drawing – but it is something else building it with bricks and mortar. I don't know anyone who has ever lived inside a drawing! However, I had to go through the process and I even got my name listed as the architect on the original plans.

All the while my focus had been to get fit and once I had fully recovered from my back operation, I started work on our new home. I did all the work myself, even excavating two fishing lakes at the wheel of my own 360 digger. My ability to put my hands to anything made the dream possible. I never earned enough money from darts to pay for a place like that but I only had to pay for the raw materials, and darts paid for those. The building skills that I had acquired during my late teens and twenties stood me in good stead – and, of course, the work of Doctor Gardiner made it all possible. I didn't buy George Hall. I built it from scratch. If it went on sale tomorrow I probably wouldn't be able to afford it.

I was very much a one-man band but I did need a few little helpers. Joey Matthews assisted me with the blocks, Keith Thomas worked on the electrics, Russell Newman did the plumbing, Archie Arnold was useful with the machinery and young Mark Furlong was like Tarzan in the trees and around the lakes.

My nephew Frankie Garcia was also very useful, cleaning up after us and doing odd bits of labouring. All the family helped in their own way. My favourite phrase at the time was, 'You don't come to George Hall and do fuck all!' Everyone came to work.

The old man always said that anyone who owned land had freedom. My nearest neighbour was a sand quarry. I had freedom, all right.

The old man was now living on his own in Barkingside but as soon as he heard about the land, he told me, 'Get me down there now. I want to live with you.' He loved all types of nature and wildlife and couldn't wait to get over and see it for himself.

I put his house up for sale and sold it within half an hour. I also put our house up for sale and sold that within two days. I didn't need the hassle of haggling for the best price, I just wanted to get over to Ardleigh and build our future. Pat loaned me a digger to clear the land of rubbish and then I got the pumps working to provide water and a generator to supply electricity. We lived on the site. I bought a Portakabin for the family and a caravan for the old man to use.

Overnight, we went from chandeliers and jacuzzis to living like Rumpelstiltskin. It was a real shock to the system but the boys loved it, and so did the old man. It wasn't so much fun for Marie. She had to run the business from there and do her daily chores with just the barest necessities. We lived like that for two and a half years.

I was regularly working from eight in the morning through to three the following morning. It was gruelling work but I was buzzing and I knew that every single day we were a step closer to moving in. I dug out the foundations, put in the footings and drains, and then laid all the floors in one hit, saving myself a lot of time and money. I did all the brickwork, put the walls in and joists across, and then worked up to the second floor and finally the roof.

The roof is the most important part of any house, because once you have got the roof on, you have got somewhere to live. When that was done and the windows were in, I could start putting the rooms into something like working order. I built a 26ft long kitchen first of all and then got the central heating done.

To be able to close a door on a finished room is a tremendous buzz. Marie spends half her life in the kitchen and so she was pleased. So too was George, my parrot. George lives in our kitchen and he became the first one of us to spend the night at George Hall.

The next room to be done was one of the bathrooms. We could now eat and wash in comfort. The bedrooms followed shortly afterwards and by the summer of 1997 – 30 months after I had started the work – my whole family had moved in to what was a very basic George Hall.

Once we were in, the rest of the work on the house was a lot easier and I could begin to concentrate on the fixtures and fittings that were to make it a really special home. The cornice work and the chandeliers make it look grand both inside and out, as you would expect from a building standing on such historic land.

I was on a mission, working towards my life's goal. I had long dreamed of waking up in the morning and looking out of my window to see my own lakes. There was so much water on the land that digging a lake looked relatively easy – so much so that I planned to dig two of them to go alongside a small fishing pond – but I encountered serious problems when the digger hit some blue clay and water rushed out at quite a pace, something like 40,000 gallons per hour. Fortunately, I managed to find the source and laid some pipes to divert the water, running them across the field to the stream, and controlling the water flow with a system of valves. It took 20 tonnes of clay to cover them up. Water always finds the easiest route, as I discovered when working on the Victoria Line underground tunnel.

When I actually dug out the lakes, I opened one valve and closed another, which enabled me to dig with no intrusion of water at all. The earth was as dry as a bone – with blue clay all around – until I unblocked the valves and let all the water in. It was a hard fortnight's work but it was a success and the water gently and slowly began to run into them. At the end, I was absolutely shattered. I went to bed feeling as though I could sleep for ever but Marie woke me up the very next morning with the words, 'Bob, you've finally got your dream.' I looked outside and both lakes were full of fresh water. It was a fantastic feeling and meant so much to me.

The lakes are the big thing for me but George Hall also has a dining room that seats 20 people, a games room and a bar area, as well as all those bedrooms, just so I can make love to my wife in a different room every night! Each bedroom is painted in a different colour so guests can choose their favourite. All the paints came courtesy of my old darts friend Tony Sontag, who is now a painter and decorator.

I wanted to incorporate darts into George Hall here and there and came up with the idea of designing the hallway ceiling in the shape of a darts flight. It wasn't easy to do but it was satisfying to accomplish and definitely gives the entrance to the property a distinctive look.

My friend Harry Kicks made me a lamppost to stand on the driveway, complete with three little darts on the top, and I also had some darts welded on to the front gates. Many Georgian houses have semicircles of glass above the front door with a design on them, so I had one made featuring the top part of a dartboard.

The Bobby George logo of a crown with three darts is featured everywhere from the tablemats and the dining-room chairs to the old pub sign by the front gates, which I picked up from the Flying Fox down the road and repainted myself.

Throughout all this, my work ethic shone through. It all comes from my dear old mum. Mum was the worker in our family and both she and the old man had made me work so hard at home, but it paid dividends. The fact that I have never been in debt in my life is due to the old man. When I bought my first house, his first words to me were, 'Forget the carpets and sit on orange boxes if you have to, just pay off the mortgage and own the fucking house.'

I couldn't get enough of the old man when I was young. I thought he was great. I really looked up to him and would hang on to every word he said. He was very much his own man but he was a real hero to me and I thought the world of him. He knew how to work me. That was his way of educating me and helping himself at the same time. The old man knew the theory but never put anything into practice himself. That is where I came in and that is what made me feel so special to him, because I carried out his work. The old man never got his hands dirty but he was the guv'nor of the house. I once asked him, when he was going to paint the hall. 'When it smells,' came his reply, but he soon had me painting for him. When it came to the doors, he told me, 'Paint all the middle panels first, then go across. Do the top and the bottom and then the sides and always check the corners because that's where you get the runs.' The old man never painted a bloody door in his entire life.

He was a real inspiration and I lived my life trying to meet his expectations. Every single day of my life up until building George Hall – when I was approaching 50 years of age – I was still working to the mantra laid down by the old man, but then I realised that he was essentially all talk. He could do the verbal bit but he wasn't able to lift a finger to help me build that house. That hit me very hard. I was totally shell-shocked. I was quite old to discover something like that and it affected me emotionally. It was the end of a fairytale, rather like a young child discovering there is no Father Christmas, only this child was well into his late forties.

For almost half a century, I had a firm vision of who the old man was. He talked such a good game that when I embarked on building my dream home, I really thought it was his chance to repay me for looking after him in his later years. When the big moment came along, though, he just hid away. Maybe he was embarrassed. All my life the old man had talked down to me and under-estimated me but I was now in the process of finally proving to him that I had become even smarter than he pretended to be. I knew things that he didn't and he just couldn't accept that.

I thought the old man could do everything because that is what he told me but when it mattered, he failed me. He made promises that he couldn't keep. He could talk the talk but was unable to walk the walk. To undertake the job of building a house, a man needs someone to lean on, but the old man couldn't give me answers to any of my questions. He was out of his depth and became quite aggressive, sometimes shouting, 'Why do you fucking keep asking me?' I think he was both ashamed and frustrated by the whole thing. I had gone out and done something that he had spent his entire life just talking about.

I worked all day and all night building George Hall and was knackered at the end of it. I kept telling myself that you only get from life what you put in, but it was hard graft. I had to push myself because often my body had had enough and the repetition of tasks did my head in. Then I had to rely on sheer willpower, talking myself through 18 hour days by saying I was a 'tart' and 'full of trap' when things got tough. That is how I got through it, mentally and physically. No doubt Linda Batten, my psychologist friend, would have been very proud of me.

A few weeks after I started, a building inspector from the Council, Dave Hart, came over to see how I was getting on and asked, 'What hat have you got on today, then?' He couldn't believe I was doing it on my own, but paying someone to do something I could do myself just seemed silly. Anyway, I had to keep the costs down.

I lost a lot of weight building George Hall but it was well worth it. The satisfaction I felt at the end was immeasurable and the tingle I get in my rebuilt spine when I drive through those gates is fantastic.

The old man never gave me any credit for building it, but then he very rarely spoke in a positive fashion about my darts either. 'You're the best-looking player and the best showman but you can be a right prick on the dartboard,' was about the only 'compliment' I remember getting from him, but he idolised my sons, Robert and Richard. I think this was because they weren't frightened of him. They stood up to him and he accepted them as people.

Make no mistake, the old man was a pretty intimidating spectacle. He was a massive bloke and quite scary to look at, particularly for a young child. Nicola and Shane were petrified of him. They had little to do with him but when they did they would always cry and Betty soon stopped allowing them to visit him. She had a good reason. Nicola was once picking flowers in the old man's garden and commented, 'I love flowers, God made them for us and they're beautiful.'

The old man was an atheist and hated to hear anything like that. He shouted back at her, 'God made fuck all. It had nothing to do with him. I planted those flowers. I watered them and fed them.' Nicola was five at the time.

He was exactly the same with Robert and Richard but they just ignored him and in return he gave them love.

The old man wrote poetry all his life and wrote about the boys in his later years. Being unable to see properly, he had to dictate the words for Marie to type. He wrote one poem called 'Bath Time' and we all knew the first two lines off by heart:

Bath time, bath time, bath time's fun.
Me and my brother are sad, when bath time's done.

The boys would cuddle him, kiss him and sleep with him in the caravan. He would tell them to fuck off but they took no notice. They just accepted him for what he was. I think they brought him a lot of love and happiness after Mum died and the difference this made to his personality was massive. They brought out a more gentle side to his character. The old man would swear in front of the boys like they were grown adults, so they swore back at him and he was fine about that.

The old man described the little peripheral vision he had as like 'looking through cracked glass', but he never admitted that he couldn't see, especially in front of visitors, and this got him and us into all sorts of predicaments. Whenever he boiled water to make a cup of tea, for instance, he would have to place his finger in the cup and then tip the kettle over it until the red-hot water burned him and confirmed he was aiming in the right direction. By that stage, boiling water was all over the place.

Mum mellowed over the years. She was a good woman at heart and when I started earning decent money from darts I gave her the odd £50 note to spend on something nice for herself. She always told me that she would keep it for a rainy day. When she died, her purse was full of £50 notes. She never saw that rainy day.

When Mum was very ill, I was up north playing in a darts exhibition. I telephoned her in hospital and she told me, 'Don't worry about me, you have your own life to lead.' That is very much how she brought me up, to look after number one. It helped me in some ways and I definitely get my determination from her.

I will always remember something she told me when I was a child – 'If you're fit, you'll always be rich, because you'll always be able to make something out of nothing.'

She kept all the newspaper cuttings from my darts career but she was disappointed that I never became an athlete. I think she had visions of me winning a gold medal at the Olympic Games. I might have done if I'd had some proper kit! Deep down, I do think that both of them were proud of me but neither of them showed it.

The old man wrote a poem about me when I first started playing darts, which I never knew anything about. I discovered it many years later. It shows love for me, and pride in my achievements.

It is fair to say that the old man was not the most hygienic person in the world and when he lived with us at George Hall, I used to hate having to go up to his dirty, smelly room. We tried to tell him about it but he would have none of it. 'There's fuck all wrong with this room,' he would say. 'I cleaned it yesterday. And it's spotless. What's wrong with you?' He must have had a sense of smell worse than his sense of sight. It was absolutely vile in there. He rarely changed his clothes and when he had a cold he would throw used tissues on the floor.

I did have a go at him on occasions but that just upset him and I felt bad for days afterwards. So I let him get on with it and allowed him to live like that. He never threw anything away and wouldn't spend a pound when a penny would do. Once I gave him some bleach to clean out his sink and toilet, and he splashed it all over himself and ruined his red shirt in the process. When he came downstairs and I told him about it, he never stopped to think about throwing the shirt out and instead asked for a red felt-tipped pen to colour in the white marks.

Marie would try and get his dirty sheets off the bed to do some washing for him and he would fight her off, saying, 'What's the point? They'll only get dirty again next week.'

I think the old man started to get depressed in the end. I would often suggest he went for a walk down to the lakes but he had no interest. 'Seen it, done it. Fuck the lake,' he would say to me. Then again if he did go for a walk, he would only insult people. One fisherman once made the mistake of calling him 'mate' only for the old man to snap back aggressively, 'I'm not your mate. I don't even know who you are. Fuck off.'

He absolutely adored Mum and was lost without her. It was sad that she went first because, after that, all he lived for were his memories.

In the last few years of his life he spent hours just sitting in his bed-room, living through his yesteryears.

The old man was an awesome size, much bigger than me. He stood 6ft 4in and weighed 24 stone when he died with not an ounce of fat on him. He never drank or smoked and remained in decent health until he passed away at the age of 75 in 2000. We cremated him and put his ashes in an urn, which we keep in the lounge at George Hall.

One good trait I inherited from the old man was his honesty. Nothing has ever scared me in life and so I have never seen any reason for lying. Trust matters to me as well. I am as good as gold with all my friends but if anyone crosses me just once, whoever they are, I am finished with them.

The old man would always say what he felt and I was the same until I became well known. Nowadays, I have an image to look after and I have to remember that it sometimes pays to keep my mouth shut. If some drunk comes up to me and has a go, my instinct is to react but I can't do that any more. I am in the public eye now, so I have to handle it differently.

The old man's big problem was that he would never allow anyone to help him. He wanted to survive all by himself. He should have been born back in the Middle Ages. In the days when he lived alone, after Mum died, I made him a beautiful bathroom with brand new units. He seemed pleased with it and thanked me. The next time I went over to see him, he had birds living in it. He never used the bath so he decided to give it to the birds. He was unbelievable. You couldn't make it up.

George Hall is everything to me. There is always something for me to do, to make or to mend. I have got my garden, my lakes, my fishing and my family. A lot of people who come to visit expect to find me fully decked out, up to my neck in jewellery, but it isn't like that at all. I am often dressed in an old T-shirt, torn jeans and working boots, doing jobs on the house or in the grounds. I love it all so much that I just hate driving through the gates and leaving the place behind. Marie, the boys and George Hall have made a huge difference to my life. In the early days, I never had anything to go home for, so I just didn't bother. Nowadays, I only leave the house to play exhibitions. I hardly ever go on holiday. George Hall is paradise to me, so why should I?

The darts memorabilia is all down to Marie. I didn't have one trophy around my old place when I met her but now I am never allowed to give anything away. Of course, I had my two winning boards from the *News of the World* championship and a few plaques from America, which had miraculously survived over the years, tucked away, but nothing else. Marie started collecting items from my past and now I have my very own room with lots of trophies, plaques and old photographs that she has managed to track down. It is like a Bobby George museum in there.

Like darts, fishing struggles to be recognised as a sport and that is not right. It takes a lot of skill to be the best and my good friend Bob Nudd was the best in the world for many years. There is no luck involved in winning world titles, whatever the sport, and fishing is no exception. Bob is totally dedicated to his sport and works at it every single day.

We have been friends since the 1970s and still fish together from time to time. Sometimes, he catches and I don't and then I have to accept that he really is something special. Bob studies different types of water and various species of fish, learning how they all feed. He has taught me a lot and I pass this knowledge on to the anglers who fish my lakes.

To start with I wanted the lakes for myself but now I share them with others. I don't see the point in having something nice and not sharing it. Guests respect the lakes, leave no litter, use proper equipment and look after the fish.

I hadn't considered opening up the lakes for business. I was happy to let fishermen use them for their pleasure but one day I popped into a local tackle shop to buy some maggots and was asked by the owner, Doug Titshall, where I fished. I explained that I had my own lakes. The next thing, Doug came down to George Hall with the idea of doing day tickets for the punters. The whole 'Bobby George Lakes' business has just grown from there.

I love it. I walk around the lakes and have a chat with the anglers. I look at the type of equipment they use, the lines and the hooks. I like to watch them catch and it is nice to see people enjoying themselves.

Some of them bring a camera and get quite a surprise when they see me in my scruffs with no glitter in sight. I have even been mistaken for the gardener.

Pat Reeve wouldn't be happy about that. She has looked after the lawns and gardens at George Hall for years and does a splendid job. Pat and her late partner Dave Clarke were heavily involved in the Essex darts scene and were regular visitors to George Hall in the early days. They always brought gifts for the boys and that got them the nickname of 'Santa and Mrs Claus'. Pat still does the gardens for us and Robert and Richard still call her Mrs Claus. She is very much part of the family and a very special lady.

Fishing is my hobby. I hate to see fish harmed in any way and I am very strict about how people fish on my land and the materials they use. When fish breed they can hurt themselves by getting cut on rubble, and if a fish suffers any form of cut or sore, parasites jump on it. If I ever find fish in distress, I immediately attend to it. I bathe it, put some TCP on the wound and then rub some honey in. TCP kills the infection and the honey acts as an antibiotic. I have saved hundreds of fish that way. That is why they call me 'Doctor Robert'.

It really hurts me to see dead fish in my lakes. Fish get stressed if things aren't right and anyone who works with them has to understand them. You need to know about bacteria, oxygen levels and water flow among other things. There is quite a lot to it.

Originally, I released different species of fish in the lakes and they have bred. Wildlife is naturally attracted to water and I have got everything from frogs to herons at George Hall. Herons live on fish and can be a nuisance but there is no mistaking that they are beautiful birds. I once had a very persistent heron on my land and was told that the best way to get rid of it was to put a plastic heron by the water. So I did and watched in amusement as the heron flew down to the lake and tried to chat up the plastic one! This went on for days and was hilarious to watch.

I held a mixed pairs fishing competition at George Hall once and entered with Marie. I was doing the fishing and it was her job to take the fish off the hook and put them in the net. We were doing well and on more than one occasion I asked Marie how many fish we had caught and she excitedly replied, 'Quite a lot,' but at the end of the competition, our net was empty. I looked quizzically at Marie and she told me that she had put all the fish back in the lake. I wasn't very happy!

Just like the old man, I love all forms of nature. Everything interests me, even flies and worms. They are all magical beings in their own little way. I think the kingfisher is the prettiest bird in this country. I have some down at my lakes and I can't take my eyes off them. They seem to change colour when they fly. People living in towns and cities never come across kingfishers and they don't know what they are missing. When I lived in east London, all I ever saw were blackbirds, sparrows and starlings, but once I moved out to where there was water and a little open space, I was suddenly surrounded with wildlife. That is how nature works. It is amazing and really beautiful.

Wild deer sometimes gather at the bottom of the land but animals mainly stay away because of the guard dogs, which live and sleep outside. They are on patrol 24 hours a day.

For many years I had two bearded collies, Dosh and Euro. We fed them, of course, but they would have been just as happy feeding themselves out in the wild if they had to. Dosh is still around but Euro sadly passed away in 2005. The two of them together were the business. They were very tough dogs, but clever as well, and would kip in the day so that they were always alert when it got dark. They had so much fur on them it was difficult to see their faces. I would clip them in the summertime but they hated it and Dosh once ran off with his coat half-clipped. The fishermen looked at me open-mouthed as the dog ran around with half his body covered in a thick, hairy coat and the other half shaved right back, but he didn't care.

All of my animals' names have a monetary theme. The latest dogs to join our ranks are tiny, so I have called one 2p and the other Visa. The three cats get similar treatment and go under the names of Penny, Dollar and Discount.

I also have two African Grey parrots – George and Charlie. We adopted Charlie a few years ago and any reference to a former Arsenal, Derby County and England footballer is purely coincidental. Charlie had his name long before we got him.

Parrots are fantastic creatures and very intelligent. They learn to protect themselves with different noises so that they can confuse possible predators out in the wild.

I first fell in love with parrots in the late 1980s when I was doing a darts exhibition at the Black Bull pub in Leicester. I went to the bar to pay my bill and no one was around so I had to shout out for some service. A voice came back, 'Get the beers in.' Presuming that the landlord could see me and was winding me up, I walked around the bar to find him and spotted a parrot. I had a conversation with the bird and decided there and then that I wanted one.

George has brought us hours of entertainment – and plenty of headaches – over the years. When I was doing the roof on the house, I would tell Marie that I needed to work for a few hours and for her not to disturb me unless it was an emergency. I would get up on the roof and start work and within a few minutes I would hear Marie's voice calling out my name. 'What can she want?' I thought. I would climb down and go indoors to find that Marie had gone out shopping. George didn't want to be alone and so he had called me down from the roof for company.

George's speciality is telephone ring tones. He can do the house phone, the mobile phone and the fax machine to perfection. He can also take off the washing machine and tumble dryer, and barks as well as he can talk. I took him down to the Lakeside one year and he went down a storm.

14 King of the qualifiers

Twelve months after those memorable matches against Kevin Kenny and Magnus Caris and my forgettable final with John Part, I was back at the Lakeside competing in my 11th Embassy world championship.

I qualified again by virtue of reaching the last four in the event but I had spent the entire year recovering from my back operation, and all my spare time had gone into drawing up plans for George Hall. I was terribly short of match practice.

Scotland captain Ronnie Sharp, a semi-finalist from the previous year, was my first-round opponent. He came on stage with a screw-driver, jokingly pretending to tighten up my back before the match to ensure there were no further problems in that area. It seemed a very long year since all that business.

I hit a 12-darter in the first leg but after that Ronnie cruised it, 3–0, which was no surprise really. I had done no preparation at all and had hardly thrown a dart in a year. My mind just wasn't on it.

Richie Burnett of Wales won the world championship that year, defeating Raymond Barneveld 6–3 in the final. It was a decent tournament and kick-started the careers of a new breed of darts player – Martin Adams, Andy Fordham, Colin Monk and Les Wallace. The BDO had survived the turmoil of the previous two years and was on the up again, but all I could think about was how much work I needed to do when I got back to George Hall.

Slowly I got back into darts. I did a few exhibitions and in the summer of 1995 I was invited up to the Dunoon Open in Glasgow to make a presentation. Once there, I was persuaded to take part in the singles competition and ended up winning it, beating Scottish international John Murdoch in the final. Someone else had to make the presentation to me! I was generally larking about for most of the time as well, attempting perfect nine-darters in virtually every leg I played.

Let me explain what I mean by a 'perfect nine-darter'. There are lots of ways to win a leg of 501 with nine darts. The tried and tested way is seven treble 20s followed by treble 15 and double 18, but that wasn't the way that Paul Lim hit the only ever nine-darter in the Embassy in 1990. He went two maximums and then treble 20, treble 19 and double 12.

All darts professionals can hit nine-darters for fun and we practise them all the time but there is one formula that I have never seen anyone throw and that is what I call the 'perfect nine-darter' – treble 20, treble 19 and bull three times in a row. I tried it in Glasgow and came within a whisker of achieving it for the first time, hitting the outer bull with my final dart. It would have brought the house down.

One funny memory I have of attempting the perfect nine-darter happened in the cabin at George Hall with my blind old man. I was stood there talking him through it, shot by shot, and when I got to my last three darts announced 'treble 20' as I hit it and 'treble 19' as I hit that. Just as the final dart was leaving my hand heading towards the bull, the old man shouted out, 'Well, it isn't that fucking hard, is it son?' and I hit a big single three.

Fun and frolics aside, I now had a big decision to make regarding darts. Since being persuaded to make a return to competitive darts in late 1992 via the Embassy play-offs, my subsequent semi-final and final appearances had qualified me for the 1994 and 1995 tournaments, but that run had now come to an end. There would be no invitation to play in the 1996 tournament. If I wanted to remain a part of it, I would have to do it through the qualifiers.

Just like the *News of the World* championship before it, the Embassy is a 'window to the world' tournament. Global TV coverage means it is able to take darts players into the homes of millions of people in dozens of countries. The world championship is just something else – the crowds are fantastic, the walk-ons are indescribable and the amount of exhibition work that one week in the limelight generates is incredible. It is enough to earn a darts player a living for a year.

I had missed being away, and hadn't realised how much until I went back, and on top of the business side of things, my desire to win the Embassy world title had been reignited by coming so close in 1993 and

1994. I even risked never being able to walk again by playing in it.

Marie and I sat down for hours to talk it through. The 1993 tournament was supposed to be a one-off but it had taken me down a completely different path. I had the fire in my belly once more and we all loved that first week of the New Year. I decided to give the qualifiers a go – it was only one night after all – but what a difference three years had made. Then I was just an old boy having a crack at a comeback, but at the Paragon Hotel in Earl's Court in late 1995, I was very much a face again and, more than ever, the one to beat.

The sponsors' invitation that got me a place in the qualifiers didn't go down too well, either. The tournament had changed a lot since the days when 24 invited players took part and now even just being invited to take part in the play-offs was seen as a very big deal.

The top-ranked 25 or so players in the world qualify for the Embassy as of right and must include, or be joined by, the previous year's four semi-finalists, which usually leaves around five places to be contested at the annual play-offs. The system is complicated by the big names being able to earn more money from exhibitions than from playing in world-ranking tournaments. However, most of the top players do enough to be listed in the world's top 25 and therefore qualify. For the rest, it is the play-offs. Over 200 top county players and internationals are joined by two sponsors' wild cards – usually Mike Gregory and me. Former world champions are also guaranteed a place in the qualifiers, and the late Leighton Rees entered every year until, sadly, he passed away in 2003.

To whittle 200 or so hopefuls down to just five means that the successful players have to come through five or six short matches – best of three sets, best of five legs – to take their place at the Lakeside. Believe me, it is as hard as winning the world title itself. The standard is so high. I got to the final round of the 1996 play-offs, where I came up against an unknown Dutchman, Co Stompe, who had a very peculiar throw.

Co's jerky action may have looked odd – in the style of Ceri Morgan – but it was very effective and he beat me in a sudden-death final leg after I missed a chance at double 18 for the match. I was out of the Embassy before I had even got in it.

Of course, Co went on to become a Lakeside legend in the late 1990s and was just one of many talented players to emerge from the low-lands of Holland, but that was little consolation to me. Access to the 'window to the world' was via a one-off qualification event with no cameras or spotlights, and I had failed the task.

Obviously, not playing in world-ranking events was a big disadvantage. I used to play competitive darts every night of the week for years but now I was playing in a tournament just once every 12 months and it was much harder to find any sort of rhythm.

I still went down to the Lakeside for a few days during the world championship but it was very odd. I wanted to get up on the stage and couldn't. Red Rum was paraded around Aintree at the Grand National each and every year after his retirement and I used to wonder how he felt. Now I knew. The whole thing was very hard to stomach but the experience gave me a real hunger to make sure that I got back on that stage and soon.

If I wanted another crack at the Embassy, I had to put a lot more work into it and I accepted that, but what I didn't expect was for the BDO to invite female players into the mix. Half-a-dozen ladies took part in the 1997 play-offs and I had to play one of them. Francis Hoenselaar, of Holland, was the best female player in the world at that time and she was drawn in the same qualifying group as I was. It was a no-win situation – if I beat her, it would be expected, but if she beat me, I feared that I would never live it down. It felt very similar to when I played Maureen Flowers in the Santa Monica Open in 1980, but this time the stakes were much higher.

I had felt for a long time that ladies should have their own world championship but there wasn't one and the problem for the BDO was that a growing number of talented female players were demanding a crack at the world title. There is now a ladies' world championship – won every year since it began in 2001 by the excellent Trina Gulliver – and this has encouraged a further growth in the ladies' game.

Francis was a very talented player and easily capable of getting through at Earl's Court that night. The match format was so short that anyone could beat anyone. In terms of publicity for the ladies' game, what could be better than Francis beating Bobby George in the play-offs? I had a bad feeling about the whole thing.

Everyone was stood around our board to watch the match. Francis had a lot of support – half of Holland seemed to be packed around that dartboard – and I had visions of negative headlines the following day should she beat me. Unlike the year before, TV cameras were there and they were filming our match. In terms of pressure, this was honestly as bad as anything I had ever known in darts. I was completely messed up by it all.

To make things worse, Francis started really well and took the first set off me with a 15-dart leg before the shock of what was happening sunk in and I managed to get my head together. I didn't lose another leg as I fought back to beat her, 2–1, but it was a close shave and I hated the whole experience.

Next up was John Walton, a very good county player who had represented England. I had once played pairs with John and knew him well. He was a powerful scorer but a poor finisher, and he struggled badly with his doubles against me that night. I beat him comfortably and faced Stefan Nagy of Sweden in the final round for a much-wanted place back on the Embassy stage.

By now it was approaching midnight and just a handful of fans, players, BDO officials and a solitary TV crew remained amid all the litter that was strewn across the floor. It wasn't a pretty sight – a far cry from the glitz and glamour of the Lakeside – but this is what it had all boiled down to, and a very long day was about to be topped off by the longest three-set match of my career.

Stefan is well known as one of the slowest players in the world. He is a good player and very precise but he is also boring to watch and very frustrating to play against. I was prepared for him. My driver at the time, George Sutherland, suffered from 'dartitis' – the inability to release a dart – and I had practised with him just days before the qualifiers. I was used to waiting around on the oche as my opponent took his time.

However, just as in my match against Francis, my concentration faltered. I lost my rhythm early on, gave away silly legs, and – eventually – Stefan threw for the match. He had darts to win at both double top and double ten but missed them. I stuck in and landed double 18 to secure my place back among the world's élite.

It had been a long and difficult match – the same could be said for the whole procedure of qualifying – but I was going back to Frimley Green and I was going to savour the atmosphere like I had never done before. Now I knew just how difficult it was to qualify, I would always think about my next match at the Lakeside as possibly my last.

I met another qualifier, Mick Brooks, in the first round. It is fair to say that Mick was a bag of nerves on his Lakeside debut – many players are – and it was no contest. My second-round match was a different story. Roland Scholten was one of the top names in Holland and always a dangerous player in the world championship. He beat me 3–0 in a scruffy match that had a lot of double six finishes for some reason.

Les Wallace won the tournament by wiping the floor with everyone. It was no surprise. He had a lot of talent and had been very unlucky in the previous two years. In 1995, Les had the highest average of the championship – he hit ten maximums – but still lost to Raymond Barneveld in the first round, and in 1996 he blitzed his way to the semi-finals but lack of sleep the night before his match with Richie Burnett affected his game.

Les took no such chances in 1997 and no one could get near him. He was magnificent and I was so pleased for him. He is a proud Scotsman and I nicknamed him 'Les McDanger' due to his heritage and his darts ability with his awesome left hand.

Les is a shy bloke and he hated doing interviews but, despite that, he tried to give himself some sort of image in the game. Bagpipes greeted his entrance into the hall and he wore a great kilt, but I never quite understood the fisherman's jumper.

After winning the Embassy he was struck down with glandular fever and was never the same player again. Exhibitions didn't suit him so he decided to pack it in and went back to plastering. Les later told me, 'In this game, you go from hero to zero overnight,' and that is how it can be, as I know from my own experience. One minute you are up there and everyone wants to shake your hand and the next no one wants to know you. That is the game of darts.

For me, a last-16 place was not a bad return, considering this was the only tournament that I entered, but it meant that if I wanted to come back, I would have to do it the hard way again, so I did. After another gruelling day and night in the play-offs in Earl's Court, I qualified for the 1998 tournament and hardly dropped a set in the process.

I was rewarded with a good draw and met a real Red Indian in the shape of Braulio Roncero in the first round. Braulio was of Spanish origin but represented Holland. He looked like he had come straight out of a John Wayne movie but his appearance was misleading and there was no mistaking his ability as a dart player. The boy didn't say much during the match and the only word I said that he understood was 'cojones', which translates as 'bollocks' in his native tongue – well, my wife is of Spanish descent – but Braulio could play. He hit seven maximums but missed a few important doubles. I beat him, 3–1.

I was in the last 16 again and this time I faced Sean Palfrey, one of the latest names to emerge in Welsh darts. A lot of people from his home town of Newport were there to support him that night and I had a few fans in as well, which made for a good atmosphere and a lot of noise in the hall. It was tailor made for me and I had a real opportunity to get to the quarter-finals but once again I let myself and my fans down when it mattered by missing simple, stupid doubles.

A poor workman blames his tools but I made a fatal mistake by allowing my darts to be sharpened by a friend just before the match. The points were left too short and my arrows were bouncing back at me throughout the game, which was annoying. Sean is a capable player but he is also a beatable player and he was very beatable that night but he won, 3–2. I was gutted.

Raymond Barneveld won the title that year and that was the final piece of the jigsaw for darts in Holland. The game had been bubbling for a while and now it exploded. Barney was voted Dutch sports personality of the year in 1998, beating footballer Dennis Bergkamp into second place. Holland had three world-class players in Raymond, Roland Scholten and Co Stompe, and Dutch fans turned up in their droves to exhibitions. Even today, many British players do a lot of work there. The Dutch have the right attitude to enjoying life and the emphasis is on fun and entertainment.

The qualifiers for the 1999 Embassy were switched to Frimley Green.

They always precede the Winmau World Masters and with the Masters moving from Earl's Court, so did the play-offs. I didn't like the new set-up at all. The Lakeside was not cut out to host the play-offs and every room had to be used as a result. Some matches were played in dining rooms, with big chandeliers touching your head. Players had to take the bulbs out before they were able to throw.

There wasn't any room for anything. There were people eating fish and chips just a few inches from the oche and when the TV cameras arrived to film a match, you could hardly move. Spectators were climbing over players to get a view of the board.

I beat one guy in that room and all he did was moan and swear throughout the match. He had some mates with him, all with a drink or two inside them, and the whole thing looked like kicking off. To be fair, we shouldn't have been trying to qualify in such a room. The play-offs mark a culmination of a lot of hard work for a lot of players and this was no way to decide things.

I went out to Wayne Jones in the third qualifying round. This was the first time I hadn't got to the final qualifying round in six attempts and it meant that I wouldn't be celebrating a third successive appearance at the Embassy. But Mum always told me that 'when one door closes, another one opens' and this turned out to be true when BBC Sport offered me the role of guest in the TV studio for the 1999 championship, which I was happy to accept.

The year 2000 marked the 20th anniversary of my first-ever appearance in the tournament and I desperately wanted to compete for that reason, and because it was the millennium, I wanted to be part of that history.

As it turned out, the 2000 play-offs were a breeze. In fact, the biggest problem I had was a bit of goading from Ronnie Baxter, the previous year's runner-up. I couldn't be bothered with 'Rocket Ronnie' that night. I was too old for all that.

He said it was a 'fix' how I kept qualifying for the Embassy through the play-offs. It was a ludicrous claim and one he should have put to some of the talented young players I beat that night, including Lee Harlow and Ray Jones. I was buzzing and consistently hit 140s in virtually every leg that I played. I was so focused on getting to the millennium championship that everything just went right for me.

The standard at the play-offs is always very high and can often be better than the main event at the Lakeside and 2000 was possibly the strongest line-up yet. Richie Burnett, Mike Gregory and Roland Scholten all tried to qualify and all failed. Both Richie and Roland left the BDO for the PDC shortly afterwards. The World Darts Council had by now changed its name to the Professional Darts Corporation.

The year 2000 marked my fourth successful world championship play-off attempt and earned me a new nickname in the process – 'King of the Qualifiers'. I don't know what it is that helps me perform so well in the play-offs. When the whistle blows, I am just one of 250 hopefuls and it is a case of every man for himself. There is no such thing as a favourite in that environment.

Shorter matches are difficult to play but one thing I never do is panic. No match is over until the winning double. That attitude has got me through on a few occasions. It is always possible to turn games around. Make no mistake, I prefer to play longer matches – all the top players do – but circumstances have dictated that I haven't played in many of those in recent years.

Joining me en route to the Lakeside was a young lad from Dagenham called Wayne Mardle, nicknamed 'Mouth of the South' at the time. This was before his Hawaiian makeover and his new nickname of 'Hawaii Five-O-One'.

I had known Wayne since he was a kid. He was a very good youth player and whenever I did exhibitions down his way he would always ask me for a game. Wayne has that rare combination of being both a player and an entertainer. He has a bit of flare about him and likes to jump around and put on a show, which is always good to see.

The 2000 Embassy was the first sporting event of the new millennium. I saw it as historic and had a new cloak made for the occasion with 'Darts 2000' embroidered on the inside. My cousins Valerie and Phyllis made it for me.

I really fancied my chances of winning the title. I felt so focused and my form was as good as it had been since I broke my back six years earlier. I saw what the other players had to offer and felt that I was head and shoulders above all of them.

Denis Ovens was my first-round opponent, a very experienced player who had played for England but surprisingly never qualified to play in the world championship before. Denis was ranked ninth in the world and was therefore regarded as the best unseeded player in the draw, but the pressure was something new to him and I took my chances to beat him, 3–1.

At 54 years of age, I was now the oldest man ever to win a match at the Embassy, and I loved every second of it. I blew kisses to the crowd and the support I received was fantastic. It was great to be back. Two years was a long time to be away but I had no intention of leaving the place just yet. I really believed I could go all the way.

My next match could hardly have been more difficult. I faced the number two seed and the 1999 runner-up, Ronnie Baxter. Ronnie and I have never been the best of friends, and that goes back to long before he made those disparaging remarks to me during the play-offs. But I can't knock his darts. He is a fast player and heavy scorer and will always prove to be a difficult opponent because he can check out on big scores. That is his biggest weapon. The only real difference between the two of us in 2000 was that Ronnie played darts 52 weeks a year while I spent most of my time working on my house and lakes.

We had a few scores to settle – his comments at the qualifiers were still fresh in my mind – and I was more than happy to play him. It all made for what was to be an extraordinary match. The needle started early on with Ronnie pointing to his watch as soon as we got up on the stage. I think he must have been making a point about my walk-on taking longer than his. So what? I am the game's entertainer and I have my fans to think about! This set the scene for the match. There was no banter, no fun and no warmth. In fact, it was as cold as it could have been up there on that stage.

He took the first set against the darts and muttered to me, 'Two more to go,' at the start of the second set.

'You're a long way from winning it, yet,' I replied.

Ronnie knows the rules. He has been in the game a long time but I have been in it a lot longer and I know the rules too. He wasn't going to affect me like that. I knew that I really had to win the second set to stay in the match and did so in the fifth and final leg, whipping the crowd into a frenzy and cupping my ear to generate even more noise from them. It was a flashback to my match against Mike Gregory in 1993 and Ronnie didn't like it one bit.

The third set also went down to the wire and I took it on my third attempt at double five after putting each of my previous two darts above the wire. I jumped up in the air for the first time since that fateful leap in 1994 while playing Kevin Kenny. It was just one of those moments. I was ahead for the first time in the match and there was total pandemonium in the hall around me. I glanced over to Marie and then looked at the crowd and realised that I was again on the verge of something special. I stood one set away from a place in the last eight.

Ronnie raised the pace of the match in the fourth set and a 133 checkout levelled the score at two sets all. We went into the fifth and deciding set with not so much as a handshake. Any protocol simply went out of the window. There was no respect on either side.

I was now so focused it was untrue but I had to keep my concentration. I took the first two legs of the final set on double ten and double 18 and stood on the threshold of the sweetest of victories. I glanced over to my opponent and I swear he was a beaten man. I had the darts in the third leg but I wasted that opportunity and allowed Ronnie back into the game.

However, in the next leg I had six darts to hit 178 and win the match. I nervously scored 92 with my first three darts, leaving 86 for victory. Ronnie scored well to put the pressure on but I still very much held the upper hand. Two darts – treble 18 and double 16 – would give me victory and shut him up once and for all.

My first dart hit single 18, and it stood at such an awkward angle that the treble bed was obscured and almost impossible to hit. I was left on 68 with two darts for the match. The normal shot would be 18 and bull but often in exhibitions I just play on the doubles and so I thought I would go out on double 18 and double 16 instead.

There should be nothing to those shots. I do them all the time, but I found out that the world championship is no exhibition. I missed double 18 by the width of a wire with my next dart and despite getting it with my last dart to leave 32, Ronnie checked out to win the leg and take the match into a tie-break.

The rest of the match became a slow, painful death. I knew I had thrown it away and Ronnie did as well. I still had the darts but I knew deep down that I had let him off the hook. My mind was dancing and I lost concentration. All my form suddenly disappeared and Ronnie scraped through into the quarter-finals. I hadn't been behind in the match since the end of the second set but I lost it 3–2 in sets after a sudden-death tie-break.

The final set had more twists and turns than an Alfred Hitchcock movie. When MC Martin Fitzmaurice came on stage at the end to say a few words, he said that Ronnie had got out of jail, and my opponent must have thought so too because he applauded me off the stage.

I had missed another great opportunity in the world championship. I had raised my game for four and a half sets and then thrown it away at the end. It was sickening.

I thought nothing more about my fanciful exhibition double-double attempt until I turned up to work for the BBC the next day and found that it was all the talk. Questions, criticisms, e-mails and faxes rained down throughout the day, and I even had to go out on to the Lakeside stage and talk through the shot live on the afternoon show.

I had no regrets about going for that combination and if I had pulled it off it would have been regarded as one of the most extravagant and fantastic winning checkouts in the history of the event. Instead, it became known as the costliest trick shot that had ever gone wrong.

At the time, I considered it nothing more than a missed opportunity but my unorthodox scoring was set to become a major talking point in the world of darts, again. I had to think quickly during that match and my brain went into exhibition mode. I took a chance and I came unstuck. That shot did cost me the game but I was confident that I could hit it. That is the gamble that I often take, and it makes me the type of player that I am. I suppose playing that shot, at that time, sums me up very well.

Ronnie went on to reach the final again that year, where he was thrashed 6–0 by Ted Hankey in a brilliant 46-minute performance that ended with a 170 checkout. I honestly think that had I beaten Ronnie, I would have gone all the way to the final, although in that sort of form, Ted would probably have beaten me.

For months I beat myself up badly over that match. I had fought so hard to get through the qualifiers and play in the millennium championship and then to have such a glorious opportunity and waste it was difficult to live with for a while. But I dusted myself down and gave the play-offs another go later in the year. This time I wasn't successful. Ray Jones gained revenge for losing to me in the previous two qualifiers and knocked me out, leaving me with just my TV work for the 2001 championship.

I took that opportunity with both hands and did a lot of homework on the players involved so that I could put much more into my developing role on the box. On the opening day of the tournament, BBC presenter Ray Stubbs asked me who, in my estimation, would win the title. Quick as a flash, I replied, 'John Walton.' It was some punt. His name was at the bottom of the list and his odds were 50–1, but I did have some inside information. John had telephoned me during the summer to ask advice about his trouble with scoring doubles, something that had dogged him throughout his darts career.

'Go around the board in doubles from one to twenty in forty darts,' I told him, 'and then ring me back.'

A few weeks later, he rang back to tell me he had done it in 40 darts.

'OK, now do it in thirty,' I said.

A month or so later I was lowering his target to 25 and after he had achieved that, I gave him the ultimate task of going around the board in doubles in just 20 darts. It took him another month to do it but he eventually came back on the phone with the news that he had achieved it. He asked what he should do next.

'Go and win the Embassy,' I told him.

I knew that if John could hit his doubles, no one would be able to get close to him and he proved me right at the end of that week. He annihilated everyone that he played.

John hated the fact that I kept tipping him that year but he had his lucky mascot in Kevin, the teddy bear. All that nonsense with the teddy bear came about in Amsterdam of all places. I was rooming with John at the time and one night all the players fancied a bit of the red-light district but my room-mate decided that wasn't his scene and opted for an early night instead.

I had noticed the teddy bear and mentioned it to some of the lads, who almost fell into the canal on hearing about it. 'John Boy's tucked up with his teddy bear' was the chant that night. Kevin Painter later gave it a name by kicking it in the air when we all piled into our hotel room. John did the best thing he could in the circumstances and played along with it. He had the last laugh when it turned into something of a lucky omen for him.

In 2001, he went on to win virtually every tournament he entered. That summer he came over to visit me at George Hall and I told him that he had to make a name for himself to secure his future. I tried to tell him that winning all these tournaments wouldn't make the slightest bit of difference in ten years' time. Touring the country and selling his name could do, but that isn't his scene. Lovely fellow that he is, his moment in the limelight came and went in a flash. I suppose the bloke played to his strengths and, at the end of the day, he is not cut out to be on the stage with a microphone in his hand.

John Boy winning everything in 2001 had a knock-on effect on the world rankings. Fewer players reached the requisite points total and therefore better players had to attempt to qualify for the following year's Embassy. It was a unique situation. In the past, a player would need maybe two tournament wins under his belt to qualify but in 2001 he needed just one Open quarter-final appearance. John topped the world rankings with a massive 75 points and some players qualified for the Embassy with as little as seven points. It was ridiculous.

While all this was going on, Croatian tennis player Goran Ivanisevic was handed a wild card at Wimbledon and went on to win the championship, breaking British hearts in the process by beating Tim Henman in the semi-finals. I felt that Goran had a lot in common with me. We were both popular players in our respective sports and had been beaten finalists on more than a few occasions. I telephoned Olly Croft. If the All-England club could allow wild cards at Wimbledon, surely the BDO could do the same for me at the Lakeside. We spoke long and hard about it but Olly told me that he couldn't give me a wild card because such a decision would be unpopular with the BDO. Well, it was worth a try.

The 2002 tournament was further turned upside down when a

host of BDO players – Ronnie Baxter, Steve Beaton, Andy Jenkins, Peter Manley and Kevin Painter – left to sign for the PDC on the eve of the qualifiers. Despite that, there was no u-turn from Olly and the BDO about my wild-card proposal. If I was going to play at the Lakeside, I was going to have to practise hard and qualify again, even though the mess with the rankings meant that it would be harder than ever.

Before I could take my place in the qualifiers that autumn, though, I had to find a solution to another problem. Suddenly and surprisingly, I didn't have a county to put my name under. I had played county darts for Essex, London and Suffolk in my time. I was captain of Essex for ten years before signing for Suffolk in the late 1980s, and when I returned to competitive darts in 1992, I did so under the county banner of London. In 2001, it got messy. London refused to sign my registration form on account of me not playing Super League for them. I told them that I hadn't played Super League since the mid 1980s and I wasn't going to start again now. The stand-off ended in a big row and I walked out on them. My view was that if London didn't want me, I would play for a county that did, but it wasn't as easy as that. I contacted both Essex and Suffolk and they replied in a similar manner. If I wasn't prepared to play Super League for them, I wasn't going to be registered by them.

My place in the Embassy qualifiers came courtesy of the BDO and a sponsor's invitation but I needed to represent a county and none of the three that I had played for wanted me. I didn't understand the reasons but feared there was some sort of conspiracy going on. Obviously, there was a backlash to me entering the qualifiers in this way and regularly winning through to the world championship, and someone, somewhere was trying to put an end to it.

Then I had an idea. Through my exhibition work I had friends in darts all over the country, including the Highlands of Scotland. The town of Fraserburgh in Aberdeenshire had made me honorary president of its Super League team. It was time to ask if I could call in a favour.

I telephoned them, explained my plight and asked if I could sign up for them. The next day, I received a registration form and a stamped addressed envelope and within a week I was registered as a Fraserburgh player. Importantly, this meant I could play in the qualifiers for Grampian. I wore the flag of St Andrew on my sleeve to acknowledge the fact and as a sign of gratitude.

My mother was born in nearby Aberdeen and so I do have Scottish blood. The whole situation was coming full circle from the time when I almost signed up for Scotland in the early 1980s and was denied by an overnight rule change by the BDO.

Another change for the 2002 qualifiers was my appearance. I had weighed 21 stone 7lb at the start of the year and was experiencing increasing pain in my knees. Marie put me on a special diet and I managed to lose a few stones but I had started to put weight back on again, mainly through eating junk food on the road.

I started to smoke the odd cigar and found that this helped to take the pain away. I hadn't smoked for years but needs must and all that. I would wake up in the morning with searing pain in my knees and when painkillers couldn't shift it, I turned to the cigars and found that they really helped. Smoking affects your appetite and before I knew it I was down to 16 stone 7lb. I lost five stones in less than a year. That's the way to do it! Smoking may not be good for your health but the choice was between smoking and walking, or not smoking and not walking. I decided to stay on the cigars.

So a slimline Bobby George was going to the Lakeside in an attempt to qualify for the Embassy for a record fifth time in late November 2001.

I practised like never before in the weeks leading up to the play-offs. I hate practising but overcame that with my determination to succeed, and I left George Hall for the 125-mile journey in very good spirits, just as the sun came out, accompanied by my own little band of merry men – Lance Hardy, big Olly Forster and my loyal driver and MC of many years, Roly Bright.

A lot of Scottish players asked me why I was wearing the cross of St Andrew and they all wished me the best of luck when I told them. I am a man of principle and I wanted to get to the Embassy for the good people of Fraserburgh. They had allowed me the chance to compete in the greatest darts tournament still around. The least I could do was wear the country's flag on my sleeve.

I was handed a difficult start when I was pitched against the Welshman Alan Reynolds in the opening round. We both played really good darts and upped each other's standard. I won 2–1, but it was some encounter. Alan is easily the best player I have come up against in the play-offs, and that match ranks as the hardest qualifier I have ever played. The pressure was constant and we were both consistently winning legs in 11 and 12 darts.

It was a great way to warm up, and the draw was opening up for me because in the second qualifying round I got a bye. Neither Les Hodkinson, whom I had played under those infamous chandeliers a few years earlier, or George McLean turned up to register in time, so I automatically progressed to the third round. In over 25 years of playing darts this had never happened to me before. The odds on neither of them turning up must have been huge. It meant that I had to wait five hours between winning my first match and playing my next, against Glen Toms.

Luckily, what with knowing the Lakeside so well, I found an air-conditioned area away from the autograph hunters and other players, where I could relax and mentally prepare for the match, and a private practice room, which allowed me to throw darts on my own. This was a completely new approach for me but it paid handsome dividends.

I beat Glen and then defeated Tab Hunter to set up a clash with my old mate Geoff Wylie from Northern Ireland. Geoff took a set off me but I managed to get through to face up-and-coming Finnish player Marko Kantele in the final round. Marko played on the 19s throughout the match and hit 171 a few times. On one occasion, he left himself double four to finish. It was interesting to watch but I beat him 2–0 and for the fifth time qualified for the world championship through the play-offs. At the end of a long but great day I was again King of the Qualifiers.

It was all due to the work that the four of us had put in as a team – Lance, Olly, Roly and me – both on and off the oche. The long journey home was one to remember. I was two weeks off my 56th birthday and we sang all the way back to George Hall. It was like we had the Embassy trophy on the back seat with us, just like the good old days in the 1970s. It was great.

It felt like we had pulled off the perfect bank job. All the nastiness I felt from the counties beforehand had been swept aside by what amounted to a very effective business plan. For once in my life, I had used my brain. I had been as good as gold and got my head down to the job in hand. Linda Batten would have been very proud of me.

I like to think the mother I don't remember would have been proud too, because officially I had qualified as a Scottish player. In doing so, I became the first man to compete at the Embassy under the flags of two countries – 14 times for England and now once for Scotland.

To celebrate qualifying for the 25th Embassy, I contacted Tony Leggett and Alan Parker to see if they fancied recording a new version of '180' with me. I was the only remaining player from the original 1980 recording and thought that the time was right to do a remix because the game was now in a completely new era. Tony and Alan were keen to be involved again and we wrote out some new words together, featuring current players Ted Hankey and John Walton.

Vince Williams was lead vocalist again and I did my own rap on the new version, which seemed to impress my son Robert more than anything I had ever achieved in darts. Franky de Wildt did a chorus in Dutch for all the boys and girls in Holland who love darts so much. All of us sang along to 'Honderd en Tachtig' and it was hilarious.

Pop music was suddenly coming into my life in a big way. At the same time, an all-girl group from Liverpool called Jezebelle recorded a song about me on their album *Circus Life*. It was called 'Bobby George' and included the line, 'When Bobby George plays darts, he does it from the heart.' It was a catchy tune and Marie loved it so much that we had the CD on in the house for weeks after it came out.

A few days after getting through the qualifiers, the draw for the world finals was made live on TV and my name was pulled out next to Raymond Barneveld's. It was the hardest match I could have asked for. The BBC immediately announced it would be shown live on the evening of the opening Saturday.

That was some occasion and some standard of darts, watched by over two million viewers. I had four darts to win the opening set but couldn't take them. I missed doubles at vital moments and allowed Raymond to punish me by moving into a two-set lead.

At one stage I was on for a nine-darter. It would have been the first to be shown live anywhere in the world and carried a cash payout of £52,000. I hit two maximum 180s to leave 141 with three darts. The crowd was jumping when I went up to the oche to throw for a third time. My plan was to go treble 19, treble 20, double 12 but I changed my mind at the last moment and aimed for treble 20 first. I lost my focus and hit bloody five. I always go 57 first, so why I changed my mind at that crucial time, I don't know.

The Dutchman came back to win that leg. I won just the one set and that was against the darts, which is typical of me, but I went down fighting. Barney needed 32 to win the match and I was left way back on 202 when it suddenly hit me that this could be my last-ever moment on the Embassy stage. I was determined not to go out on a whimper and pulled out a maximum to get the crowd on their feet. Raymond wobbled and I hit double 11 to crown a memorable ten-darter. I just had to give the fans something to remember me by.

The standard had been high. Barney hit the highest first-round average (33.36) in Embassy history to beat me and after a week of the event, I still had the third-highest average and I had gone out of the tournament on the opening day.

Later that year, the Dutch TV channel SBS-6 put on its own tour-nament, the World Darts Trophy, in a huge skating rink in Utrecht and offered me a wild card for the event. I hadn't done too much exhi-bition work in Holland and decided that I should take advantage of the invitation to put on a show for the Dutch, to show them what they were missing.

Martin Adams was my first-round opponent and I played up to the crowd something rotten. George Noble was refereeing the match and I was commentating as I hit treble 20s, 'That's for you, George, that's for you, Martin, and this one's for me.' The crowd loved it and I loved larking about on stage for them, but perhaps I tried too hard to play the clown. Martin punished me where it mattered, on the dartboard.

I took the first set but threw away the next two sets and lost the match, 3–1. It was a close contest and had I concentrated I might eas-ily have won. Martin took it all in good spirit but, looking back, it was ridiculous. I got too carried away with entertaining the crowd, and the more they wanted, the more I gave them. It was a buzz but it backfired. This was a world-ranking event, live on TV, against the number two player in the world. I was a fool to myself again.

Marie was furious with me for wasting such an opportunity. She did have a point. I had finally been given a wild card into an international event and I tossed it away. She punished me by taking me shopping the next day. After walking miles around Utrecht, I had blisters on my feet for a week. It taught me a lesson, at least until the next time!

I felt the Dutch wanted some showmanship in the event and that is why they invited me to play. I felt duty-bound to put on a show for them but probably overdid it. I can't help it. Darts is about entertainment and that is what I love to do. I would much rather put on a show and lose than grind out dull victories. Maybe that is where I have gone wrong but at least I have followed my heart.

I have always put the fans first and I think I always will. I couldn't get up on the stage without a smile on my face. No one would cheer then, and why should they? That is why I enjoy exhibitions so much. I am a winner every night of the week.

Tony David won the inaugural World Darts Trophy to add to his emotional win in the Embassy a few months before. Tony has come through a lot in his life due to serious illness and it was great that everything went so right for him in darts that year.

After four years at the Lakeside, the BDO switched the world qualifiers and the Winmau World Masters to the North Yorkshire seaside resort of Bridlington at the end of 2002. I didn't play too well there, losing to Dave Evans in the second qualifying round of the play-offs and going out in the first round of the Masters the following day after hitting the highest number of treble ones I had ever hit in a match in my life.

The main reason for such a sorry display was severe pain. Ever since my back operation in 1994, my loss of height and extra upper body weight had combined to put a lot of pressure on my knees. Basically, the knees buckled and eventually I required a replacement knee operation to enable me to walk. I also had to have a toe amputated as my condition worsened. My weight had knackered my toes too, and they had all spread outwards, making my feet look like something out of *Alien*.

By now, no matter how many cigars I smoked or how much rum I consumed, I couldn't get rid of the pain. I kept this to myself in the hope of pulling off some sort of miracle but I was in no state to play darts. I couldn't even get up the stairs at our seafront hotel.

After the tournament, I had new X-rays done on my spine and discovered that it was three inches shorter than when I first damaged it in 1994. The situation was only going to get worse, so I booked myself in for a replacement knee operation. That involved having the middle part of my right knee cut out and a metal joint inserted into the marrow of the bone. It is amazing to think that surgeons can now almost cut off your leg and then sew you back up again. The pain afterwards was something else, especially if I tried to put any pressure on my foot, but gradually it got easier and it is fair to say that the operation changed my life.

In the meantime, darts was a waste of time for me. I entered the world qualifiers for 2004 and 2005 as a token gesture. It was only after recovering from the knee operation that I felt able to mount a proper challenge again, in the final year of my fifties.

I accepted another invitation to play in the International Darts Trophy in Holland n 2005, which had become a round-robin event and was held in The Hague, and had a great time. I did myself proud, beating Tony West, losing to Shaun Greatbatch by just one leg and putting up a decent display against Stephen Bunting. I put on a show for the punters as well, but the main thing the tournament gave me was a return of self-confidence.

A few months later it all came right for me on the first day of the Winmau World Masters at Bridlington, when I made it through from over 200 hopefuls to the last 16 on the stage.

I always receive a sponsor's invitation to play in the Masters, which works well for me because I am up there working for the BBC anyway and it coincides with the world qualifiers. I found myself winning for fun in the early rounds of the 2005 tournament and beat both Vladimir Lavrentiev and Martin Atkins without dropping a set.

In the evening, I defeated Mario Robbe and John Henderson, both

3–2, to qualify for the televised stages against Sweden's Goran Klemme, who was a dangerous player and had already knocked out Co Stompe. I was turning the clock back once more. The only catch was getting up at eight in the morning to prepare for a ten o'clock start – not an ideal time to play darts for a night owl like me. Full of eggs and bacon, I never got into any sort of rhythm and was well beaten by Goran, who finished as runner-up.

Bridlington Spa is a very difficult place to play darts. The hall is quite tight and can become easily crowded. The place is made for shocks and, of course, everyone wants to turn over someone like me. But that is where the world qualifiers are held and that is what I have to come through if I am ever going to walk out on that marvellous Lakeside stage again, and maybe even lift that trophy.

The whole experience in 2005 convinced me that there was life in the old dog yet, and although I have still to do the business at Bridlington, my dreams aren't ready to be killed off. I came close to qualifying for the 2007 world championship when I defeated Ray Campbell, Connie Finnan, John Roberts and Kevin Simm before going out in the penultimate qualifying round to Preben Krabben of Denmark.

I took the first four legs against Preben and missed five darts to clinch the match before losing 5–3 on a final set tie-break. It was the same old story. I did the hard bit and then let the prize slip away just as it was getting close, but it proved that on my day I can still do it. Out of some 256 players who entered the 2007 world qualifiers for four guaranteed places, I got down to the penultimate qualifying round and could have gone further. In all honesty, I should have gone further.

The qualifiers come around late in the year, leaving little time to prepare for the main event, but that is just the way it is. Five times I have got through those play-offs but it is so very difficult and it isn't getting any easier. I have told the BDO on numerous occasions that I don't agree with the way the world championship is organised, and I have put forward a proposal that the top 16 players in the world should be joined in the main event by 16 qualifiers. That idea has more to do with creating a better tournament than with me being in the finals. Getting through those play-offs is as hard as it used to be getting through to the final of the *News of the World* championship. The standard is that good, and I should know.

Nevertheless, I will continue trying to qualify for the Lakeside the hard way. I just can't let go, even now. You can't buy the buzz you get from that crowd. You can't order a pint of it from behind the bar. That is what helps make the event so special. I still dream of holding that trophy above my head and while there is air in my body I will not give up on it, although I have to admit that the sand is running out on me.

15 Star of the small screen

Television made darts and as the game got bigger, all sorts of TV spin-offs started to come the way of the players. One of the biggest to come my way was the opportunity to appear in *Superstars*, the show where all types of sportsmen battled it out to prove who was the best. It was competitive, exciting and it made great TV.

In the early 1980s, darts players were beginning to be criticised for being 'pot-bellied', 'beer-swilling' and 'unhealthy slobs', which was getting on my nerves, particularly as I didn't fit into any of those categories. The *Russell Harty* show and the *Not the Nine O'Clock News* sketch hadn't helped but they were just the tip of the iceberg as darts got kicked from pillar to post. I wanted to do something about it and shut the critics up once and for all. Sid Waddell, who worked in TV at that time, had been pushing me to do *Superstars* for a while and I made the pledge that I would get myself into shape and take part, just to show the public that darts players were also sportsmen.

I met Brian Jacks, the Olympic judo star who had won *Superstars* a number of times. We did some weights together and discussed what was required and he was very supportive. I was working on a specialised training programme when I suffered a ruptured spleen and had to withdraw. My chance was gone. It was such a shame because I was fit and strong and, at 35, still relatively young. I think I would have done all right. We will never know.

Superstars was big news in the late 1970s and early 1980s. Everyone who was anyone in the world of sport wanted to take part. Famously, Kevin Keegan, who was the most famous footballer in England at the time, injured himself in a cycle race for the programme, and that seemed to affect who was allowed to take part in the show. Also after that incident, more of the top stars became reluctant to risk injury.

Kevin was very much the David Beckham of his day. I met him a couple of times. He had a bubble perm just like me – only mine was natural – and was the biggest star in English football. Kevin made his name at Liverpool before moving to Germany and playing for SV Hamburg. It was during his time there that I first met him. I was at a trade fair in Cologne playing darts and he was giving away signed footballs.

Despite Kevin's fame, I didn't have a clue who he was. I have never had much interest in football. I don't watch it on the TV and I don't read any of the newspapers. It is possible – even in this day and age – to have a life away from all that.

We got chatting and I asked him, 'Don't you ever get fed up selling footballs?' He explained that he was a sportsman, not a salesman. I was a bit embarrassed but we had a game of darts and enjoyed a good laugh together.

A year or so later, I was invited to Wembley Stadium by sponsors for a game between England and Spain. I took my seat in the stand and looked down on the pitch to see that Kevin was captaining England. The penny finally dropped. He was the main man.

Luckily, footballers seem to know more about darts than I know about football. I have met David Beckham, Michael Owen and Alan Shearer in recent years and have been impressed by how much they all knew about the game.

One TV show that I did go on in the 1980s was the live children's programme, *Saturday Superstore*. David Icke, who presented darts for the BBC at the time, used to do a sports round-up spot and invited me on because I was European singles champion. I always liked David. I found him to be a decent man and very knowledgeable about darts. He was respectful of the game, and all the players appreciated that.

I was asked to perform a simple trick shot involving a newspaper with presenter Keith Chegwin. We rehearsed it with five copies of the same newspaper covering the dartboard and I soon learned that the crossword covered treble 20 and that the horoscopes were over the bull, that sort of thing. Live on air, Keith asked me to hit the bull and proceeded to cover the board with a completely different newspaper from the one that we had practised with. As he put the newspaper over the board his eyes met mine and we seemed to read each other's mind, but it was too late to do anything about it. I did my best and luckily hit two bulls and a 25. That simple error made an easy trick shot pretty difficult.

I went on a pop panel with the all-girl group Bananarama. We played Hit or Miss and the songs were so awful I started playing my own game of Take It or Leave It. When I was asked my opinion, I kept telling host Mike Read, 'I'll leave it, thanks.'

The fact that I was on a show like that underlines just how big darts had become within a short space of time. The game was included across a broad spectrum of TV programmes, both for adults and children. It is a far cry from the rather insular world darts inhabits today.

TV and darts went hand in hand and after the TV tournaments dried up, guest appearances by players on the box became very rare. My first TV appearance for a long while – other than darts – came in the late 1990s when I was the mystery guest on *Through the Keyhole*. Lloyd Grossman came over to George Hall and was amazed to discover that I had built the place with my own hands. He walked around the house and grounds by himself and told his camera crew where to film as he sat down and worked on his script. He was very particular about what he ate. Marie offered him all types of sandwiches and he wouldn't touch any of them, but his crew gratefully gobbled them up. The panel of Bobby Davro, Kris Akabusi and Anna Walker eventually guessed it was my house after Anna saw my wardrobe and suggested it was Elton John's gaff!

I found Sir David Frost a master at interviewing in the studio. He let me do all the talking but somehow got all the answers he needed. I would have loved to have sat in that chair and been interviewed by him for a whole hour. The programme was filmed in front of a live audience in Leeds. The agent Eric Hall was on the show with me and I have never seen a bloke spray himself with so much aftershave in one go, from head to toe. I should have got him to have a word with the old man.

At around the same time, I also featured on the *Live Obituary Show* on Radio Five Live with Jim White, which was fantastic – a whole hour devoted to my life and my favourite music. Jim was a really nice guy and I got to play songs by The Beatles and The Kinks during the interview. Thankfully, I didn't have to be dead to appear on the programme either!

In the autumn of 1998 I may not have done too well in the world championship qualifiers, but that early exit opened up a whole new world for me in the role of TV pundit. The BBC rang me up just days after I found myself at a loose end to ask if I would be interested in working for them at the Lakeside as a studio guest. I jumped at the chance. It would be a steep upward learning curve but I couldn't wait to give it a go. As well as the new experience, it was another way of keeping my name in lights.

I had always got on with the boys from the BBC – and ITV for that matter – and it was nice to get this opportunity to work alongside professionals whom I considered friends. I knew the backroom staff very well from all the many interviews I had done and I knew that I would be in safe hands with them.

Over the years, I have developed into much more of a TV animal and in addition to the studio work, I now go out on stage and film master classes or play a popular 'Leg with Bobby' against famous fans of darts. I have also turned my hand to features and interviews, most memorably cooking with darts player-come-chef Jez Porter and being Ted Hankey's chauffeur in a stretch limo. My favourite film of all was a fabulous *Through the Keyhole* spoof with the two fat refs, Martin Fitz-maurice and George 'The Puppy' Noble, who always share Room 180 at the Lakeside every year. They both loved it.

While working at the Lakeside, I have to watch each match like a hawk, memorising averages and finishes. The very first year I did it, Chris Mason came from 4–1 down to beat Martin Adams 5–4 in the quarter-finals in one of the greatest matches ever played in the world championship. The pair hit more trebles than doubles – 29 between them – and Chris won the match on double one after Martin had missed double one, which says it all. It was magnificent drama, and fascinating to see it from a different perspective and to be able to comment on it in my new role in the studio.

Earlier that day, in our afternoon show, Chris had picked his favourite Embassy moments – including my win over Magnus Caris –

and ironically, just a few hours later, his win over Martin would join them as one of the true classics in the history of the event.

Darts wouldn't be darts without a story and after that epic quarter-final, Chris had a row with his missus and had to sleep on the refs' hotel room floor before playing his semi-final the next day.

A few of the players had a negative view about my TV role at first and didn't like me doing it, but most of them were kind enough. They admired me for having a go, and for trying to take the game to a new audience. As time has gone on, I have received more respect from the other players. I try to make them feel at ease when they come into the studio and my relationship with many of them has improved as a result. I also think they now realise how hard TV can be.

Once I started working all day long, I could no longer have a drink during the day and that was hard to cope with at first. I had to work on my vocabulary as well and try not to repeat myself on screen. TV work is challenging in that respect, but I always have an opinion. I know all about the game's history and I can analyse matches. I have done eight years in the role now, so I must be doing something right, and I seem to be regarded as the elder statesman of the game. I realise that I have a big responsibility in what I say and I consider it a privi-leged position to be in.

I once told Richie Burnett off in the studio after he went out in the first round. It was just a natural thing to do. Richie was a tremendous talent but was sulking after a shock defeat to Leo Laurens. I got a lot of admiration from the players that night, but my most famous moment concerned Mervyn King in 2004. I took a stand after watching his match with Rick Hapstra, and accused him of gamesmanship. We didn't speak for the rest of the tournament, or the rest of the year.

Mervyn had won the opening two sets against a young boy making his debut in the tournament and then started to complain that the oche was short and asked for it to be measured. The oche was meas-ured and was found to be the correct length, and as if to prove it, Mervyn then produced a 12-darter. I said live on air that he had 'done the boy up like a kipper'. That is still my opinion today.

It all got a bit silly. In his TV interviews, Mervyn started accusing me of gamesmanship myself. The last thing I needed was to get into a public slanging match, so I didn't take the bait, but I stood by my comments and repeated the assertion when asked.

Mervyn seems to be one of those players that has to have everything right so that he can focus on his darts. If it isn't the air conditioning that's wrong, it's the lighting. If it isn't the height of the board, it might be the length of the oche. It is a great shame because the man is undoubtedly a very talented darts player. If he could just remember that and forget all the other rubbish, he would be world champion in a shot. I know that and he knows that.

Eighteen months after the incident, Mervyn came up to me during the International Darts League event in Holland and apologised for his comments. He asked if we could bury the hatchet.

'If you're man enough to say sorry,' I told him, 'I'm man enough to shake your hand and accept that.'

Of course, we still disagree about all the oche business – we both stand firm about that – but we have moved on and our relationship is a professional one.

I am now seen as a true authority on the game, not just by TV viewers but also by many of the players themselves. Raymond Barneveld calls me 'The Master' and many of the younger boys ask me how to stand and want advice on certain out-shots. I have definitely come full circle from the early days when I was accused of not being able to count.

The BBC has had a broad spectrum of darts presenters over the years and I have got on with all of them very well. Peter Purves was the first one I knew. He was a big fan of the game and used to get very excited. He understood it and loved to get involved.

David Icke was always good to me. I know he has gone off and done other things that may not be to everyone's liking but I got on well with the bloke. Dougie Donnelly paved the way for what I am doing now, even though he often used words that I didn't understand and was a bit quick for me at times. His interviews were short and sweet but he was very professional and put you at ease at once.

Ray Stubbs has guided me through my days as a studio guest over the last few years and I have a lot to thank him for. The two of us go back a long way – we first met at the Unipart British Masters in the

1980s – and we have had some good times together. He once joined me on a trip to Germany to entertain the troops. He loves darts and it is a great thrill for me that all these years on we now work together on the box.

Clare Balding was the first woman to present darts on TV and the two of us got on like a house on fire. It was a difficult environment for her and she did very well and was a good giggle. She told me to make sure that I put all my gold in the safe at night and I told her that I put it in the fridge, because it was made of chocolate! She had a good sense of humour and I enjoyed working with her very much.

The BBC invited me down to Royal Ascot one year, which was a terrific experience. I took Marie along and she was in her element. It was Ladies' Day and I had to comment on all the hats, and try to pick out some winners. I looked the part in my top hat and tails and had a great time talking about the fashions of the day with designer Jeff Banks. Unfortunately, I struggled on the races and kept picking one loser after another. It was just a shame that John Boy Walton wasn't running!

Back on the box a few weeks later, I appeared as a mystery guest on *They Think It's All Over* with cape and candelabra, and got felt up by Jonathan Ross!

Interactivity is a big part of TV these days and we receive e-mails and texts about all sorts of things at the world championship, some serious and some not so serious. I love the e-mails more than anything. I find having to think on my feet quite demanding and communicating with the public in that way is great fun.

Viewers once requested a special Bobby George package and the BBC got permission from ITV to run my 1979 *News of the World* win against Alan Glazier. It was the first time that either Marie or myself had seen the footage and it meant so much to both of us. It brought all the memories flooding back to me and once again underlined the power of TV in darts, both then and now.

In 2001, one viewer e-mailed to ask if I had ever considered appearing in the soap *EastEnders*. My response was that the only part I could possibly see myself getting was that of an East End gangster.

The next week, I received a telephone call at home from a young film director, Lee Pavey. He had written a screenplay called *Dog* and wanted me to play the lead role of gangster Tony Barton in it. I told him that I had no acting experience at all but he was undeterred.

'You've done live TV,' he said. 'You look the part and you speak the part. You are the part.'

Lee had apparently been looking for someone to play the role for months and one day his mother rang him up and said, 'Turn BBC Two on now.' There I was. He loved my jewellery, he loved my accent and he so desperately wanted an East End feel to the film that he said he would allow me to put a bit of Cockney rhyming slang into the script. It was to be a low-budget film set around a prized greyhound and by the end of our telephone conversation I had agreed to play the role of Tony Barton.

Tony is a butcher in the day and a butcher at night. Anyone who gets in his way usually ends up in a pork pie. I filmed a trailer at an abattoir in south east London, and in late 2002 I filmed half a dozen or so scenes at Catford dog track and the Asylum pub on the Old Kent Road. The hours were unbelievable. I was up for 6 a.m. starts and finished the day at midnight. The onus was on making the most of the little time we had.

It was a decent cast list, including Billy Murray (formerly of *The Bill* and now *EastEnders*), Paul Danan (once of *Hollyoaks* and now more famous for trying to get his leg over on the reality TV show *Celebrity Love Island*) and the lovely Danielle Brent (currently appearing in *Bad Girls*). I even got Ray Stubbs a part as one of my gang. He was cast as Mickey the Mouth and couldn't speak a word because of a bad scar across his chops.

And I had my own porn star in the shape of Teresa May. Teresa has appeared in a lot of movies and magazines and has her own website. She plays the part of my moll in the film and manages to keep her clothes on throughout, which is just as well, otherwise Marie might have had something to say about it.

We had an impromptu rehearsal at George Hall one afternoon and Teresa turned up with her portfolio. She laid all these photographs out on the snooker table in the games room. I had never seen anything quite like it, but I was an actor now and nodded along with a professional eye as she showed me her work.

It was such a drawn-out process, making the film. I thought that TV was slow until I made the movie. It can be quite boring but it is very rewarding work. I had to be on my mettle throughout. If I made one single mistake, the whole scene would be ruined and we would have to go for another take. I felt a lot of responsibility on my shoulders, particularly because I was an amateur among professionals. I was anxious not to make any mistakes and hold up filming. Memorising certain words, or making adjustments to the script in any way, was very hard for me. Marie and I spent days rehearsing scenes so that I was ready when the cameras rolled.

The original plan was to make a short movie but in the end it became a full feature-length film, running for 80 minutes. The cast list became quite long and included a few real life criminals who were actually tagged. They were all decent blokes and I became friends with some of them. I found these guys very interesting to talk to and enjoyed speaking to them about my own experiences as a nightclub bouncer in the 1960s. Making *Dog* brought back a lot of memories and those recollections helped me to fall into that mode again to play my part.

The film was a great experience for me. I had never dreamed that I would ever get such an opportunity and it was an honour to be asked to appear in it. Whether it leads anywhere is irrelevant. It is just nice to say that I have been in a movie.

I only learned the lines I had to, so I wasn't totally sure of how the film ended until I saw the finished product. It isn't too dissimilar in its format and feel to *Lock, Stock and Two Smoking Barrels*. That would be the best comparison I could give. There is a lot of subtle humour in it. For instance, my gang wear gold and my rival's gang wear silver. Stuff like that, which film buffs can't get enough of.

Tony Barton loves darts and in one scene he is seen throwing a maximum in a pub. It is very reminiscent of my meeting with Kenny the Mouth at the Old Maypole all those years ago but no one on the set knew about that story. It was just total coincidence, and it makes it into the final cut.

I never got to Cannes or Hollywood but the film, which has now been retitled *One Man And His Dog*, quickly led to another spin-off when I received a phone call in the summer of 2005 from rappers The Mitchell Brothers, asking me to appear in their pop video 'Excuse My Brother'.

The boys are good friends of Mike Skinner, the man behind The Streets and a big darts fan himself. All three of them were involved in the video and wanted me to play the same type of role as I had in *Dog*. I was happy to oblige and had a good day out with them on the set. They are all diamond geezers. I got dressed up as a gangster again, with all the jewellery and everything, and did the film in one day at an old warehouse in London. After filming *Dog*, it was a breeze.

In the last few years I have been inundated with requests to appear on live celebrity shows – *Celebrity Love Island* aside – but I have had to decline many of them, due to the state of my knees or my back. *I'm A Celebrity, Get Me Out Of Here* was the biggest disappointment. I talked with the producers about going into the jungle the year that Johnny Rotten of the Sex Pistols appeared in it. Now, that would have been a laugh. My health let me down – I was about to have a knee replacement. Actually, it was just as well because there is no way I could have coped with any of those tasks apart from maybe eating some of the bugs and lying down with the water rats.

When the opportunity came for me to do *Celebrity Fit Club*, I felt that the time was right. It had been two years since my knee operation and I needed to get fit and lose a bit of weight anyhow. I was 60 years of age and time was against me in the fitness stakes. I went on the show and made some good friends, but the dieting was hard work and by the end of it I couldn't wait to get a few pounds back on my waist-line.

My weight went down to under 14 stone, which is the lightest I had been in nearly 50 years, apart from the time when I almost died after rupturing my spleen. I felt like an old man, I looked like an old man and Marie said she was living with an old man. We took all the mirrors down from the walls in George Hall for the duration of the show but I stuck at the task and did it all properly, just as the doctors ordered.

A lot was made about whether Anne Diamond cheated on the programme. Anne had a gastric band fitted before filming began and didn't tell anyone about it. We all had to fill in a form before we signed up for the show and there was plenty of space for her to include details of the operation but she decided not to.

It was not what *Celebrity Fit Club* was meant to be about. The whole idea of the show was to lose weight sensibly, through eating properly and exercise and meeting weekly targets set by a team of experts.

Everyone who took part in the series did very well. Losing weight isn't easy. I made friends with the whole gang, a lot of good people from different walks of life. Russell Grant is a nice man with not a bad bone in his body. We had to play tennis together at Bisham Abbey and he was an absolute scream that day.

I got on with Mick Quinn like a house on fire. We share the same sense of humour and even though he is almost 20 years younger than I am we had a good laugh together. Mick was one of the youngest contestants and once he started shedding the pounds, it was evident that he used to be a professional sportsman. He lost a lot of weight and was a worthy winner of the show.

Carole Malone is a lovely lady, even though she never takes a breath and can talk for England. When we speak on the telephone, I make sure she is the one paying for the call. Sharon Marshall was also in my team and great fun to be around. She put a lot of hard work into getting fit and it paid dividends. She looked fantastic at the end.

Dale Winton is the ideal host for the programme, working so hard to get fit and look good himself, and Dr Adam Carey, the show's nutritionist, is a gentleman.

I even made my peace with Sergeant Major Harvey Walden IV, the fitness instructor on the programme, who wouldn't have been out of place at Gearies Secondary School in the 1950s! Harvey made fun of me for looking like Mr T the first time we met, but he had to concede that the language barrier between the two of us was one of the biggest challenges he had ever faced in his line of work. Lovely jubbly.

The whole experience showed me a new way of life. First thing in the morning, I would get up and go to the gym, do the bike, the cross trainer and walk on the treadmill. Then I would finish off with some leg exercises and weights. I would get home and have kippers for breakfast. Lunch would be very light and my evening meal was generally chicken or fish with plenty of salad. I lived on fruit and vegetables, including the beetroot that I vowed never to touch again following my childhood. For three months I ate no bread, no chips and no potatoes. All carbohydrates were out, as were chocolate, crisps, alcohol, fizzy drinks and takeaways. It is common sense to lose weight that way, but it is bloody difficult to carry it off.

Drinking a pint or two can put four pounds back on and that could be my weekly target. If I was going to have a go at doing it, I had to do it properly.

I think going from 17 stone to less than 14 stone was too much for me. I didn't like the way I looked at the end. I even stopped getting wolf whistles from the old ladies, and I can't be having that.

After filming the final show in Sheffield, I treated myself to some cans of beer and a Kentucky Fried Chicken takeaway. It was delicious. I just can't tell you. I loved it. It is nice to be thin and fit but it is even nicer to be a little fatter and a little happier.

16 Treble twenty and beyond

Now that I have turned 60 it seems a good time to reflect on my life, half of which has been spent playing darts. There is no doubt about the most important event, meeting Marie, and that was through darts.

I suppose that, emotionally, I was a lost soul until I met her. She gave me a purpose and I certainly wouldn't be where I am today without her. My wife and family are everything to me. I only understood what love was when I met Marie and later had my boys with her. That was, and still is, real love. I found it when I found her. I was 38 years old and consider myself very, very lucky.

When a man gets older, he isn't into the chase so much. He finds a mate, forms a partnership, matures and starts a family with the woman he loves. Well, that is how it happened to me anyway. Love really does take over, and life becomes centred on your family. I realised that quite late in life, but better late than never. Every man needs the love of a good woman. You just can't make it on your own and it must be pretty sad trying to.

While Marie and darts changed my life, my personality has remained the same all the way along. That comes from the old man. I am a gentle, trusting person until I am wronged, and then I turn. He taught me to look after myself. When I was a boy my motto was if someone wanted trouble and put a bullet in a gun, I would happily pull the trigger. If they didn't want trouble, there were no bullets and therefore no need to pull the trigger. I have been like that all my life, from school to the nightclubs and throughout my darts career. I still believe it today. I haven't changed a bit.

The old man always believed that to judge a man all you had to do was look straight into his eyes. 'You can see everything there is to know,' he once told me. He was spot on. He also taught me never to listen to anyone who gives advice on life unless they have suffered. I believe he was right about that, too. Until a man has been hurt, he knows nothing

Mum was the one who brought me up to say what I believed and I have always done that, even if it has upset some people along the way. The old girl had a lot of sayings. My favourite was, 'If you're not yourself, then you're no one. But if you're yourself, then you'll always be someone.' I have held that one close to my heart and now I have passed it on to my boys.

Mum had a big impact on how I turned out. She had strong beliefs and taught me that to get anything out of life I had to go out and grasp it. 'Nothing ever comes to you if you sit on your backside and wait for it,' she would say. That is very true as well.

Materialistically, everything I have in my life today has come from either my hands or the game of darts. George Hall is an example of that. Darts may have paid for the raw materials but I turned the dream into reality with my own bare hands.

I only got to travel through darts. I had never been on a plane until the BDO took me to America at the age of 32, but since then I have travelled far and wide, from the Gulf to the Falklands. I have visited many wonderful countries to play darts, and of all the places I have seen, San Francisco is way above the rest. But ask me what my favourite place in the whole wide world is and my answer is simple – my garden.

When I was a young boy with a stutter, hardly able to read or write, I couldn't have imagined, even in my wildest dreams, that one day I would be the star of a film or a face on the BBC. My stutter was a massive hurdle to get over, but almost as soon as I got out of school, it improved. The more confidence I gained from working with my hands, the more I forgot about it until one day I found it had gone for good. Thankfully, it has never once come back.

Everything seems to happen late to me. I didn't start playing darts until I was 30, I got a job on the TV when I was well into my fifties and I landed an acting role when I was close to 60. Every door has led to another new opening – darts into TV and TV into film – and long may that continue. Through it all, I have remained true to myself. I am still the same bloke who knocked out the schoolteacher, worked on the nightclub doors, dug the Victoria Line underground and laid those concrete floors. I have always given my best and I have always tried to get on with people. That is all a man can do. The rest has to take care of itself.

My first-ever darts exhibition was for Ford motor company in Romford, a few months after I took up the game in 1976. I remember that I was asked to do a talk and answer questions from the floor. I still wasn't too confident with my speech in those days and found it the most terrifying task that I had ever undertaken. At the end of the night a chap came over, shook my hand and said, 'You're the Henry Cooper of darts, you are mate. Never ever change. Just believe in yourself and keep on being yourself.'

I have never forgotten those words. I sometimes think back to the bullying I suffered at school, due to my stutter and lack of education, and shake my head at what I am now doing on TV and film. It has been a truly incredible journey and darts made it all possible.

The stuttering and lack of self-confidence didn't leave me overnight. I was very shy well into my teens and early twenties and would go bright red with embarrassment whenever my speech impediment returned to haunt me. Darts changed all that.

My ambition on taking up darts in 1976 was to be the best in the world and I achieved that when I won the *News of the World* championship three years later. That ranks as my greatest single achievement in darts, simply because it meant everything and made my name in the game. I didn't drop a leg in ten months of that competition and I looked the part. It was long before the glitter and the gold, but live TV coverage turned me into a pop star overnight.

Once again, it is important to acknowledge that for over 50 years the NOW championship was recognised as the world title in darts. The televised success of the Embassy (now called the Lakeside) world championship and Phil Taylor's domination of PDC events have blurred this fact in recent years. All the players wanted to win it. George Bristow – Eric's old man – famously remarked that his son could 'now be accepted as a proper darts player' when he lifted the NOW crown for the first time in 1983, and Eric had won the Embassy twice and the World Masters three times by then.

I won the NOW championship twice – in 1979 and 1986 – and they remain my two biggest triumphs. The 1978 North American Open, the 1979 and 1980 Butlin's Grand Masters, the 1982 European singles and my 25 England caps come a long way down the list. Strangely, the one event that I am most closely associated with these days is the one tournament I never managed to win.

A lot of people ask me how many times I won the Embassy world championship, and the answer is none. If you talk about the glory days of darts, the names of Eric Bristow, John Lowe, Jocky Wilson and myself are those that trip off the tongue, but I am the odd one out when it comes to lifting the Embassy trophy.

I had my chances. I could have beaten Eric in 1980 and I believe I was the best player by a mile in 1993. I could have won it in 1982 and 1994 but was affected by illness and injury. It is my own fault that I never won it. I had the talent to do so – I beat Eric, John and Jocky in so many events – but I was never able to put enough into it when it mattered.

I am still my own worst enemy when it comes to darts. Entertainment has always mattered more to me than achievement. It drives Marie mad but it's just the way I am. The only time I put any consistent concentration and effort into my game at the Lakeside was in 1993 when I was invited into the qualifiers after a five-year absence. I desperately wanted to prove a point that year – particularly with the WDC split on the cards – and I got all the way to the semis where I threw it away against John Lowe. I believe I was the best player in the field again the next year too, only to break my back at a crucial time. You couldn't write a script like that. Sometimes I wonder if it just isn't meant to be.

In the early days, I felt that the Embassy was just another tournament and there was always next year. Now, nearly 30 years on, it is the only one that counts. It is the one that I enter year after year, and the only one that matters to me.

Apart from the Embassy and a few tournaments here and there, I haven't played competitive darts for over 20 years. With too little money and too much hassle involved, there is no real reason for me to do so. Darts is a single man's game. It is very difficult to travel the world picking up ranking points here and there if you have a wife and family at home.

I played darts for England 25 times but never got paid a penny. All my earnings came from the exposure I got through appearing on TV. National pride soon wore off and all those international matches became just another vehicle to provide me with a living. When TV coverage dried up, it was a no-brainer to quit.

I could see two roads ahead of me. One was full of darts players trying to win a few quid and the other had all these pubs and clubs offering good money to be entertained. Entertainment was my living and so the exhibition circuit was perfect for me. It can be hard work and quite demanding. No one wants to play a pissed-up professional who struggles to hit the board. You have to be on your game at all times to make it pay on the exhibition circuit. Many players have tried and failed. They all want to get their hands into that tiny pot of gold but their problem is that I got mine in there first and they just can't get it out of the way.

Eric Bristow used to give me stick about my exhibition work and I would tell him that we are all made differently. He was into beer, fags and darts, and nothing else seemed to matter to him. I was always the total opposite to that.

Any decent exhibition player needs a good MC by his side, a man who can call, compere and referee. There is quite a lot involved. An MC has to know the rules, be able to count fast and accurately, and be authoritative with a good sense of humour and a nice, clear voice. He also needs to look the part with a clean suit, clean shirt and bow tie, clean shoes and be clean-shaven. The biggest rule of all is that he must entertain but not embarrass the audience.

I have worked with many top MCs over the years and in young Richard Ashdown I currently have one of the best. I met Richard when he was a young boy of 14 and what he doesn't know about darts isn't worth knowing. He is a diamond with a brilliant brain for numbers and an obsession with unorthodox finishes, which is just as well as he works with me. I gave him the nickname of 'Bobby's Best Counter', which is quite appropriate because I got him a job as a spotter with the BBC down at the Lakeside a few years ago.

At the start of my career, I worked with both Freddie Williams and Tony Green. Freddie was one of the very first MCs and played it straight. Tony was a decent county player who became the first recognised MC on the TV and then, of course, went on to become a successful commentator.

Martin Fitzmaurice worked with me for many years as well. He is a great caller and a big personality with plenty of jokes and funny stories thrown in for good measure. He can both referee and MC with ease. Many years ago, I recommended Martin to the BDO general secretary Olly Croft and he never looked back.

I worked with Phil Jones on and off for the best part of 20 years. He is always very smartly dressed, clever with his words and has a great personality. I thought he would go on to make a great TV game show host but it hasn't happened.

Paul 'Slapper' Taylor is quite similar to Phil. He is a quiet guy but very witty and when he gets on the microphone, he becomes a real entertainer. Dave Swindells worked with me as well. He also did a lot of work for Alan Evans. He was a very reliable caller and a teetotaller, which is pretty rare in darts.

Jacque Nieuwlaat is one of the best MCs in Holland. He started off as my driver over there and then got into calling. He has since done TV commentaries and now works with the top Dutch players but he always finds time for me whenever I visit the lowlands. Another of my old drivers, George Sutherland, is a former Scottish international. I got him to do some MC work and he was quite a natural. He has since worked with a lot of the top players, including Phil Taylor. Dear old Roly Bright, who has worked with me for the past 25 years, could drive for England. He is old school, military and very much to the point, just like a scoutmaster.

George 'The Puppy' Noble is probably the best tournament caller around at the present time. I first met him when he was a youth player. He started to call games in London and I took him on the road with me. Again, I put his name forward to the BDO and again the rest is history.

I have never once regretted my decision to go down the exhibition road. I love it and don't really think of it as work. How can I after so many years spent shovelling concrete? The only drawback is it leaves me a little match rusty when it comes to the world play-offs every autumn.

In 2002, I set a new record for the oldest player to reach the final stages of the Embassy when I played a first-round match at the age of 56 years and 20 days. My aim now is to become the first man in his sixties to do the same. I still believe that I can win the Lakeside world championship and while that is the case I owe it to myself to keep trying.

One day I will have to draw the curtain on what has been a marvellous time for me in darts, but as long as the telephone rings and I have got my health, that day will have to wait. My eyesight is just about holding up. I do wear glasses in the house and one day I may have to wear them when I play darts. If that ever happens, I will get my mate Alan Marks to make me some that glitter so that they blend in with the rest of my outfit.

It is now over two years since my knee replacement operation and I feel good. I always believe that next year could be my year at the Lakeside and my performance in the 2005 World Masters in Bridlington suggests that I still have a chance. After all, I desperately wanted to play in the millennium championship and managed to do so, and I fought hard to qualify for the 25th Embassy in 2002. One goal is to get there again in 2010, when I'm 64, and walk out to that great old song of the same name by The Beatles. That would be hilarious, the best walk-on ever, although I hope I won't be 'losing my hair'.

Walking out on to that Lakeside stage is something else – every player who has done it knows what I am talking about – and I never fail to feel a little tingle down my spine when my name is called out and I enter the arena through those big double doors. That is what darts is all about for me and that is why I do my utmost to play there. Some players hate all that but I savour every step and every cheer. I love it.

For many years now, I have walked out to 'We Are The Champions' by Queen. The words in the verses tell the story of my life and the chorus sums up how I feel about darts and my fans. The words 'we' and 'my friends' represent those people in the audience who have made a success of their own lives, whatever they have done, and have come to see me and cheer me on through thick and thin. The line, 'We'll keep on fighting till the end' sums us all up pretty well.

The candles have been with me since 1980 but the cape is a relatively new addition to my wardrobe, arriving much later than the glitter and gold. I got such a buzz from my return in the 1993 tournament that I decided to do something special for the fans the following year and a cape seemed perfect. The cape has made my image in darts what it is today. A few years ago, at an exhibition in Holland, the organiser asked me if I had brought the cape and candles with me.

'Sure,' I told him. 'I'll get them out after I've played some darts.' He looked at me in total disbelief and replied as only the Dutch can.

'Fuck the darts, Bobby,' he said. 'Get the cape and candles now. That's what the fans want to see.'

Holland has been fantastic for darts during the past decade. As well as unearthing some very talented players, the fans are something else. The game just seems to suit the mentality of the Dutch. They love to have a good time. Obviously, the success the country has enjoyed in darts in recent years has been another important factor in the game going through the roof in terms of popularity. I have made a few trips to Holland over the years, both on my own and alongside Chris Mason and John Walton among others, and the atmosphere is unbelievable. The Dutch fans call me 'The Godfather', another nickname to add to my growing collection.

In Holland, and at home, I sometimes have to do two or three walk-ons with the music playing and the lights out, just to get the place in the right mood before I can start playing darts. I take a great deal of care over my outfits but I must stress that all that glitter comes out only for the stage. On occasions, I have been stopped in the local supermarket, shopping in my scruffs, by fans asking me where my cape is. I hardly wear any gold at home – not a good idea when I am digging lakes and tiling roofs all the time.

Darts is about razzmatazz nowadays and that all began with me. Every year that I haven't qualified to play at the Lakeside but have been there working for the BBC, the BDO has kindly asked me to do a walk-on for the crowd on the Friday evening. That is always a very special moment for me and the fans really get up for it.

The Embassy world championship has provided me with some very special memories from my 30 years in the game, both as a player and as a TV pundit. The best darts performance I have ever seen took place there when Dennis Priestley took five legs off me in just 49 darts in a practice match in 1993. That is really going some and I doubt I will ever witness anything like that again in my life. For that reason alone I would rank Dennis as the best darts player I have ever seen at the Lakeside, followed by Ted Hankey and then Phil Taylor.

The old man used to think that Ted was the business and when he is on song he really is something special. I love watching him play darts. He is so relaxed and, in my view, his natural, flowing action is the best around by some distance. On his day, Ted can beat anyone. In his 2000 Embassy semi-final against Chris Mason, he hit a record 22 maximums and followed that up by winning the world title against Ronnie Baxter 6–0, with a 170 checkout. That was something else.

Placing Phil third in my list may sound a little low given all the plaudits he gets, but I am basing this on my own personal experience. Despite having all the PDC records, Phil has been away from the BDO scene for so long that it is quite hard for me to judge him. Phil is an exceptional player but I ask myself how would he have fared in the game if there had not been a BDO–WDC split in 1993. We will never know but I genuinely doubt that he would have won 13 'world' titles.

For me, the true world darts champion will always be the winner of the BDO event, because he is the best player from all the competing nations in the world. I know the player I consider to be world champion and it isn't 'The Power'. He doesn't play in the same tournament as I do, so how on earth can I recognise him as being the best in the world?

I have never gone a lot on all this talk of a BDO v. PDC champions play-off, simply because I don't see the point in one. Phil Taylor won the Embassy world title twice and I take my hat off to him for those achievements. How many more he could have won will always be open to debate and opinion.

In my view, Keith Deller provided the finest moment in Embassy history when he checked out on 138 to win the title in 1983. For a young qualifier to reach the final and then finish off the world number one with such style was tremendous. Darts hit its absolute peak as a result of that.

When it comes to standard of darts thrown, I believe the best Embassy world champion was John Walton and I am in absolutely no doubt about that. John was simply awesome in 2001. He demolished the field all the way through from start to finish.

Finally, and unsurprisingly, Eric Bristow gets my vote as the Embassy champion of all time. His tally of five wins in ten final appearances is simply staggering, but then, I was around to contest only half of them! Our 1980 final really set the game of darts off and running, certainly in terms of match atmosphere and entertainment. With our different styles and personalities fans either loved or hated Eric and me, so having the two of us together on an occasion like that was dynamite for the game. We whipped up the crowd big style. I will always remember the chants of 'Bristow', 'Bobby George', 'Bristow', 'Bobby George' ringing out at Jollees. We definitely lit the touch paper that night.

Incidentally, since I was the NOW champion and Eric was the Winmau World Masters champion and world number one, even then we had two world champions of a sort without anyone giving it much attention – Eric was BDO world champion and I was NDA world champion.

Many fans have told me over the years that it was the standard of darts and the atmosphere in that 1980 final that first got them hooked on the game. I am sure that a little bit of glitter did no harm either.

Eric was an enigma. He made out that he liked to be disliked but, deep down, he didn't. His mouth could sometimes run away with him and he made some comments that he later regretted. I think a fair amount of it was hyped up for the box. Maybe Eric confused wit with rudeness and while he was rising to the top he got away with that. People haven't been as understanding with him in recent years.

I have to give the boy his due, though, he was honest and you knew exactly where you stood with him. Eric wasn't always the nicest bloke on the circuit but he didn't tell lies.

He was truly exceptional in the Embassy, particularly when you consider the other players around at that time, but the emergence of new darts talent and his personal struggle with 'dartitis' in the early 1990s killed him off as a force in the game.

'Dartitis' is a strange thing. I am lucky not to have experienced it but I have seen some players literally fall over the oche, unable to release the dart from their hand. Eric suffered badly from it and he has never been the same player since.

The two of us go back a long way. There is over ten years' age difference between us so I have always felt like his older, better-looking brother. Whenever I see him nowadays, he still reminds me of the young boy I used to play money races with all those years ago. He hasn't really changed in his heart. Eric is a true character and, like me, he gave life to darts when the game most needed it. It is impossible to imagine the glory days without him.

The main difference between us is that Eric had to win tournaments to become a star whereas I didn't. He said that himself. Maybe that is the reason why I have remained popular with the punters when a lot of my contemporaries from the 1970s have come and gone.

I never really enjoyed playing competitive darts and always preferred to put on a show instead. To enjoy darts, surely you have got to have a laugh. I hate practising on my own and find it boring. Pubs and clubs provide the atmosphere I want to play in. I have been called a clown because of that, but clowns don't win trophies, such as the NOW championship twice. My popularity is due to a mixture of talent and entertainment.

Tony Brown, Keith Deller, Alan Evans, Alan Glazier, Cliff Lazarenko, John Lowe, Leighton Rees, Tony Sontag, Dave Whitcomb and Jocky Wilson – these are the players who, along with Eric and me, helped make the game of darts what it is today. The ten of us were a unique bunch of blokes who were catapulted from the pub into the limelight. It was a crazy time and will never be repeated. What made it work was that there were enough of us to make it interesting and yet we were all different players and characters in our own right, with our own fan bases. The public never got bored and with so many TV events there was enough money in the pot for the lot of us to make a living.

Jocky was a true character and, for a while, my best friend in the game. I haven't seen him for some time and miss his company. He was always a good bloke to have a beer with.

You will know by now that the only one of the players from the golden era that I didn't get on with was John Lowe. We are like chalk and cheese. What he doesn't like about me is probably in equal measure to what I don't like about him, but John made it personal. He seemed to try to make things hard for me for me because I did things differently from how he thought they should be done.

It was a difficult time for me when John and his pals tried to set up the WPDPA in the early 1980s in an attempt to ban glitter and sequins from shirts. The writing was on the wall. Sequinned shirts, unconventional scoring and an unorthodox style made me very different from the rest and John seemed to have a problem with that from the off. I don't know what he really wanted for darts – a game with no glitter, no gold, no music and no entertainment? Who would have been interested in watching that?

John was one of the 16 players who split from the BDO and signed up with the WDC in 1993. Just like with the WPDPA, I was never asked to join the WDC but, as I have said, I would have turned down the invitation if it had come my way. I have always felt loyalty towards Olly Croft and the BDO. I don't agree with him all the time but without him the game of darts would be a lot worse off.

Before Olly set up the BDO, darts had the NOW championship and various pub tournaments but there was no commercial outlet for the game at all. Olly and the BDO created that commercial arm, got TV involved, formed an England side for international competitions and set up a Super League for 64 counties.

Once upon a time, someone invented the door handle to open and close doors. No doubt, door handles look a lot prettier today but no one gives credit to the man who made the first one. In darts, that man was Olly Croft and we should all remember that. There would be no BDO without him and, whatever your point of view, there is no denying that without the BDO none of us would be stars today.

Since the 1993 split, four Embassy champions – including four times winner Raymond Barneveld – have left the BDO to join the PDC but none of them are missed. I still believe the BDO ranks as the true world championship and every year it has been able to find a new star.

In 2006, 21-year-old Jelle Klaasen became the best-looking world finalist since me, and won the trophy with some blistering darts. He is a polite young man with a lot of talent and he will be a big star in the future. It is good to see another new face breaking through.

A few years ago, Andy Fordham became one of the most popular ever world champions and his success put darts well and truly back on the map. Andy did more with the world title than anyone else in recent years. Being such a big guy, 'The Viking' was instantly recognisable and had an all-important image. Generally speaking, though, darts doesn't have the characters that it used to have. People come to watch the stars entertain them, and some players seem to have forgotten that.

I don't blame any of the boys who decided to leave the BDO for the PDC. They exercised their freedom of choice, and every man has to answer only to himself. It just wasn't for me. It is up to the individual which side of the fence he chooses to play his darts. What annoys me is the criticism that is hurled over that fence. There is no need for it. We all come from the pub and play darts, so it is sad that there is still such nastiness around. Maybe too much has happened, too much has been said and too many people have been hurt for the scars ever to heal fully. There was a TV documentary about it all a few years ago called *Blood On The Carpet* and I was left shaking my head at how messy the whole situation had become.

In 2001, the BBC invited Phil Taylor to the Lakeside for an interview in an effort to explain the BDO–PDC situation fairly and properly to the public. Phil agreed to the interview and ended up staying around for a few days and doing some TV commentary for the BBC alongside John Part, another former BDO player who has since won the PDC event. At that moment, the two organisations seemed to be as close as they have ever been. Phil drank and joked with BDO players at the hotel bar and that was nice to see, but it seems a very long time ago.

John Part is an excellent commentator and I consider him to be the best in the business now. He is also the only one who understands why I leave 121 as a favourite finish.

One of my best friends today is a PDC player. Keith Deller agreed to appear as a live studio guest on the BBC afternoon show in 2003 to talk about his great win at the Lakeside 20 years before. Keith didn't once attempt to talk politics and that deserves respect. Never mind the BDO and the PDC, at the end of the day we are all darts players and should be friends.

I remember in the early days of my career, when prize money and tournaments were coming out of our ears, thinking that in the year 2000, the Embassy world title would probably carry a winner's cheque of around £500,000. It was actually £44,000. My point is that all the players believed that the glory days were there to stay and that the future meant mega money for us all. Things didn't quite work out like that and very few of those players managed to make a decent living out of the game in the end.

Since I built George Hall, I have moved well away from the darts circle but the times have also changed a lot. I honestly don't think that the players of today enjoy the crack in the same way that we did in the late 1970s and early 1980s. That is mainly because there is far less money about today. Fierce competition has bred a rivalry that has replaced the friendships. It just isn't the same any more, all the camaraderie has gone, but I suppose that is life.

I don't have too much in common with today's darts players – I am twice as old as half of them for a start – but through my son Richard, I have recently returned to the county game with Suffolk and still regularly top the averages, even in my sixties.

It was not my intention to push either of the boys into darts and neither did I, but they grew up with the game and it has come naturally to both of them. Robert once left himself 60 and had the audacity to go out on two double 15s. I told him off for that. 'Who do you think you are, Bobby George?' He replied in a flash, 'That's exactly who I am, Dad.' Talk about a chip off the old block!

Both boys have the potential to be decent players and time will tell if either of them can achieve something in the game. Robert enjoys a game of darts but Richard is quite serious about it and already plays for Suffolk under the name of Richie 'Rich' George. I don't know where he got that name from, or the money for that matter!

It would be lovely to think that either of them could go on to play in the world championship. Both of them are still young – Robert is 19 and Richard is 17 – so time is definitely on their side, but you can't push kids into doing anything they don't want to do. My boys have chosen the game for themselves.

Robert adopted a similar throw to me when he was young but he has since developed his own style. Richard was throwing darts – in a similar style to Keith Deller – when he still had his nappy on. I took him down to the Lakeside when he was at primary school and he was hitting maximums for fun on the practice boards.

He has appeared on TV many times and was interviewed by John Inverdale on BBC TV when he was just 11. He won his first tournament at 14 and a mate of mine has had a bet on for years that he will win the world championship by the time he reaches 30.

In the future, I will also be cheering on a young lad from Weymouth who is named after me. Bobby George was born in 1993 to the landlord and landlady of the town's Royal Oak pub. I have already played him at darts but I won't tell you who won, other than it was Bobby George.

The reason Richard and I play for Suffolk is that the county apologised to me for the nonsense surrounding my appearance in the 2002 world qualifiers and asked me to re-sign for them. Members of the Suffolk Super League team had been so outraged by the county's decision not to support me that they held a meeting to discuss the matter. This led to Suffolk reversing its decision and inviting me to re-sign for them after all, ahead of the 2002 Embassy. I had already signed up for Fraserburgh by then, so I declined.

It was a farce and could have had serious consequences for me but thankfully sense prevailed and due to Richard's involvement in the Suffolk Super League, I have found myself representing the county again. The Suffolk lads were genuinely upset by it all and explained to me that they never voted on the issue. I decided to let bygones be bygones. They have been great with Richard, giving him his first chance in senior darts and he is now repaying them with good performances for the A team. Richard has already been selected for England Youth and is now seriously considering playing on the Open circuit when he turns 18 in December 2007.

I hadn't played competitive darts in pubs for years so the county system was very much a blast from the past for me and it has knocked a few cobwebs off. I don't think it will necessarily improve my game but I have become reacquainted with a corner of the darts scene that I had long forgotten.

Incidentally, there has been no backtracking from either Essex or London since our fallout in 2001, despite the sponsorship deals that I have earned for both of them over the years. Both counties have very short memories but mine is long and strong and what goes around eventually comes around.

I know, deep in my heart, that I can still win the world championship. I wouldn't be going through the hassle of trying to qualify via the play-offs if I didn't think I could. If you are in it, you can win it – simple as that. Look at Keith Deller, John Walton and Jelle Klaasen – all unknowns who swept aside all in front of them to win the world title. That is why I still believe I can do it, if I can just manage to qualify again.

England has been the leader in many sports over the years but eventually the rest of the world catches up, and darts has been no exception to that. The top prize has gone to players from Australia, Canada and most notably Holland in recent years. No foreign player won the Embassy in its first 15 years, but since then the title has gone overseas on seven occasions and an Englishman has won it just four times. The complexion of the game has totally changed. I expect that the next countries to make a charge on darts will come from Asia and Scandinavia.

I would still love to win the world title for Marie and the boys but I would also love to win it so that I could do something for the growth of darts. I really would do that, from touring schools and colleges to appearing on chat shows and selling the game worldwide. We have had a succession of one-week wonders. It has often been a case of sweeping the Lakeside stage after the final and forgetting about it until the following year.

It annoys me so much that I haven't won it because I see all the opportunities that these guys waste year after year. With the exception of Andy Fordham, they have done absolutely nothing with it. They may as well have had 10,000 fags with no matches to light them. It is very sad and frustrating.

The way I see it, it doesn't matter if you are world champion or world number one, if your telephone doesn't ring, no one wants to book you so essentially you are no good. Trophies alone don't earn darts players a living. They never have. I have always tried to put entertainment and laughter into darts and when I do finally pack this game in, the one thing I hope people will remember me for is my smile.

Life is all about timing and I have been very lucky in that respect. If I had been born 20 years later and got into darts in the 1990s, things would have been quite different for me with fewer tournaments, less TV coverage and many more players on the scene.

A few years ago, I decided to return to Kinsale, in southern Ireland, and visited the Lobster Pot, the pub that opened the door to my darts career on that stormy day way back in the summer of 1976. Funnily enough, the pub no longer has a dartboard.

Life really is all about timing.

I am leaving the last page of this book to the old man and the only poem he ever wrote about me. It would make his day to know that his work had been published!

My Son Bob
BY FRANCIS J. GEORGE (THE OLD MAN), 1976

Do you know my son Bob?
He can do any sort of job
He works with all sorts of sands
And is clever with his hands
He'll build you an extension or a bar
He'll mend, spray or weld your motor car
He has every sort of tool
And he'll even build you a swimming pool
He's good at woodwork and painting
And he'll weld things while you're waiting
Plumbing, bricklaying, anything in the building game
That's what I'm saying
There's one thing more
He can plaster and lay a granite floor
So, if there's anything you want done
Why not nip round and see my son?
Oh, there's another thing
Did you know he's the Essex dartboard king?
So, if there's any little job
Nip round and see my son Bob

May the darts be with you!

Index

Chapman, Peter, 65, 92
Charlie (BG's parrot), 217
Checkpoint Charlie, 169
Chegwin, Keith, 243–4
Chelmsford, 203
Chigwell, 4, 40, 51, 63
Chile, 21
Chingford, 67
Chris' Club, Vallejo, 150
'Circus Life', 236
Clacton-on-Sea, 64
'Claire', 109
Clark, Tony, 120
Clarke, Dave (Courage
    employee), 87, 159
Clarke, Dave (Essex darts
    player), 216
Clayton Lodge, Stoke-on-
    Trent, 98–9
Cochrane, Terry, 128
Colchester, 205
Cologne, 243
'Combine Harvester', 1
Confessions of a Window
    Cleaner, 44
Connaught Rooms, London,
    148
Coombes, Lil, 57
Copenhagen, 93, 94, 95,
    110–11
Cosnett, John, 142
Costa del Sol, 97
Cottee, Roy, 73, 86
Cottee, Tony, 73
Cottee, Will, 73
Courage brewery, 86, 87,
    142, 143, 148, 159–60,
    166
Covent Garden, 31
Cowen, Richard, 46
Crafty Cockney, The (pub),
    Santa Monica, 79–80
Crayford Open 1977, 65
Crest Hotel, Stockton-on-
    Tees, 126
Croft, Lorna, 121
Croft, Olly, 130, 132
  American trip, 74, 75
  and third-place play-offs, 96
  and BG's outfits, 100, 107
  and Russell Harty show, 108
  and BDO Sports Personality
    award, 119

joins in recording of '180',
    121
invites BG to take part in
    qualification play-offs for
    1993 Embassy, 174
and WDC, 175, 186, 265
and public relations for
    1994 Embassy, 187
refuses to give BG a wild
    card for 2002 Embassy,
    232, 233
BG recommends Martin
    Fitzmaurice to, 259
important role in develop-
    ment of the game, 265
Cromwell, Oliver, 205
Croucher, Gordon, 83, 85, 98
Croucher, Kay, 82–3
Croucher, Sandra see Adams
    (née Croucher), Sandra

Dagenham, 34, 41
Danan, Paul, 249
Danish Open, 154
  1979, 92–3, 94, 95
  1980, 111
Daphne (Phyllis George's
    daughter), 10
Darts World magazine, 109,
    144
David, Mario, 21
David, Tony, 238
Davies, Malcolm, 148
Davis, Barry, 89
Davis, Mr (headmaster), 130
Davis, Steve, 159
Davro, Bobby, 244
Del Carmen Tanti, Camelia,
    162
Del Carmen Tanti, Marie see
    George (née Del Carmen
    Tanti), Marie
Del Carmen Tanti, Salvador,
    162
Deller, Keith, 264, 268
  in pub match against BG,
    81–2
  in America, 116–17
  attends 1982 Embassy, 131
  in 1983 Embassy, 81, 137,
    139–41, 198, 263, 269
  in area finals for 1986
    NOW championship, 155

joins WDC, 173
  appears as BBC studio
    guest, 267
Demag, 47
de Mandeville, Geoffrey, 205
de Wildt, Franky, 236
Denmark, 93–5, 148, 154
Dexy's Midnight Runners,
    121
Diamond, Anne, 252
Discount (BG's cat), 217
'Dog' (later retitled 'One
    Man and His Dog'),
    249–51
Dolenz, Micky, 146
Dollar (BG's cat), 217
Domesday Book, 205
Donnelly, Dougie, 178, 179,
    190, 247
Dors, Diana, 84, 91, 157–8
Dosh (BG's dog), 217
Dowsett, Jim, 158
Dubai, 135
Duke Gardens, Barkingside,
    14
Dunn, Barry, 96
Dunoon Open 1995, 219
Durrant, Paul, 70, 73, 82
Durro, 70, 73, 75, 82
Dyke, Peter, 187

Earl's Court, 163, 221, 222,
    225, 226
East Berlin, 168–70
EastEnders, 42, 248–9
Eastern Counties area final
  1978, 70
  1979, 81–2
East Germany, 168–70
East Ham, 73
East Ham Memorial
    Hospital, 7
Edinburgh, 88
Ellis, Malcolm, 1–2, 3, 4, 51,
    52–3, 54, 55, 56, 57, 64,
    67, 85
Elm Park, 41
Embassy world championship
    (now called Lakeside
    world championship), 86,
    159, 173, 256, 257, 262,
    263, 264, 266, 269
  1978, 101